Modern Irish Poetry

*This book is dedicated to
my mother and her people,
the Mallons/Ó Mealláin,
'keepers of St. Patrick's bell'.*

Preface

This study provides (in English) a close reading and evaluation of poetry by the four leading twentieth-century Irish language poets: Seán Ó Ríordáin and Máirtín Ó Direáin who emerged in the late 1940s and wrote mainly between the 1950s and 1970s; and contemporary poets Cathal Ó Searcaigh and Nuala Ní Dhomhnaill who emerged in the late 1970s and have been writing and publishing mainly from the 1980s to the present.

To indicate social and literary shifts between these two generations, chapters turn from Ó Ríordáin to Ó Searcaigh, back (in time) to Ó Direáin and forward again to Ní Dhomhnaill. This path best highlights some of the most significant trends and developments in Irish language poetry in the latter half of our century. In all cases, translations are provided.

My approach to these poets is to take them on their own transgressive terms which necessitates that they be considered in the light of their own eclectic influences, and alongside their peers and contemporaries with whom they are often engaged in a far-reaching intertextual dialogue. While focusing on each of the four's own individual concerns, this critical study of minority but national language poets necessarily raises some of today's key questions facing cultural commentators on Ireland: the relationship between the writer and his/her public; between the writer in Irish and her/his English (and other) language colleagues; between the writer and tradition, the writer and modernity; between the writer and the city, the writer and the nation.

The four poets whose work I have selected are craftspeople who extend the tradition of their country's art by building *anew* from the scattered signs, materials, and resources around them modern stanzas or, literally, 'rooms'. Combining elements and techniques from home and abroad, past and present, they make the literary estate of the Irish language and the Alhambra of Ireland's art look lived in: 'chomh beo beathúch is a bhí sí ina seanléim'.

Acknowledgements

Modern Irish Poetry: A New Alhambra began life as a PhD thesis supervised by Professor Robert Welch whose own work has inspired and encouraged me. I wish to thank Professor Welch, Dr Anne McCartney, and all other University of Ulster academic, library staff, and students who helped in my researches. A belated thanks goes to staff of the English, Slavonic, Irish Departments, and library of the University of Belfast who first set me off on this particular academic path, especially Professor Edna Longley and Professor Marcus Wheeler. Penultimate thanks go to the authors whose work is the subject of this research: to Seán Ó Ríordáin and Máirtín Ó Direáin who, I felt, kept an otherworldly gaze on my endeavours; and to Cathal Ó Searcaigh and Nuala Ní Dhomhnaill who corresponded with me, sharing some previously unpublished poems. Finally, I wish to thank my friends and family for their encouragement throughout.

The following authors and publishers have kindly permitted me to reproduce or quote from previously published material: excerpt from 'Field of Vision' and excerpt from 'Squarings' from *Opened Ground: Selected Poems 1966–1996* by Seamus Heaney. Copyright © 1998 by Seamus Heaney. Reprinted by permission of Farrar, Strauss and Giroux, LLC. *Seeing Things* by Seamus Heaney, Faber and Faber Ltd. *All That is Solid Melts Into Air: the Experience of Modernity* by Marshall Berman (London and New York: Verseo, 1983, 1995). Gabhaim buíochas go háirithe le Nuala Ní Dhomhnaill, Cathal Ó Searcaigh, An Clóchomhar Sáirséal · Ó Marcaigh agus Cló Iar-Chonnachta. Bail, beannacht agus rathúnas orthu.

Contents

LIST OF ABBREVIATIONS   x

Introduction: Ireland's Alhambra   1

1. Seán Ó Ríordáin: Between Corkery and Joycery   9

2. Cathal Ó Searcaigh: Zig-zagging All Over Creation   54

3. Máirtín Ó Direáin: Departures You Cannot Go Back On   104

4. Nuala Ní Dhomhnaill: Journeying to the Shrine   149

Conclusion: A Polish Perspective   199

APPENDIX: TRANSLATIONS   203

BIBLIOGRAPHY   216

INDEX   229

Abbreviations

1. SEÁN Ó RÍORDÁIN: BETWEEN CORKERY AND JOYCERY

ES   *Eireaball Spideoige* (Dublin: Sáirséal agus Dill, 1952, 1986)
B   *Brosna* (Dublin: Sáirséal agus Dill, 1964, 1987)
LL   *Línte Liombó* (Dublin: Sáirséal agus Dill, 1971, 1980)
TÉB   *Tar Éis Mo Bháis* (Dublin: Sáirséal agus Dill, 1978, 1986)

2. CATHAL Ó SEARCAIGH: ZIG-ZAGGING ALL OVER CREATION

MC   *Miontraigéide Cathrach* (An Fálcarrach: Cló Uí Chuireáin, 1975)
SS   *Súile Shuibhne* (Dublin: Coiscéim, 1983)
S   *Suibhne* (Dublin: Coiscéim, 1987)
ABB   *An Bealach 'na Bhaile/Homecoming* (Indreabhán: Cló Iar-Chonnachta, 1993)
NBB   *Na Buachaillí Bána* (Indreabhán: Cló Iar-Chonnachta, 1996)
OO   *Out in the Open* (Indreabhán: Cló Iar-Chonnachta, 1997)

3. MÁIRTÍN Ó DIREÁIN: DEPARTURES YOU CANNOT GO BACK ON

FB   *Feamainn Bhealtaine* (Dublin: An Clóchomhar, 1961, 1971)
D   *Dánta 1939–1979* (Dublin: An Clóchomhar, 1980)
SP/TD   *Selected Poems/Tacar Dánta* (Newbridge: Goldsmith Press, 1984)
CD   *Craobhóg Dán* (Dublin: An Clóchomhar, 1986)
CMC   *Cime Mar Chách: Aistí ar Mháirtín Ó Direáin* ed. Caoimhín Mac Giolla Léith (Dublin: Coiscéim, 1993)

4. NUALA NÍ DHOMHNAILL: JOURNEYING
TO THE SHRINE

DD   *An Dealg Droighin* (Dublin and Cork: Mercier Press, 1981)
FS   *Féar Suaithinseach* (Maynooth: An Sagart, 1984)
SP/RD   *Selected Poems/Rogha Dánta* (Dublin: Raven Arts Press, 1988; repr. 1991)
PD   *Pharaoh's Daughter* (Loughcrew: Gallery, 1990)
F   *Feis* (Maynooth: An Sagart, 1991)
AC   *The Astrakhan Cloak* (Loughcrew: Gallery, 1993)

Introduction: Ireland's Alhambra

I'm talking to you—but it isn't
my fault if you can't hear me.

Joseph Brodski[1]

This critical study is designed to provide (in English) an introduction
to the work of four of the main modern Irish-language poets: Seán Ó
Ríordáin and Máirtín Ó Direáin who were writing mainly from the late
1940s to 1970s; and Cathal Ó Searcaigh and Nuala Ní Dhomhnaill who
have been writing mainly from the late 1970s to the present.

The need to focus, at length, on these four poets has forced me to
omit others who could have been included: Máire Mhac an tSaoi,
Eoghan Ó Tuairisc, Michael Davitt, Liam Ó Muirthile and Biddy
Jenkinson, to name but a few. All of the aforementioned have made
valuable contributions to Irish literature and I can only hope that my
study of four of their number will encourage readers and critics to inves-
tigate, for themselves, work not only by the poets whom I have selected
but by their 'comrades in Irish'.[2]

Irish literature, a dual tradition,[3] continues to be written in both the
country's majority and minority language: English and Irish. Bilingual
readings of that literature become all the more necessary as the two
languages keep up their 'dynamic interaction'[4] despite prolonged cases
of 'bodhaire Uí Laoghaire'/deaf ears being turned upon writing in Irish.
For example, even the perspicacious poet and critic Eavan Boland once
failed to notice the presence, or even the existence, of the Irish language
poet, and potential foremother, Máire Mhac an tSaoi: 'if I had looked
closely . . . I might have noticed that there were no women poets, old

---

[1] Joseph Brodski, quoted by Anna Czekanowicz in 'Travel Poem'. See Pirie, D. (ed.),
Young Poets of a New Poland (London: Forest Books, 1993), 76.
[2] A phrase borrowed from the Belfast poet Pádraic Fiacc.
[3] See Kinsella, Thomas, *The Dual Tradition: An Essay on Poetry and Politics in Ireland*
(Manchester: Carcanet Press, 1995).
[4] Kinsella, Thomas (ed.), Preface, *The New Oxford Book of Irish Verse* (Oxford:
Oxford University Press, 1986), xxvii.

or young, past or present in my immediate environment.'[5] However, at this time (late 1950s, early 1960s), Mhac an tSaoi's work and reputation were at their peak.[6] How then does one overcome such deaf or blindspots, threshold difficulties or 'dividing idiocies'[7] between Irish literature in English and that in Irish?

Simply by tuning in not only to writing in English but to the pre- and co-existing 'stáisiún forleatha'/broadcasting station[8] of Irish language and literature—*at least*, in translation and via transgressive, bilingual, bipolar criticism for a more comprehensive representation and understanding of this country's art. Thankfully, a growing number of writers and critics *are* continuing the genuinely pluralist tradition of Irish literature by adopting an inclusive approach to the various languages, dialects and forms that even one art in one country can take.[9] Therefore, whereas in some quarters an Anglo-Cyclops' view of this country's poetry still exists,[10] recent studies of contemporary work recognize the need to account for the polyphony of voices[11] which make up the 'fuaim na habhann'/riversound[12] or living stream of Irish writing.

For their part, Irish-language poets have almost always been culturally open and pluralist. Their very bilingualism, and sometimes more, is not often shared, for example, by some of their detractors[13] or by those who

---

[5] See Johnston, Dillon, *Irish Poetry After Joyce*, 2nd edn. (New York: Syracuse University Press, 1997), 286–7.

[6] In 1956, she had published her first, and best, collection: *Margadh na Saoire* with the memorable, pre-feminist lyrics 'AthDheirdre'/Another Deirdre, 'Gan Réiteach'/Unresolved and 'Ceathrúintí [Quatrains of] Mháire Ní Ógáin', as well as translations from Lorca and Shakespeare. See Mhac an tSaoi, Máire, *An Cion go dtí Seo* (Dublin: Sáirséal - Ó Marcaigh, 1987, repr. 1988).

[7] Kinsella, Thomas, 'Another Country', in *The Pleasures of Gaelic Poetry*, ed. Seán Mac Réamoinn (London: Allen Lane, 1982), 178.

[8] See Ó Ríordáin, Seán, 'Na Blascaodaí'/The Blaskets, *Eireaball Spideoige*, 2nd edn. (Dublin: Sáirséal - Ó Marcaigh, 1986), 94–6 (p. 96).

[9] See, for example, Cronin, Michael, *Translating Ireland: Translations, Languages, Cultures* (Cork: Cork University Press, 1996).

[10] ' "Irish poetry" means what most of the English-reading world recognizes: poetry written in English, from or pertaining mostly to Ireland. Johnston, D., *Irish Poetry After Joyce*, xix. Johnston does, at least, make some amends in the second edition of his text. See 'Afterword', 286–98.

[11] See, for example, Walshe, Éibhear (ed.), *Sex, Nation and Dissent in Irish Writing* (Cork: Cork University Press, 1997); or Kiberd, Declan, *Idir Dhá Chultúr* (Dublin: Coiscéim, 1993).

[12] Ó Ríordáin, 'Éist le Fuaim na hAbhann'/Listen to the River-sound', *Eireaball Spideoige*, 47.

[13] Including, unfortunately, Patrick Kavanagh who, in two letters printed in the *Irish*

choose to avoid, ignore, or play them down.[14] Yet, ironically, the openness
of modern Irish-language poets to influence (from home *and* abroad), the
keenness with which they have experienced modernity and change,
precipitated, in the first generation whose work I want to discuss, the
ontological insecurity which characterizes much of their work.

Seán Ó Ríordáin, most anxious to find the way to put 'mise ins an
rud a bhí le rá/"I" in what I had to say',[15] raised a question which is
central to the identity-crises of many modern individuals and peoples:
'what can one do when things outside the [native] tradition have gone
into one—when the person is wider than the tradition?'[16] Influenced by
James Joyce, Ó Ríordáin was open to encountering the reality of experience, to imaginative transgressions between the borders of self and the
outer world of things and ideas but, also influenced by Daniel Corkery,
he was always aware of the danger of losing himself or his 'true' self on
the way, of not being able to return/'fill arís'; of tumbling into
madness/'gealtacht', 'hunself',[17] or of simply drowning (with only a
'poem-straw' to hold onto[18]) in the drunkenness of things—and *self*—
being various.

Máirtín Ó Direáin, in 'Solas'/Light, may have found a way round Ó
Ríordáin's difficulty of containing, within the self, native and un-native
elements and influences:

> Ariamh níor dhiúltaigh solas
> Ó na ceithre hairde nuair tháinig;

Times (24 January and 2 February 1972), referred to Irish language poetry as merely 'the
doodlings and phrase-making of mediocrities'. See Ó Coileáin, Seán, *Seán Ó Ríordáin:
Beatha agus Saothar* (Dublin: An Clóchomhar 1982, repr. 1985), 249.

[14] Peter McDonald has stated that 'some Irish language poetry has created a
"dialogue" of sorts in recent years, though I think it's tempting to overrate the significance of this'. See 'A Writer for his Kind: Carol Rumens talks to Peter McDonald', in
Brangle: Essays, Reviews and Poetry from N. Ireland and Beyond, No. 2 (London: Brangle
Publications, 1997), 31–43 (pp. 32–3). On the contrary, the significance of cross-language
dialogue in Irish poetry is too often *underrated* or not picked up.

[15] Ó Ríordáin, 'Línte Liombó', *Línte Liombó* (Dublin: Sáirséal & Dill, 1971, repr.
1980), 9.

[16] 'Ach cad tá le déanamh nuair a bhíonn nithe lasmuigh den tráidisiún dulta i
nduine—nuair a bhíonn an duine níos fairsinge ná an tráidisiún?' See Ó Coileáin, *Seán
Ó Ríordáin*, 210.

[17] Ibid. 155–6. See also Ó Tuama, Seán, 'Synge and the Idea of a National Literature'
(1972), *Repossessions: Selected Essays on the Irish Literary Heritage* (Cork: Cork University
Press, 1995), 219–33 (p. 230).

[18] 'Greim an fhir bháite . . . an súgán seo filíochta.' Ó Ríordáin, 'Cnoc
Mellerí'/Mount Mellery, *Eireaball Spideoige*, 64–7 (p. 67).

Ach iarraim ar an solas iasachta
Gan mo sholas féin a mhúchadh.

I never knocked back light
from anywhere when it came
but I ask the foreign light
not to put [drown] out my own.[19]

Yet, to read Ó Direáin's oeuvre from beginning to end is to witness the candle of his creativity burn down and out. Overwhelmed by the foreign light of modern cities, overshadowed by sky-scrapers and the deluge of American-English language and values, he re-directed his own light onto the receding past of his Aran island childhood home more than onto his present—the 'cathair fhallsa'/deceitful city which, like Eliot's abyss, he could not bear to look at for long[20] as it signalled to him the decline of all he valued.

Cathal Ó Searcaigh, a generation after Ó Ríordáin and Ó Direáin, has benefited from their examples and also from the freewheeling modernity and internationalism of the *INNTI* group to which he contributed.[21] His early interest in American Beat poetry and also his Russian studies at Limerick provide an Eastern dimension to his thought, culminating in his recent fascination with Nepal.[22] Sufficiently well-versed in his own country's language, song and poetry, Ó Searcaigh is mystically confident of his own individual light, that of his tradition and that of all existences. Therefore, he manages to blend or synthesise different, but essential, lights—the old and new, the native and foreign—and he does so, in the timeless manner of Néde, by 'ag nochtadh an fhocail'/making naked the word:

Fercheirtne:

a question, o young man of learning
what art do you practise?

---

[19] Ó Direáin, Máirtín, 'Solas'/Light, *Craobhog Dán,* (Dublin: An Clóchomhar Tta, 1986), 23.

[20] See Gardner, Helen, *The Art of T. S. Eliot* (London: The Cresset Press, 1949, repr. 1968), 79.

[21] *INNTI* was founded as a poetry broadsheet by students at UCC in March 1970 and relaunched as a journal by Michael Davitt, a founding editor, in 1980. The movement was characterized by youthful vigour, modernity, and internationalism, including a post-1960s interest, among some contributors including Gabriel Rosenstock and Cathal Ó Searcaigh, in Eastern mysticism.

[22] See Ó Searcaigh, Cathal, 'Kathmandu', *Out in the Open* (Indreabhán: Cló Iar-Chonnachta, 1997), 194–9.

to which Néde replied:
> not hard to answer
> I bring blush to face
> and spirit to flesh
> I practise fear's erasure
> and tumescence of impudence
> metre's nurture
> honour's venture
> and wisdom's wooing
> I shape beauty to human mouths
> give wings to insight
> I make naked the word [. . .][23]

When, at an early stage, home ground became too narrow for Ó Searcaigh, he hightailed it out of there like 'An Bó Bhradach/The Braddy Cow' of his poem by that name,[24] and became a 'rucksack romantic', an on-the-road poet in the manner of Basho, Raftery, and Kerouac. However, he has repeatedly and insistently brought 'an solas iasachta'/the foreign light back home, brought his present, self and light to bear on home, tradition, and on the past so that each of these could continue to 'go itself', grow like one of the many plants or trees in his poetry rather than ossify in a Medusa-like lock.[25] Ó Searcaigh, like Yevgeny Yevtushenko, seeks the truth in himself and shares it with others, seeks the truth in others, from people to pink lilies, from Donegal to Nepal, and stores it up in himself.[26]

Nuala Ní Dhomhnaill has also spent a number of years 'ar seachrán'/'astray', living or travelling abroad. In her home, three languages co-exist (Irish, Turkish, and English) which shows the degree to which different lights and languages *can* live and let live. Similarly, there are two essential and contiguous aspects to her work: 'an ionspioráid phearsanta'/personal inspiration and béaloideas/oral lore or learning. Combining these two elements, the poet has described her

---

[23] See 'The Dialogue of the Two Sages', trans. Williamson, in Stewart, R. J. and Williamson, R., *Celtic Bards, Celtic Druids* (London: Blandford/Cassell, 1996), 91–6 (p. 93).

[24] Ó Searcaigh, *An Bealach 'na Bhaile/Homecoming* (Indreabhán: Cló Iar-Chonnachta, 1993), 126.

[25] See Welch, R., *Changing States: Transformations in Modern Irish Writing* (London: Routledge, 1993), ix.

[26] Yevtushenko, Y., *A Precocious Autobiography* (Harmondsworth: Penguin, 1965), 124.

objective as 'forbairt ar an traidisiúin trína phearsanú, agus saibhriú an duine trí mheán an traidisiúin'/development of the tradition through personalization, and enrichment of the person through tradition.[27] This is made possible by the fact that she finds a bond between her own modern-day predicaments (or worries) and everything that comes down to her through the language and béaloideas/'tá nascadh mar sin idir mo thrioblóid féin agus gach a thagann anuas chugam trí mheán na teanga agus trí mheán an bhéaloidis'.[28] This bond, as evidenced by her work and progress, does not limit but enables her to transgress (literally, step beyond) the psychic traumas and hindrances caused, for example, by sexual and linguistic marginalization due to forces such as patriarchy and colonialism. For Ní Dhomhnaill, keeping going the tradition means keeping going the self; telling the tale to live means, as it does for the sculptor Louise Bourgeois,[29] living to tell the tale.

For Irish writers in English, the Irish language dimension of their tradition has not only proved to be a rich source for translation but has widened the range of voices—and, therefore, choices—in contemporary debates: for example, awareness of what comrades-in-Irish such as Seán Ó Ríordáin and Nuala Ní Dhomhnaill were writing has directly influenced comrades-in-English such as Seamus Heaney[30] and Paul Muldoon in the working out of their own individual positions and viewpoints, methods and techniques. Indeed, it is a measure of Ní Dhomhnaill's success and influence that she can transform the world from the Parish of Ventry to the 'Pennington car wash', providing no less a figure than the maverick Muldoon with, allegedly, the only image 'worth a fuck' in *Prince of the Quotidian*:

> As I coasted into the tunnel
> of the Pennington car wash
> I glanced at my copy of *Feis*
> by Nuala Ní Dhomhnaill:
>
> a wave broke over a rock
> somewhere west of Dingle;
> my windshield was a tangle
> of eel-grass and bladderwrack.[31]

[27] See Ó Tuairisc, E. (ed.), *Rogha an Fhile/The Poet's Choice* (Dublin: Goldsmith Press, 1974), 57–8.   [28] Ibid.
[29] Meyer-Thoss, C., *Louise Bourgeois: Designing for Free Fall* (Zurich: Ammann, 1992), 195.   [30] See Seamus Heaney regarding Séan Ó Ríordáin in Chapter 1 Part 2.
[31] Muldoon, Paul, *Prince of the Quotidian* (Loughcrew: Gallery Press, 1994), 38–40.

For other writers, the linguistic plurality of Ireland's literary heritage has provided not only a dual source but an alternative medium: Michael Hartnett, Eithne Strong and, more recently, Celia de Fréine and Eibhlís Lordan are among a growing number of bilingual writers each attempting to become 'a threader/of double-stranded words'[32] in English and/or Irish as opposed to being silenced or 'torn between two languages'.[33]

World poetry in English and other languages has also, naturally, influenced and informed Irish poetry. American poets such as T. S. Eliot, Robert Frost, and Adrienne Rich, as well as Russian poets, including Alexander Blok, Yevgeny Yevtushenko, and Marina Tsvetaeva, have particularly inspired one or other of the poets in this study. Where this influence is most discernible and revealing, I explore the nature of the exchange.

Some familiarity with several literary traditions has convinced me that poets in every country touch on the personal to embrace 'that which is common to many';[34] scan the local, parochial, regional, or national to span the international; focus on the particular to envisage the universal. To say so is to state an obvious and often repeated fact. In Ireland, however, there are times when this fact must be repeated. I wonder if it would be necessary in any other country to explain that a certain poet was, say, 'cosmopolitan-*and*-Russian' or 'Polish-*but*-universal'. In Ireland, however, the poet and critic Theo Dorgan recently felt compelled to present, or rather defend, Irish (and, therefore, world) poets as 'cosmopolitan-and-Irish'.[35] Unfortunately, Dorgan's defensiveness is warranted due to recurring suggestions from some critical quarters that to be or sound like an 'Irish poet' is somehow to be 'less' than *a* poet.[36]

Ó Ríordáin, Ó Searcaigh, Ó Direáin and Ní Dhomhnaill are Irish poets and, therefore, world poets. By contributing to their country's literature, they contribute to world literature. Each one has added to

---

[32] McGuckian, Medbh 'The Dream-Language of Fergus', *Selected Poems 1978–1994* (Loughcrew: Gallery Press, 1997), 48–9.

[33] Ó Ríordáin's description of himself. See Ó Coileáin, *Seán Ó Ríordáin*, 301.

[34] Yevtushenko, *A Precocious Autobiography*, 10.

[35] Dorgan, 'Looking Over the Edge', in *Irish Poetry Since Kavanagh*, ed. by Theo Dorgan (Blackrock: Four Courts Press, 1996), 147–58 (p. 156).

[36] 'Mahon seems to have chosen to work hard at sounding like an Irish poet. This is a lesser thing, and it is everybody's loss.' Peter McDonald, 'Incurable Ache' (review of *The Yellow Book*, Derek Mahon, Gallery, 1997), *Poetry Ireland*, 56 (Spring 1998), 117–19 (p. 119).

what I would describe as the Alhambra of Ireland's art. The original Alhambra, in Spain,

stands on the hills overlooking Granada, and was built by the Moors in the thirteenth and fourteenth centuries. It was a fortress and also a palace, and is the most striking example of Moorish architecture in the world. It is entered by the Gate of Justice, and its two greatest courts are the Court of the Lions and the Court of the Fishpond. Its rooms are decorated with sculptures, columns, carvings, etc., of the most exquisite kind.[37]

In an Irish context, Joep Leerssen has stated that 'one should be able to have the courage and acknowledge the difference between present-day Ireland and its pre-nineteenth-century roots. The only simile I can think of is the Alhambra destroyed and the same rubble used to rebuild a different building according to a different architecture.'[38] While I acknowledge the differences between then and now, if one uses the same rubble to re-build, then one builds anew the Alhambra which, as a metaphor for Irish art, was never (I believe) completely destroyed. This 'Alhambra' was sometimes obscured and/or went unrecognized; all along, however, it expanded because generations of Irish artists kept extending it in their own fashion.

Today, therefore, the Alhambra of Ireland's art is open to all visitors as should be the Alhambra of every country's art. It is entered (just like the original thirteenth-century Moorish Alhambra) via the Gate of Justice. Inside, there are many different courts, rooms, and features, including sculptures, columns, carvings, and manuscripts produced in a variety of modes, media, and languages by generations of the nation's artists. Before entering the gate to visit the four installations on my itinerary, I pray that my exposition does them justice.

[37] See Alington, C. A., Revd., DD, *The New Standard Encyclopaedia and World Atlas* (London: Odhams Press Ltd., 1932).
[38] See Ó Muirthile, Liam, 'Rebuilding the Alhambra: A Discussion with Joep Leerssen', *Poetry Ireland Review*, Issue 49 (Spring/Earrach 1996), 28–36 (p. 33).

CHAPTER 1

Seán Ó Ríordáin: Between Corkery and Joycery

There is no continuing direct line;
there is rather a departure,
a pushing away from the known point [. . .]
Any literary succession is first of all a struggle,
a destruction of old values
and a reconstruction of old elements.

Yuri Tynyanov, 1921[1]

INTRODUCTION

In 1950, Seán Ó Tuama edited *Nuabhéarsaíocht*,[2] an anthology of 'new verse' in Irish. This calculated mid-twentieth-century intervention was designed to secure recognition for the three most innovative poets of that generation—Máirtín Ó Direáin, Seán Ó Ríordáin and Máire Mhac an tSaoi. The emergence of these three individual writers heralded a revolution in Irish verse:

it was [. . .] the fact that Máirtín Ó Direáin, Seán Ó Ríordáin and Máire Mhac an tSaoi began, opportunely, to write almost simultaneously which marked those years as a new beginning in poetry. While each of these wrote in an individual vein, their work taken together realized the desire for an authentic modern voice in poetry. Their use of the language in response to experience established the validity of modern poetry in Irish.[3]

[1] Tynyanov quoted in Rylance, R. (ed.), 'Versions of Formalism', *Debating Texts: A Reader in Twentieth-century Literary Theory and Method*, 3rd edn. (Milton Keynes: Open University Press, 1990), 31–65 (p. 34).
[2] Ó Tuama, S. (ed.) *Nuabhéarsaíocht: 1939–1949*, 5th edn. (Dublin: Sáirséal agus Dill, 1974).
[3] Ó hAnluain, E., 'The Twentieth Century: Prose and Verse', additional chapter in

One must try to imagine the impact of their poetry at the time: Ó Tuama wrote that poems such as Ó Ríordáin's 'Adhlacadh Mo Mháthar'/My Mother's Burial (*ES* p. 56) 'astonished' readers in 1945 because 'they were straight away in a territory of the imagination which poetry in Irish had not previously entered'.[4] Ó Direáin's comment on the period further accounts for the surprise:

In matters of form and style, we were greatly handicapped by having no proper models of the kind we needed badly, that is, some authoritative poet attempting to deal with contemporary problems in contemporary style. If our poetry had been at full flood, rather than at an ebb, from, say, 1900 onwards, such a poet would have existed and the change would not have appeared so strange when it came.[5]

No one caused more surprise and controversy than Seán Ó Ríordáin, born on the third of December 1916 in the West Cork semi-Gaeltacht of Baile Bhuirne.

Unfortunately, illness and the threat of illness were never far from Ó Ríordáin's life: when the poet was only ten years old, for example, his father died from tuberculosis, a disease which claimed many lives in his family and surrounding area. It was impressed on Ó Ríordáin at a very early stage, therefore, just how thin a hold humankind can have on a life that itself can be prone to major upheavals. Ó Ríordáin himself was soon forced, for example, to take extended periods of leave from school[6] and, later, from his clerical job in Cork City Hall, due to tuberculosis. His life from then on was plagued by illness, leading to financial worry and increasing loneliness. At times, his affliction, and particularly that of others, blackened his vision. A diary entry for April 1940 tells of a meeting with a young woman suffering from TB whose visibly imminent death hurt him into despair and rage: 'poverty is largely responsible for this disease. And people are afraid that Hitler will destroy this

---

A. de Blacam, *Gaelic Literature Surveyed*, 2nd edn. (Dublin: Talbot Press, 1929, 1973), 387–405 (p. 387).

[4] Ó Tuama, S., 'Seán Ó Ríordáin', in S. Mac Réamoinn (ed.), *The Pleasures of Gaelic Poetry* (London: Allen Lane, Penguin Books, 1982), 129–41 (p. 129).

[5] Quoted and translated by Greene, D., in *Writing in Irish Today*, Irish Life and Culture Series, XVIII (Cork: Mercier Press, 1972), 39–40.

[6] 'I suffered pneumonia when I was thirteen in Baile Bhuirne—three times in succession [. . .] That's when this solitariness began, perhaps.' Quoted in S. Ó Mórdha (ed.), 'Seán Ó Ríordáin ag caint le Seán Ó Mórdha', *Scríobh 3* (Dublin: An Clóchomhar Tta, 1978), 163–84 (p. 170).

civilisation! If he does it won't be soon enough. Puffed-up Christianity with no conscience!'[7]

One cannot exaggerate the toll of physical suffering on Ó Ríordáin's life: 'was there ever a heart as hate-filled as mine? If I could sit outside, this feeling would go. It's unhealthy to be hemmed in like this; spaciousness is healthy.'[8] Physically fenced in by TB, he was also to some extent socially fenced out by its taboo at the time.

Ó Ríordáin began writing both poetry and his diary in 1935. Writing, for him, sprang from a natural life-source, and constituted a defiantly creative act, a stand against the negative forces of pain, death, and oblivion. However, he had published only two books of poetry by the time he gave up his job in 1965 due to ill-health. There are several reasons why Ó Ríordáin was not a prolific writer: illness; severe criticism from certain outspoken figures (including, notably, Máire Mhac an tSaoi) which shook his confidence in himself, his aesthetic and, most detrimentally, his ability to use Irish; also, in later life, he channelled much creative energy into journalism, writing regularly for the *Irish Times* from 1967 to 1975. Looking at his work in its entirety, one may also suspect that the enormous effort that went into his first (huge) collection, *Eireaball Spideoige* (1952), considerably drained his pool of inspiration.[9]

Nevertheless, Ó Ríordáin is, as Heaney has stated, 'a significant voice in modern Irish writing'[10] who lived to see his achievement recognized when, for example, he was awarded an Honorary D. Litt. from the National University of Ireland in April 1976. He died from TB a year later in St Stephen's Hospital, Cork—a loss which was lamented by Seán Ó Tuama as that of 'a modern Gaelic poet who, more than any other, managed to combine the vision of European writers from Baudelaire to Beckett with the Irish language tradition—the result of which was poetry unequalled in the language for hundreds of years'.[11]

Ó Ríordáin was certainly a central figure in the new wave of Irish

---

[7] Seán Ó Coileáin, *Seán Ó Ríordáin: Beatha agus Saothar* (Dublin: An Clóchomhar Tta, 1982, 1985), 125. All prose quotations (in English) from this book are my translations.

[8] Ibid. 274.   [9] Ibid. 266.

[10] Seamus Heaney, 'Forked Tongues, Céilís and Incubators', in *Fortnight*, 197 (September 1983), 113–16 (p. 115).

[11] Ó Tuama, Seán, 'Seán Ó Ríordáin agus an Nuafhilíocht', *Studia Hibernica*, 13 (1973), 100–67 (p. 167).

language poets this century. Declan Kiberd refers to him as 'far and away the leading poet of the period' when modern poetry in Irish began to flower.[12] Yet, it is my contention that there was, for Ó Ríordáin, a price to pay for attempting to span the national and international (and also the physical and metaphysical) elements and influences in his work. I agree with Ó Tuama that his combination of these is at the source of his success but only because it provided the necessary conflict or set of contraries which made (as Blake has argued) progression possible. This left the poet feeling lost on home ground, utterly divided, not possessing the best of both worlds but considering himself to be, like one of Muldoon's 'Mules', 'neither one thing nor the other';[13] or, as Ó Ríordáin himself once grimly described, a 'neamh-fhile ag neamh-scrí neamh-fhilíochta trí neamh-Ghaeilge do neamh-phobal'.[14]

1.1 *EIREABALL SPIDEOIGE* (1952)

Ó Ríordáin's oeuvre contains few homages. He eulogizes *things* in 'Cláirseach Shean na nGnáthrud'/The Ancient Harp of Common Things (*ES* p. 48), Peig Sayers (in passing) in 'Na Blascaodaí'/The Blaskets (*ES* p. 94), and the stud stallion 'Tulyar' (*B* p. 29)—the latter only for the purposes of satirizing Ireland in the unbecoming times. His two main eulogies, however, are for the diverse figures of Daniel Corkery and James Joyce.

> Do Dhomhnall Ó Corcora
>
> Éirigh agus can ár mbuíochas croí dhó,
> Do mhúin sé an tslí,
> Do dhúisigh eilit ár bhfilíochta
> I gcoillte blian.
>
> Do dhein dá anam cluas le héisteacht,
> Is d'éist gan trua
> (Dó féin, ná d'éinne mhúnlaigh véarsa),
> Gur thit anuas
>
> De phlimp ar urlár gallda an lae seo
> Eoghan béal binn,

---

[12] Kiberd, D., 'Introduction', *An Crann faoi Bhlath/The Flowering Tree*, ed. by Declan Kiberd and Gabriel Fitzmaurice (Dublin: Wolfhound Press, 1991), xxxiv.

[13] Muldoon, Paul, 'Mules', *Mules* (London: Faber and Faber, 1977), 52.

[14] 'An unpoet unwriting unpoetry in unGaelic to an unpeople.' Quoted in *Cnuasach 1966*, ed. by Breandan S. Mac Aodha (Dublin: Scepter, 1966), 79.

Aindrias mac Craith, Seán Clárach, Aodhgán,
Cioth filí.

Do leag méar chiúin ar chuislinn Aodhgáin,
Do chreid a luas,
Do gheal an lá ar intinn aosta
Dúinn ba dhual.

D'fhill sé leo an bhuíon filí seo
An staighre suas,
Is do shiúil sé bóithre lán de Mhuimhnigh,
É féin 's Eoghan Rua.

Do ghoid sé uathu cluas an chine,
Cluas spailpín,
Níor fhullaing dán ar bith a thuilleadh
Ach gin gan teimheal.

Braithim é gan sos ag éisteacht
Mar athchoinsias;
Tá smacht a chluaise ar luth mo véarsa,
Trom an chuing.

Tráthnóna na teangan in Éirinn,
Is an oíche ag bogthitim mar scéal,
D'éist sé le creagar i véarsa,
Is do chuala croí cine soiléir.[15]

This poem, it must be stated, is a very public panegyric written to commemorate Corkery. Contrastingly, Ó Ríordáin's diaries show him as not always grateful for 'Korkery's' interference. In January 1948, the poet was 'seeking a gospel that will refute'[16] the professor and complaining that the latter's insistence on the traditional as opposed to the personal note has left him 'tormented'. Reading *The Hidden Ireland*[17] makes Ó Ríordáin's own self-doubt spread like a cancer: 'I'm neither Christian nor Gael, Irish nor English. I don't go to Mass or the theatre. That's my life. Perhaps Prof. Ó Corcora is right. Lack of tradition. Too much ego.'[18] He begins to conceive of his writing as 'very thin', not earthed in the actual 'rich soil' of tradition like that of Máirtín Ó Direáin to whom he felt inferior at times.[19] Despite the poet's own fears,

---

[15] *ES* pp. 51–2. Translation A in Appendix.
[16] Ó Coileáin, *Seán Ó Ríordáin*, 220.
[17] Corkery, D., *The Hidden Ireland: a Study of Gaelic Munster in the Eighteenth Century* (Dublin: Gill and Mac Millan, 1924, 1970).
[18] Ó Coileáin, *Seán Ó Ríordáin*, 221.   [19] Ibid., 314–15.

however, his biographer Seán Ó Coileáin regards the final quatrain of the poem in praise of Corkery as a superb 'example of the two traditions uniting. A sensitive, perspicacious account of an English-language book [*The Hidden Ireland*] in the terminology of the ancients.'[20]

Nevertheless, later references to Corkery in Ó Ríordáin's diaries turn to bitter resentment on the grounds that the former set unworkable limits for the writing of modern poetry in Irish:

Corkery told me once not to write a single line that wasn't based on a line of the old poetry. But what can one do when things outside the tradition have gone into one—when the person is wider than the tradition? [. . .] It's OK staying within the understanding of Irish but it's something else to leave some of yourself out of the equation. Nativeness ['an dúchas'] must be broadened however dangerous that is.[21]

Ó Ríordáin also accused Corkery of distracting him from forming his own version of Irish which could have helped him to be more true to himself. Nativeness, for Ó Ríordáin, was more a state of *being* than of *becoming*: 'as for being native ['dúchasach'], it is without your own knowing it, if you like, in spite of yourself, you'll be native [. . .] Nativeness is rooted in life. It's not an overcoat or a kilt.'[22] The poet argues that it is necessary to *be* what you are and move on, to 'go' yourself and not to be held or always harping back. Corkery, therefore, is deemed guilty of leading Ó Ríordáin into the greatest possible sin against his aesthetic and religious philosophy of 'selv-ing' à la Gerard Manley Hopkins and Joyce.[23] Indeed, Ó Ríordáin even believed that Corkery suffered from this inability to *be* himself:

Daniel Corkery from Anglo-Ireland, always on about a nativeness he never had. But is it really a question of nativeness? It's a question of lack. It's not nativeness that Daniel Korkery wants but Daniel Korkery himself. That's the Hidden Ireland—namely Daniel Korkery himself.[24]

By 1960, the hand that he had earlier eulogized as having amplified the pulse of Gaelic poetry had apparently killed it: 'Poetry was being

---

[20] Ó Coileáin, *Seán Ó Ríordáin*, 226.
[21] Ibid., 210.   [22] Ibid., 314.
[23] See Hopkins, Gerard Manley, 'As Kingfishers Catch Fire', *Selected Poems of Gerard Manley Hopkins* ed, by J. Reeves, 5th edn. (London: Heinemann, 1959), 52; and Joyce, J., *Portrait of the Artist as a Young Man*. See *The Essential James Joyce* ed. by H. Levin (London: Jonathan Cape, 1950) 176–367 (p. 327 and p. 361).
[24] Ó Coileáin, *Seán Ó Ríordáin*, 258.

written in Irish until Dónall Ó Corcora laid his dead hand upon it.'[25]

Behind all this scapegoating of Corkery, however, is Ó Ríordáin's anger at himself for ever heeding the purist, 'fíor-Gael' contingent, a weakness which confounded his ability and duty to be native, honest, and true to himself as was the prostitute whom he praised for such in his minor eulogy 'Do Striapach' (*TÉB* p. 50). In Ó Ríordáin's view, a better guide than Corkery for the path of self-determination was James Joyce, as his most remarkable praise-poem shows:

Joyce

Chuireas a thuairisc im aigne—
A raibh de im chuimhne scagaithe—
Tá sé ina chuid díom chomh dearfa
Le soiscéal Chríost nó an aibítir.

Tá a chéimseata sho-aitheanta
Ag eúiclidiú m'aigne—
Ní hé a thuilleadh é chomh fada liom,
Is mise é ó alpas é.

Ag triopallacht a fhriotalú táim treascartha,
An fhoirmiúlacht laideanta,
Ní mé mé le linn dom machnamh air,
Ach é siúd—tá lagú ann.

Do chomhraiceas le focail i bhfarradh leis,
Tá sé 'om thionlacan—an t-aingealdeamhan:
Scigshagart é ag rá scigaifrinn,
In éide scigaifrinn ifrinn.

Eiriceacht an creideamh a theagasc sé.
Mhúin sé na deich scigaitheanta,
Droim ar ais a ghairm scoil',
Is chothaigh claoine chleasaiceach.

Ciotarúnta a rún is a asarlaíocht,
Géill don bhfocal ainglí,
Loirg scéimh i salachar,
Is coisric cac le Rabelais.

Goid gach bob as leabharaibh,
Aimsigh feall fuaraigeanta,

Bí id Shátan Beannaithe,
Is coinnealbháigh an farasbarr.

Ba mhó de chleas ná pearsa é,
Foclóir bhain geit as gramadach,
Samhlaíocht a mhair ar neamhshamhlaíocht,
Fuair seilbh ar scigabdaine.[26]

This poem appeared in the 1970s at the end of Ó Ríordáin's career and proves his statement that 'the worst mistake Daniel Corkery ever made was to say that James Joyce's work wouldn't last.'[27] It reveals how essential Joyce's 'gospel' was for Ó Ríordáin. For example, part of Ó Ríordáin's own Joycean inheritance was the religious language of Catholicism which he applied to art. Following Joyce's example, Ó Ríordáin used his theological reading and religious language in his own way so that, as with Joyce, 'Catholicism [. . .] is at the source of his symbolic vision and its *imaginative constructs*.'[28] Ó Ríordáin did not provide a dictionary for *his* development of the language of Catholicism but one reason for the long introduction in *Eireaball Spideoige* was undoubtedly to explain his own combination of theology with aesthetics.

In the introduction, Ó Ríordáin inquires into the nature of poetry. In short, his view is that poetry occurs when one is transformed by something else outside of oneself. What is required, he tells us, is the open mind of a child whose vision is fresh and for whom the world appears so new that s/he can be swallowed into the atmosphere of an experience, being or thing such as, for example, a horse: 'the child tries to *be* a horse, to say the prayer of the horse, out of sheer isolation' (*ES* p. 10). Could such a child write honestly a poem from this experience or *epiphany*, it would contain the 'prayer' of the child, the horse, and of the poem itself, all combined into some purer form than is normally 'tasted' (a favourite word of Ó Ríordáin's, in Irish 'blaisigh') or uttered. Ó Ríordáin seems to share the view of the Russian Formalist critic Viktor Shklovsky that literature necessarily combats habitualization and algebrization which 'devour works, clothes, furniture, one's wife, and the fear of war' until 'we see the object as though it were enveloped in

---

[26] *TÉB* pp. 21–2. Translation B in Appendix.
[27] Ó Ríordáin, S., *Mise* (Dublin: Arts Block, UCD, 1987), 19.
[28] Schlossman, B., *Joyce's Catholic Comedy of Language* (University of Wisconsin Press, 1985), xi (my emphasis).

a sack. We know what it is by its configuration, but we see only its silhouette.'[29]

Ó Ríordáin had a further method for writing which he termed 'iarracht réasúnta' (the reasoned or conscious attempt) to step outside of the self into the unknown, the darkness, to find (God willing) some thing there that would make the seeker appreciate how wonderful a 'thing' is. Ó Ríordáin called this discovery or rediscovery method 'glanadh' or 'athnuachaint'/'cleansing [. . .] renewing or restoring' (*ES* p. 12). Again his ideas mirror those of Shklovsky who said that all poetry contains 'material obviously created to remove the automatism of perception' through, for example, *ostranenie*/defamiliarization.[30]

One example from Ó Ríordáin's oeuvre is 'Cláirseach Shean na nGnáthrud'/The Ancient Harp of Common Things (*ES* p. 48) in which he celebrates ordinary things such as a hen-call, a cat warming itself on a hearth, and pins-and-needles. This alertness to, and affection for, the otherness of common things calls to mind the poem 'Kerr's Ass' by his contemporary, Patrick Kavanagh:

> The straw-stuffed straddle, the broken breeching
> With bits of bull-wire tied;
>
> The winkers that had no choke-band,
> The collar and the reins . . .
> In Ealing Broadway, London Town
> I name their several names
>
> Until a world comes to life . . .[31]

Both Ó Ríordáin's and Kavanagh's poem share the same risk (trying to render extraordinary the ultraordinary) but also the same delight which sets 'the God of imagination waking' from the fog of dulling and contemptuous familiarity into a freshly savoured re-acquaintance.

Ó Ríordáin also insisted that tradition was a necessary requirement of poetry. For him, tradition ensures that a poem is formally precise and native to the language in which it is written. Yet, to be native does not necessarily mean to be insular, to dam the ebb and flow of migratory influences. Therefore, along with Irish literature in both languages, he read widely from abroad including English, American, and Latin poets

[29] Shklovsky, V., 'Art as Technique', in R. Rylance (ed.), *Debating Texts*, 48–56 (pp. 48–9). [30] Ibid., 54.
[31] Kavanagh, P., *Collected Poems* (London: MacGibbon and Kee, 1964), 135.

such as Eliot, Hopkins, Hardy, cummings, Frost, and Virgil. At the time of his first volume's publication, he did not fear any ill-effects of his bilingual reading and background on his ability (or right) to write in Irish. He was confident that if a poet was 'praying' in a Gaelic 'temple', s/he could only stir to life a 'Gaelic' poem (*ES* p. 25).

However, some conservative critics worried about possible 'muddying of the linguistic waters'.[32] These included Máire Mhac an tSaoi who wrote at the time that Ó Ríordáin's language 'wasn't Gaelic at all' and that 'as long as his Irish is stuffed with English, he'll only have a kind of Esperanto!'[33] Could he possibly have anticipated such criticisms in his 'Apologia'?

Do chuir an saol thar maoil,	*Life was overflowing*
Bhí an uile ní ina chúr,	*and everything foaming,*
Den lacht do dheineas im	*I made butter of the cream,*
Chun ná raghadh aon bhainne amú.	*no waste would I leave.*
Gidh olc an chuigeann ním	*However badly I churn,*
Is annamh saol a chrú,	*to milk life is rare,*
Is bíonn éileamh ar gach im	*and every butter is needed*
Le linn an drochshéasúir.	*in the poor season.* (*ES* p. 27)

The question of strict adherence to Gaelic tradition versus an individual by-any-means-necessary approach continued to pester Ó Ríordáin and was no doubt exacerbated by the extreme sensitivity with which any innovation was greeted. In *Scríobh 2* (1975), he talked of wholeheartedly following the traditional line in his teens and early twenties but then, to his surprise, acquiring a kind of freedom of speech and rejecting traditional regulations for poetry. No sooner had he done so than he wished to return again to tradition:

Is mar sin a bhíonn an duine; anonn is anall ag leanúint a phearsantacht féin scaitheamh, agus scaitheamh eile ag leanúint an traidisiúin. Pé ceann a leanann sé bíonn an ceann eile á thionlacan chomh maith. 'Sé tionlacan na n-óinseach é.[34]

---

[32] A phrase used more positively by Mary O'Connor, 'Lashings of the Mother Tongue: Nuala Ní Dhomhnaill's Anarchic Laughter', in T. O'Connor (ed.), *The Comic Tradition in Irish Women Writers* (Gainesville: University Press of Florida, 1996), 149–70 (pp. 152–3).

[33] Ó Coileáin, *Seán Ó Ríordáin*, 241.

[34] Ibid., 212. 'That's what people are like; sometimes following the Self, sometimes following tradition. Whichever one you choose, the other one accompanies you. It's the fool's escort' (Seán Ó Ríordáin).

Not so much foolish, Ó Ríordáin's personality and loyalties were such that he felt himself to be pointed and pulled initially in two directions and later apart into many strands. His poetry charts a career zigging and zagging between Corkery and Joycery.

Conflict between self and tradition or convention extends beyond writing into day-to-day and spiritual life. This conflict affected Ó Ríordáin keenly as man and poet, and constituted the most important theme of (and source for) his first collection, *Eireaball Spideoige.* Many poems in this collection dramatize the choices and difficulties which Ó Ríordáin felt he faced in life, especially regarding his relationship with poetry, the community, and Christianity.

'Ualach na Beatha'/Life's Burden (*ES* p. 33) shows Ó Ríordáin looking for signs as to how to live. First, he consults 'writers' but finds (with perhaps his two main influences, Joyce and Corkery, in mind) that the path which one faction/'drong' rejects, another recommends. He tries to judge for himself only to find that each way is clouded over and that it is only in passing through that the nature of one's choice will be revealed. The poem is reminiscent of Frost's 'The Road Not Taken' except that in Frost's poem the roads offer little to choose from in appearance.[35] In Ó Ríordáin's poem the more travelled road is the most attractive. However, in his role as poet-cum-scholastic philosopher, he knows that the lonelier road of abstinence and contemplation could lead him to a truer appreciation of the form (in Plato's sense) of beauty than the 'illusion' of flesh ever could. The poem ends neither with Frost's contentment nor with Eliot's regret at missing the 'rose-garden',[36] but with the poet crippled by doubt, indecision, and 'lack of courage'. The final image of Ó Ríordáin, exhausted and fenced out, painfully characterizes the uncertainty which hounded him.

Ó Ríordáin's record of his pilgrimage to 'Cnoc Mellerí'/Mount Mellery (*ES* p. 64) which as Kiberd has justly stated to some extent anticipates 'Heaney's "Station Island" in tone and theme by decades',[37] is characterized by paradox, questioning, switches of viewpoint, and a generally restless spirit which echoes metaphysical poets such as Donne

---

[35] Frost, *Complete Poems of Robert Frost*, 7th edn. (London: Jonathan Cape, 1966), 129.

[36] Eliot, T. S., 'Burnt Norton', in *Collected Poems: 1909–1962*, 2nd edn. (London: Faber and Faber, 1974), 189.

[37] Kiberd, Introduction, in D. Kiberd and G. Fitzmaurice (eds.), *An Crann faoi Bhlath/The Flowering Tree* (Dublin: Wolfhound Press, 1991), xxxi.

and Herbert. The tension in the poem derives from Ó Ríordáin's guilt-ridden belief that the worldly self is necessarily a wicked Caliban whose lusts must be purged like the 'laethanta ba leapacha de shonaschlúmh an tsaoil/is dreancaidí na drúise iontu ag preabarnaigh ina mílte'.[38] However, the poet is only part-puritan: he first views the monks as living a pure, sheet-white life ('chomh bán le braitlín') while that of the pilgrims is beetle-black ('chomh dubh leis an daol') but he later refers to the cloister as an ever-praying graveyard ('reilig ag síorphaidreoireacht'); the monks' way of life appears to him as an insult to God ('masla ar choimirce Dé') where Death is freezing over life ('an bás ag cur seaca ar bheatha') and is the Abbot whom they serve; he even recognizes that the end of such abstinence and servitude could mean 'charging the birds with lust/and filling the world with shame',[39] and laments that the young novice will never taste 'tréanmheisce mná'/the intoxicating power of woman or the freedom of a mind like Dante's which caught a vision of Heaven when the angels landed in the form of verses/'nuair a thuirling na hainglí i riocht véarsaí'.

The poem's perspective changes again, however, from that of the 'ego a bhí uaibhreach easumhal'/arrogant and rebellious ego when the poet-speaker reflects that the 'tréad' or community is worth more than the individual or 'duine' and that his own life has, far from being more productive, been an ugly 'waste'/'fásach', 'díomhaointeas'. When he looks again at the cloister-life, he immediately (with his allusion to Dante still in mind) recognizes it as a 'poem' with 'metre, purity, profundity, vigour, and rhyme'.[40] Yet his conversion to the Latin dance ('rinceas sa Laidin') after confession is brief. Soon religion again feels like a rope around his and the 'eunuch-priest's' neck ('sagart do ghlao-fainn coillteán'). The chain of beads clasped in his sweaty hand with which he had earlier clung on to faith is dramatically transformed in the end to 'a poem-straw in a drowning man's grip on Mellerí/greim fhir bháite ar Mhellerí an súgán seo filíochta'. Ó Ríordáin's obvious attempt at resolving the conflict between the worldly instinct for personal self-determination and the felt need to become a common servant of God within organized religion ends, as Seán Ó Tuama noted, in greater

---

[38] 'The feather-bed days of life/when fleas of lust leapt in thousands'. From 'Cnoc Mellerí', *ES* p. 64.

[39] 'Do chuirfeadh coir na drúise in intinn na n-óan / Is do líonfadh le náire an domhan.' 'Cnoc Mellerí', *ES* p. 66.

[40] 'D'aithníos dán ar an dtoirt,/Meadaracht, glaine, doimhinbhrí is comhfhuaim'. Ibid.

doubt than ever. The poet-speaker remains characteristically torn between spiritual independence and traditional, communal belief.

Ironically, Ó Ríordáin's poetic imagination seems to flag when he thinks that he has resolved his spiritual conflict and proclaims faith or obedience. For example, some of the physical details in 'Oilithreacht fám Anam'/A Pilgrimage Through My Soul (*ES* p. 70) referring to the poet's metaphorical possession by demons of knowledge, guilt or sin are graphically conveyed: in one line the devil is pushing his feet through the poet's veins to wear them as trousers. Strong physical symbols are employed to express total revulsion:

Mar ghadhar ag déanamh caca	*Like a dog shiting*
Ar fud an tí istoíche,	*at night all over the house,*
Nó mar sheilmide ag taisteal	*or a slug trailing along—*
Do bhréan an fios mo smaointe.	*knowledge sullied my thoughts.*

One is convinced that Ó Ríordáin really experienced feelings which require such diabolical force in their retelling, yet when it comes to the side of the angels, the language becomes characteristically, but unconvincingly, airy:

Is fánfaidh aingeal óg id chroí	*A young angel will stay in your heart*
Ag iompar ceoil,	*bearing [gestating] music,*
Is chífir aingeal i ngach gnaoi	*and you'll see an angel in every shape*
Go deo na ndeor.	*[and/or form] forever and ever.*

(*ES* p. 73)

Together with these weaker lines, the last section of the poem relies on biblical sounding exhortations: 'Deamhan a rá, sin deamhan a chloí'/to name a devil is to overcome him. Are the devils more convincing in this poem because, in truth, Ó Ríordáin knew more of spiritual suffering and torment than he did of salvation and peace? In *Filí faoi Sceimhle*, Seán Ó Tuama dislikes Ó Ríordáin's philosophical poems in general and believes that 'the strongest proof of Ó Ríordáin's sensitive and fitful disbelief in his own philosophy is that his best poems are those which speak out from the depths of the abyss'.[41]

'Oileán agus Oileán Eile'/One Island and Another (*ES* p. 78) is a much stronger religious or philosophical poem. Here, Corkery's threads of 'creideamh', 'náisiúnachas', 'talamh'/religion, nationality, and land are

---

[41] Ó Tuama, S., *Filí faoi Scéimhle: Seán Ó Ríordáin agus Aogán Ó Rathaille* (Dublin: Oifig an tSoláthair, 1978), 77.

as inextricably knotted together as Joyce's 'language, nationality, and religion'.[42] The poem is successful, I believe, because abstract thoughts are 'earthed in the actual' (as Heaney once said of Kavanagh's best work[43]):

> Tá Sasanach ag iascaireacht sa loch,
> Tá an fhírinne rólom ar an oileán,
> Ach raghad i measc na gcuimhne agus na gcloch,
> Is nífead le mórurraim mo dhá láimh.
>
> *An Englishman is fishing on the loch.*
> *Truth is too plain on the island.*
> *But I will go among memory and rocks*
> *and wash with reverence my hands.* (*ES* p. 78)

Ó Ríordáin is almost always more positive about the inanimate and non-human, and it is by scanning the physical world that the spiritual and artistic inspiration and enlightenment he seeks come to him on St Barra's Island:

> An ceol a ráid sé leis an mbith   *The music he gave to the world*
> Dob shin oileán an éin,   *was that bird's island.*
> Níl éinne beo nach bhfuair oileán,   *No-one is born without an island.*
> Is trua a chás má thréig.   *Pity any who desert.* (*ES* p. 80)

The poet goes on to employ ancient technical skill to strengthen the litany of his deeply held convictions in almost overpowering language and rhythm. Many of the ideas come from the philosophical writings of St Augustine who had his own guilt-ridden reasons for espousing them:

> Mar níl ionat ach eascaine   *You are only a lie*
> A dúirt an saol,   *the world gave out;*
> Níl ionat ach cabaireacht   *you're just gibberish*
> Ó bhéal go béal: *from mouth to mouth;*
> Cé gur cumadh tú id phaidir gheal   *though Jesus sang you*
> Ar bhéal Mhic Dé   *like a prayer,*
> Do scoiltis-se do thusa ceart   *you lost your self*
> Le dúil sa tsaol,   *in worldly desire;*
> Ach is paidir fós an tusa sin   *but that true self*
> Ar oileán séin,   *stayed on an isle*

---

[42] Kiberd, D., 'Seán Ó Ríordáin—File Angla-Éireannach?', *Idir Dhá Chultúr* (Dublin: Coiscéim, 1993), 261–87 (p. 266).

[43] Heaney, S., 'From Monaghan to the Grand Canal: The Poetry of Patrick Kavanagh', *Preoccupations: Selected Prose 1968–78* (London: Faber and Faber, 1980), 115–30 (p. 119).

A fhán go ciúin ag cogarnach   *whispering softly*
Ar bheolaibh Dé   *through God's smile*
Nuair do rincis-se go macnasach   *while you danced crudely*
Ar ghob an tsaoil.   *on the snout of life.*

                                                (*ES* p. 81)

Preaching done, Ó Ríordáin returns to the physical presence of the island which again provides him with the signs he seeks: in the stirring imagery of the trees twisted like 'a body being burned alive', he finds the image of Gandhi, of Barra's struggle with his earthly and spiritual self, of rebellion and service, of Barra's 'island'. However, he ends the poem with an ironic promise to return to worldliness and concealment like everyone else; after all, 'tá an fhírinne ró-lom ar an oileán'/truth is too plain on the island.

    Ó Ríordáin's struggle with orthodox beliefs makes for a great poem. The problem is that the reader's enjoyment of the poem may be partly diminished or increased depending on his/her ability to sympathize with such beliefs. Moreover, the most effective passages are not the ones which seek to chastise and convert but those with strong physical metaphors such as the lurid 'scríbhinn seo na gcrann'/writing of the tree-shapes denoting the individual's struggle with the self of God and the self of Self.

    The cocktail of themes swirling and heaving in this poem are made all the more potent by the positioning of one self awkwardly alongside a contrasting other: the 'Sasanach'/Englishman who has a right, it seems, to fish on the island but for whom the place may mean less. Who is this Sasanach? He is not just distinguished from but linked with Ó Ríordáin. They both fish for nourishment of a kind: one, perhaps, just for physical, the other for spiritual, aesthetic, and native nourishment. The Sasanach may also represent a part of Ó Ríordáin himself: the part that stands at life's surface with 'bréithre gan bhrí'/spiritless words, buried thoughts ('thuirling clúmh liath ar mo smaointe . . .'), a tired heart/'tuirse im chroí', hiding truth like everyone/'ag ceilt na fírinne mar chách', babbling on in life/'ag cabaireacht sa tsaol'. The poem shows that one has to plumb the depths of, and perhaps pass through, another element to reach one's true spiritual, national, and linguistic island or selfhood. An abiding image of Ó Ríordáin's concern is to be found in the

scríbhinn bhreacaithe ar phar   *writing jotted on a page*
Is scríbhinn eile trasna air.   *and other writing over it.*

                                                  (*ES* p. 82)

These lines could refer to translation or to the eclipse of one language by another. In any case, Ó Ríordáin's faith and solidarity always lay with the fundamental but obscured language of the source and its message: 'Níl éinne beo nach bhfuair oileán,/Is trua a chás má thréig.'[44]

War between the independent self and that following convention or tradition naturally extends beyond the spiritual sphere into the area of how one lives, especially in relation to others. For Ó Ríordáin this question was further complicated by his being a poet. He would have agreed with Kavanagh that 'a poet is never one of the people. He is detached, remote, and the life of small-time dances and talk about football would not be for him. He might take part but could not belong.'[45] Ó Ríordáin saw the role of the poet in even more traditional terms, believing it to retain some of the ancient, male, priest-like qualities of the 'file'/seer:

> Ní fada bhíonn duine ag cumadh filíochta
> Go scarann le daoscar na céille,
> Is gabhann sé go huaigneach mar gabhadh leis na cianta
> Le tuairim is dínit na cléire.
>
> *Not long into the making of poetry,*
> *one departs from the sensible mass;*
> *and wanders lonely as for centuries*
> *with the air and grace of the poet-caste.   (ES p. 35)*

A very different view on the subject of the individual vis à vis the community is found in 'Saoirse'/Freedom (*ES* p. 100), one of the few of his own works Ó Ríordáin confessed to liking: 'má tá tabhacht le rud ar bith dár scríobhas tá tábhacht leis seo. Bhíos riamh i gcás idir an dá chomhairle seo, i.e. an duine aonar versus an pobal.'[46] In this poem, Ó Ríordáin speaks as though he has spent some time on the path of self, that of the egotistical artist building his own false dreams and rejecting shared systems of thought or belief; now he wants to return to the common path which he trusts (at this point) will bring comfort and order. He hardly convinces the reader, however, that within servitude

---

[44] 'No-one was born without an island,/Pity any who desert.' From 'Oileán agus Oileán Eile', *ES* p. 80.

[45] Kavanagh, P., *Collected Prose*, 2nd edn. (London: Martin Brian and O'Keefe, 1973), 15.

[46] 'If anything I have written has been of importance, it is this. The problem of relating the individual with the crowd has always been a concern of mine.' See Ó Tuairisc, E. (ed.), *Rogha an Fhile* (Dublin: Goldsmith Press, 1974), 42–7 (p. 47). Includes Ó Ríordáin's own translation.

there is only freedom ('níl laistigh d'aon daoirse/Ach saoirse on daoirse sin') as he argues in the later, companion poem 'Daoirse'/Unfreedom (*B* p. 27). Here, in 'Saoirse'/Freedom, there doesn't seem much of a choice between 'binibshaoirse'/venom-liberty and the 'bridled', 'copied', 'co-' or 'stub-thoughts' ('macsmaointe', 'snabsmaointe', etc.) which the poet-speaker still less than humbly strains to embrace. Ó Ríordáin once again winds up restless and exhausted as at the end of 'Ualach na Beatha' and 'Cnoc Mellerí' with only a poem-straw in his drowning man's grip on faith, salvation, community.

Were one to divide the poems of *Eireaball Spideoige* according to subject matter, by far the largest group would be about poetry itself. Apart from the introduction on the subject, poems repeatedly raise questions such as: what is poetry? how do you make a poem? what does making poems make of you?

Ó Ríordáin found the making of poetry a paradoxical affair. He looked upon his poems as his 'clann véarsaí', his family of verse (*ES* p. 26) which he bore like a mother but which took masculine strength to bring forth from 'memory and rock' (*ES* p. 80). Some poems on the subject are just self-dramatizations of the poet at work, glad of inspir-ation in 'Filíocht an Phíopa'/Pipe-poetry (*ES* p. 30), of respite and release in 'Sos' (*ES* p. 46) which calls to mind the 'dance at Billy Brennan's barn' which Kavanagh will not attend in 'Inniskeen Road: July Evening'.[47] Occasionally, Ó Ríordáin even shares some of Kavanagh's impatience with his consolatory but lonely sovereignty over 'every blooming thing'. In 'Na hÓinmhidí'/The Fools, the craft seems to have cut the poet off from communion with others:

Is an óigbhean dár thugas síorghean	*the girl I loved eternally—*
Níl baint aici siúd le filíocht	*poetry is not for her,*
Ach tagadh na focail isteach	*but let the words enter*
Is suídís i bhfoirm véarsaí.	*and rest in the form of verse.*

(*ES* p. 88)

A further paradox of poetry, for Ó Ríordáin, is that it is difficult to make but easy to destroy. In 'An Peaca'/The Sin (*ES* p. 41), the 'réal na gealaí'/sixpence-moon, or 'anam dea-chumtha na hoíche'/well-formed soul of the night, slips 'go mall, mall, faitíosach'/gently and shyly into a 'scamallsparán'/cloud-purse or poem-shape but the fragile vision is shat-tered by a vulgar roar from a crowd (of critics?) turning poem to prose

---

[47] Kavanagh, *Collected Poems*, 19.

and leaving a 'sin' on the night's soul. It is no wonder that Ó Ríordáin saw the destruction of poetry as sin: for him, poetry is a matter of 'Heavenly Chance' like the trick of light in the poem 'Tionóisc Ó Neamh' (*ES* p. 32); it is something handed down from the heart of each generation of one's people like the 'milking of words' he learnt from his Kerry grand-father's milking of cows ('Dán'/Poem, or Destiny, *ES* p. 113); it is, or should be, something native, natural, true, and essential like the pure 'water-speech' of the river in 'Éist le Fuaim na hAbhann'/Listen to the River-sound (*ES* p. 47); above all, poetry for Ó Ríordáin is 'a poem-straw in a drowning man's grip', his last defence against life's confusion pulling him apart by the strands in him of believer and non-believer, Gael and Gall, free individual and citizen. It is the wisp that links him to the tradition in which he recurrently feels most hopeful of finding his place, himself, and maybe even his immortality: the tradition of Gaelic poetry: 'A Sheanfhilí, Múinídh Dom Glao'/Old Poets, Teach Me the Call (*ES* p. 36).

In moments of desperate insecurity, Ó Ríordáin seems to veer closer to the prescripts of Corkery than the example of Joyce. Yet, it is my hypothesis that he could or would never entirely wash Joyce out of his system, the 'angel-demon' whom he had 'swallowed whole' and who was as much part of him 'as the alphabet and gospels' (*TÉB* p. 21). Even in the poem 'Na Blascaodaí'/The Blaskets (*ES* p. 94) where Ó Ríordáin raises a toast to the islandmen, he does so in Joycean language when he cheers them for keeping alive the mind or 'aigne' left 'paralysed' in books. Ironically, even his most ostensibly traditional material such as this *unfinished*, bardic address does not constitute Ó Ríordáin's best service to tradition. The latter he extended, and served better, by providing new and interesting work 'at a tangent', in Heaney's phrase.[48]

Some of Ó Ríordáin's best poems occur when he ceases to agonize over his religious and poetic selves, lets his 'saoirse'/freedom spill over the margins of his 'daoirse'/confinement and gets on with the business of writing, of falling 'under the spell of something else' outside himself (*ES* p. 23). *Eireaball Spideoige*'s introduction states that the latter is a requirement of poetry, and his diary, as far back as April 1949, makes it a requirement for life and sanity:

---

[48] Heaney, S., 'Station Island', *New Selected Poems 1966–1987* (London: Faber and Faber, 1990), 163–93 (p. 193). Heaney is an example of yet another Irish poet who claims to have been raised under the uplifting thumb of Joyce. See Heaney, 'Forked Tongues, Céilís and Incubators', in *Fortnight* No. 197 (September 1983), 113–16.

Féachaim ar bhuidéal agus buidéalaítear mé. Smaoiním ar mhnaoi agus beanaítear mé. 'Sé sin, ardaíonn an buidéal asam féin mé. Bainid díom an t-ualach 'misiúil' atá 'om bhrú. Deintear buidéal díom, deintear bean díom, ach smaoineamh orthu. Sórt slaitín draíochta smaoineamh. Tá an teitheadh seo riachtanach. Do raghfá as do mheabhair dá mbeifeá id thusa i gcónaí. Tá an saol agus an mise ilghnéitheach. Ní mór dúinn bheith inár mbuidéalaibh agus inár gcapallaibh agus inár bpaidreachaibh chun ná beimis inár ngealtaibh. Gealt is ea duine a tuislíodh agus a thit isteach ann féin agus nár fhéad teacht aníos . . . Agus gealt is ea duine a tuislíodh agus a thit isteach i mbuidéal agus nár fhéad teacht aníos. Sin é é. 'No Loitering.' Ní mór do dhuine bheith ag síorthaisteal ó mhise go mise.[49]

Ó Ríordáin lets fly with his unfettered imagination the superb light-handling of the poem 'Roithleán'/Whirl or Reel (*ES* p. 53) which focuses on the poet-speaker's desire to hang on to a wisp of sleep so that he can stay in the arty miracle-world of crazy dreams. The conceit of clinging to this thread is cleverly prolonged over two stanzas in the style of 'metaphysical' poets. The speaker (Ó Ríordáin himself as always) is reluctant to give up the thread when morning comes but it curls away from him like a lock of fine hair. This saves him from 'loitering' in insanity:

Do bheinn im ghealt go buan   *Only I lost my grip on that slumber,*
Ach gur scaoileas uaim an suan.   *I'd be a crazy man forever.*

In 'Scagadh' (*ES* p. 110), where his 'refined' lover becomes so refined that she refines herself away with her own refined lover, Ó Ríordáin succumbs to the magic of the very word 'scagadh' and its possible meanings including straining, filtering, separating, assorting, examining. . . . So doing, he creates a marvellously clever, humorous and original poem which stretches word-play to the limit in a way reminiscent of George Herbert's 'The Pulley'.[50] This is a good example of Ó Ríordáin's comic power and poetic dexterity in 'milking words' (*ES* p. 114).

---

[49] 'I look at a bottle and I am bottled. I think of a woman and I am womaned. That is, the bottle and the woman lift me out of myself, take away the burden of "me-ness". To think of them is to be bottled, womaned. A thought is a kind of magic wand. This flight is necessary. You'd go insane if you were always yourself. Life and self are multifarious. We have to be bottles, horses, prayers or else we'd be mad. A lunatic is someone who has tripped and fallen into himself and can't get out . . . or into a bottle and can't get out. That's the way it is. "No Loitering." A person must keep travelling from self to self.' See Ó Coileáin, *Seán Ó Ríordáin*, 155–6.

[50] Herbert, G., *A Choice of George Herbert's Verse*, ed. by R. S. Thomas, 5th edn. (London: Faber and Faber, 1967, 1981), 68.

'Siollabadh'/Soundings (*ES* p. III) is also successful because Ó Ríordáin lets himself become immersed in word and scene: in a hospital ward, a nurse takes the patients' pulses pulsing beneath her fingers then pulses out of the room, leaving behind her a choir of pulses pulsing to the Angelus. At the end of the prayer, the pulse goes on in the monastery of the flesh 'mar mhanachaibh/ag siollabadh na nónta'/like monks sounding the nones. This type of poem loses a lot in explication and translation (the pun on 'syllabling') but I want to suggest that Ó Ríordáin's puns and conceits are as ingenious as any found in earlier Irish poetry or among the Metaphysicals.

Yet, why didn't Ó Ríordáin take flight and become 'bottled', 'womaned' or 'syllabled' more often?

Tá fairsingeacht smaointe	*There are miles of thought*
San abairt is lú,	*in the simplest phrase,*
Tá síneadh don intinn	*the mind stretches out*
I mbeag is i mór	*with a little or a lot,*
Tá iascaireacht machnaimh	*there's fish for thought*
Sa tsolas máguaird,	*in the light all around*
Ach tá m'anamsa i gcarcair,	*but my soul is trapped*
I bpeaca beag duairc.	*in a sin, small and dark.*[51]

For all his love and use of Joyce, he remained trapped in the nets that Stephen Dedalus said were flung at a man's soul in this country to keep it from flight. His is a voice from within the tangle of nets: language, nationality and, especially, religion. The interest of his poetry is its delineation of the resulting struggle.

1.2 *BROSNA* (1964)

I was heavily criticised for my Irish or lack of Irish when *Eireaball Spideoige* came out. That made me concentrate more on the language in *Brosna*. When I first began writing, I wasn't thinking about Irish at all, I was thinking about poetry. I had just encountered Yeats and that crowd, and was using whatever Baile Bhuirne Irish I had left in my head. In *Brosna*, I was nurturing Irish ['ag cothú na Gaeilge'], perhaps.[52]

---

[51] Ó Ríordáin, from 'Ifreann'/Hell, *ES* p. 105.
[52] 'Seán Ó Ríordáin ag caint le Seán Ó Mórdha', in *Scríobh* 3 ed. by Ó Mórdha, 174. My trans.

Language has long been recognized as a major theme in the literature of Ireland whether it appears as a net to be flown past but traversed and transformed on the way (Joyce), or as an essential ingredient of definition for an emerging nation (Corkery), or as a means of open self-exploration (Heaney). For Ó Ríordáin, the net of language was unavoidable and became all the more entangled and burdensome *because* he wrote in Irish.

For example, the poet Máire Mhac an tSaoi was most prominent among a number of critics who claimed that it was 'impossible to understand Ó Ríordáin without English and Ó Direáin without Irish'.[53] She believed that, early in his career at least, the influence of English language and literature had thrown a discordant spanner into the works of Ó Ríordáin: 'when Seán Ó Ríordáin's poetry was first published, I couldn't read it . . . it was like something a computer would write'.[54] A petty but bitter war ensued between these two poets over which words one or the other knew or used in which context. Mhac an tSaoi found fault, for example, with the poem-title 'Tionóisc ó Neamh'/A Heavenly Accident or Chance—the phrase taken directly, it seems, from English (*ES* p. 32). Also, in the poem 'Saoirse'/Liberty (*ES* p. 100), she found suspect both the meaning and syntax of the line '*tá* ag liú anseo', suggesting either that freedom '*is* yelling here' or simply that 'there is yelling going on here'. Grammatically, the first word should read as '*tá*' or '*atá*', referring to the freedom '*which* is yelling here'. The mistake is, most likely, due only to a slight misprint.

Such criticism, focusing not on his thoughts but on his use of Irish, left Ó Ríordáin feeling as exposed and threatened as the language itself. In *Feasta* March 1953, he said that he was 'afraid to write even a word of Irish' since he had been reviled by 'experts'.[55] Only one year before the publication of *Brosna*, Ó Ríordáin's diary shows him as regretting the choice of Irish as his literary medium. Luckily, however, the assault on his linguistic competence and confidence did not silence the poet entirely. Instead, language became a theme developed in poems strategically placed in the new collection.

Brosna opens with Ó Ríordáin addressing the 'Gaelic in my pen'/'A

[53] Mhac an tSaoi, M., 'Scríbhneoireacht sa Ghaeilge Inniu', in *Studies*, No. 44 (1955), 86–91 (p. 89).

[54] Ó Coileáin, *Seán Ó Ríordáin*, 366.

[55] Ó Ríordáin eventually satirized these experts or authorities in 'Údar'/Author, or Expert (*TÉB* p. 20). See Poem and Translation C in Appendix.

Ghaeilge im Pheannsa' (*B* p. 9). He questions the language ironically in the aisling mode of eighteenth-century vision-poems: are you beautiful as of yore? how have you come down to us? are you all there? what is our relationship? The poet himself answers immediately:

Do d'iompar atáimse,	*I am carrying you,*
Do mhalairt im chluasaibh,	*hearing only your opposite*
Ag súrac atáirse	*while you suck*
Ón striapach allúrach,	*from the foreign whore*
Is sínim chughat smaointe	*and I slip you thoughts*
A ghoideas-sa uaithi,	*I stole from her:*
Do dhealramhsa a chímse,	*I know your beauty,*
Is do mhalairt im shúilibh.	*see only your travesty [opposite].*

These lines may sound harsh towards the English language but they are spoken by a poet whose concern is the condition of his nearly drowned-out language; by someone who feels desperately divided, 'without roots, torn between two languages'.[56] Sorely tempted to abandon Irish along with its more conservative custodians, Ó Ríordáin is racked with unease over the uneven power-relations between Irish and English.

However, he develops the theme of language in *Brosna* by arguing in 'A Theanga Seo Leath-Liom'/Language Half-Mine (*B* p. 25) that poet and language are mutually dependent. To express the fear that unless they are united or fully committed to each other, each will lose the other, he employs a wonderful milling metaphor: 'Ní mheileann riamh leath-aigne'/A half-mind grinds nothing, suggesting that the poet must become immersed in the language, difficult or painful as that might be. At the same time, the poem is a call for commitment also from the language itself, an invocation. The next question is: how much of the Irish nation will heed the call or even recognize it?

Ó Ríordáin does not feel any superiority to the 'crowd' who have 'turned a deaf ear to Irish' ('tá an slua bodhar don teanga Ghaeilge') for it is a minority swamped within the majority of himself that tunes in to that particular frequency in 'Éisteacht Chúng'/ Minority Audience (*B* p. 38). In this way, he portrays himself not as part of a dying breed but part of the Irish 'crowd' in whom the language will not die despite the Irish people's infidelity to it.

Believing that language shapes a people as if they were the marrow

---

[56] 'Duine gan rútaí á stracadh idir dhá theanga ab ea mise riamh.' See Ó Coileáin, *Seán Ó Ríordáin*, 301.

of its skeleton bones (*B* p. 40), Ó Ríordáin concludes his discussion, and collection, with a stirring exhortation (for himself, although the second person singular of the poem tends to ripple out towards a wider Irish audience) to go native or, rather, return to the purity of formerly native and, therefore, 'natural' ways:

> Fág Gleann na nGealt thoir,
> Is a bhfuil d'aois seo ár dTiarna i d'fhuil,
> Dún d'intinn ar ar tharla
> Ó buaileadh Cath Cionn tSáile,
> Is ón uair go bhfuil an t-ualach trom
> Is an bothar fada [. . .]

> *Leave the Glen of the Mad behind*
> *and what's left of this year of Our Lord*
> *in your blood. Close your mind*
> *to what has happened since Kinsale,*
> *the heavy burden and the long road.*[57]

That is not all that Ó Ríordáin wants to forget in this poem. A troubled Seamus Heaney translated the following section in *Fortnight*:

> . . . bain ded mheabhair
> Srathar shibhialtacht an Bhéarla,
> Shelley, Keats is Shakespeare,
> Fill arís ar do chuid,
> Nigh d'intinn is nigh
> Do theanga a chuaigh ceangailte i gcomhréiribh
> 'Bhí bun os cionn le d'éirim [. . .]

> *. . . unshackle your mind*
> *Of its civil English tackling,*
> *Shelley, Keats and Shakespeare.*

> *Get back to what is your own.*
> *Wash your mind and wash your tongue*
> *That was spancelled in a syntax*
> *Putting you out of step with yourself.*[58]

The poem ends with Ó Ríordáin urging himself (and, I feel, the reader) to go to the Gaeltacht and sap up sun and subjunctives in order to find true self and expression.

---

57 From 'Fill Arís'/ Return Again, *B* p. 41.
58 Heaney, 'Forked Tongues', 115.

Sunny Corca Dhuibhne does make for something of a tourist picture, however, the reference to thriving subjunctives and vocatives shows that Ó Ríordáin's primary concern here was linguistic.[59] He wanted to purge his Irish language of English influence believing it would otherwise be 'spancelled' in 'syntax'. A student of any second language will understand Ó Ríordáin's objective: not to impose the speech patterns of one language on to another and end up writing with '*la plume de ma tante*/the pen of my aunt'.

Ó Ríordáin, however, also wishes to edit out what he views as the worst nightmares of Irish history, to cut the cloth of history to suit himself, to free his *present* from the burden and shame of Irish defeat, colonization and Anglicization. Understandable as this wishful thinking might be, it is impossible, if not dangerous, to rewrite history—no matter how horrible—according to one's own plan. Rather, it is necessary not just to wake from but to work through the nightmare of history and its 'back kicks'.[60] Heaney, for example, learnt a valuable lesson from Ó Ríordáin's false historicism:

If he would obliterate history since Kinsale, the loyalist imagination at its most enthusiastic would obliterate history before Kinsale. If Ó Ríordáin needs to unshackle his tongue of its English harness in order to create a secure and true spiritual home, the anti-Ó Ríordáin would exclude all taint and acquaintance with the Irish dimension of his experience in order to ratify the purity and liberty of his stand [. . .] But the very strenuousness of this maintained effort constitutes its negative aspect. Just as the Ó Ríordáin poem, in its sectarian application, would refuse to recognise history and language other than its *own espoused versions of them*, just as it would turn a vision of fulfilment into an instrument of coercion, the same *neurotic intensity* is in danger of turning conceptions and loyalties within the unionist tradition into refusals and paranoias.[61]

Ó Ríordáin himself was well aware of this apocalyptic tendency in his thinking:

Moderation was never a good chief—it is said. Neither was the *via media* [. . .] Bernadette Devlin is no *via media*. Perhaps they'll say to me that Ian Paisley is no *via media* either. Pearse, Connolly and Daniel Corkery were no *via media*. Capt. O'Neill was. What is his example worth now? Where is he now? Paisley

---

[59]   His reading of Ó Ríordáin may have *partly* prompted Heaney's later poems which use the mechanical nuts and bolts of language as material; likewise his digging for original place-names.

[60]   Joyce, J., *Ulysses* (Harmondsworth: Penguin, 1969), 40.

[61]   Heaney, 'Forked Tongues', 116.

is always getting his message across however horrible it is. Perhaps it's necessary that he has his say to get the truth to the top. He's certainly part of the drama and bringing forward the debate.[62]

In 'Fill Arís'/Return Again, it is sheer desperation that makes Ó Ríordáin go to the extreme of wanting to purge not just English imperialism but even English writers such as Shelley, Keats and Shakespeare from his cultural map. However, in his desire to, as Eliot put it, purify the dialect of his tribe, could he really have rejected these and other English-language writers? Had he forgotten e e cummings to whom he felt closer in some ways than to Seathrún Céitinn,[63] his diary's declaration (although he is still Irish) to 'read Joyce, not Eoghan Rua Ó Súilleabháin',[64] his early apprenticeship to Hopkins and Eliot, his admiration for Dante (in whose verses the 'angels landed'),[65] and his 'new Bible' in which Ibsen was his Christ, and Tolstoi, Chekhov, Strindberg, and Turgenev his four Evangelists?[66] Ó Ríordáin read these authors in English and could not have forgotten them if he tried. Unfortunately, in 'Fill Arís'/Return Again, he was simply advocating desperate means to reach an end which he desperately needed to reach, and that is to come home, to get back to where, and the ways in which, his people once belonged. Heaney's response is worth noting:

I did respond to a sense of homecoming at the end of the poem, a sense of release and repose when the poet goes on to describe his destination: for as well as being polemic, this is a poem, an expression of the writer's inner division and of his repining for that universal, paradisiacal place where our conflicts will be resolved. Nevertheless, while the curve of the feeling is true, for me the line of the argument had to be untrue.[67]

Homecoming is the main theme in *Brosna*, the need (as Ó Ríordáin saw it) for the individual to return to his/her native 'island' of original and essential selfhood if they have abandoned it. This idea dates back to the poem 'Oileán Agus Oileán Eile'/One Island and Another (*ES* p. 78) and the introduction to *Eireaball Spideoige*. However, does Ó Ríordáin do anything new with these old and rather conventional ideas or merely repeat himself and them?

---

[62] Ó Ríordáin quoted in Ó Coileáin, *Seán Ó Ríordáin*, 359.
[63] Ibid., 316.   [64] Ibid., 219.
[65] Ó Ríordáin, 'Cnoc Mellerí', *ES* pp. 64–7 (p. 66).
[66] Ó Coileáin, *Seán Ó Ríordáin*, 134.
[67] Heaney, 'Forked Tongues', 116.

'Múscail do Mhisneach'/Stir [or Wake] your Courage (*B* p. 19), for example, begins conventionally enough with a sincere and intimate plea to the reader to guard the soul more than the body. The poem proceeds dangerously along the lines of a sermon and is just about saved by the fact that the poet/speaker in the poem convinces the reader that his is the voice of experience recounting the error of his ways out of genuine concern. The metaphors Ó Ríordáin chooses of rain, fog, and sea are consciously traditional and the success of the poem is that he manages to extend the central conceit, consistently mirroring the physical with the spiritual voyage. 'Sea-motion and mountain-stance' are taken by Tadhg Ó Dúshláine, for example, to refer to the natural 'conflict between transience and permanence'.[68] The search for truth in the poem could also refer to a poet's need for small-talk to subside and thought to take shape in more profound wording or form like the strong image of the submerged rock.

Taken as a whole, however, these near-sermons about coming home to the true self are rather abstract and too polemical. The preaching in 'In Absentia' (*B* p. 20) to be always at home in and/or with oneself is banal and contradicts the poet's earlier warning that 'you would go insane if you were always yourself'.[69] Moreover, one senses that the poetic imagination is tired after the much more emotional handling of this theme in *Eireaball Spideoige*. We don't have 'a poem-straw in a drowning man's grip' in *Brosna* but a poem-straw as a drowning man's whip driving us 'home'; and home is always backwards to a prelapsarian innocence akin to a fantasy island where, anyway, the flocked black sheep of the self will always suddenly bolt for their lives in all directions to the would-be shepherd's dismay.

In 'Tost'/Silence, Ó Ríordáin confesses to having been untrue to himself by losing the key to his own mind and to the 'sanctuary' where he believed memories crystallize into the substance of art:

> Ná bain le dul isteach,
> Tá an eochair in áit mhaith,
> B'é gur folamh bheadh do thearmann beag iata;
> Cuir as do cheann ar fad
> An fharraige is a slad,
> Is bí sásta leis an aigne neamhscríte.

---

[68] Ó Dushláine, T., *Paidir File* (Indreabhán: Cló Iar-Chonnachta, 1993), 87.
[69] Ó Coileáin, *Seán Ó Ríordáin*, 155–6.

> Don't bother going in,
> the key's in a good place;
> your little locked-up sanctuary was empty,
> so put out of your head altogether
> the sea and its theft [destruction],
> be resigned to a silent, unwritten mind.
>
> (*B* p. 28)

Ó Ríordáin, however, could not let go for long of the poem-straws with which he held on not just to Cnoc Mellerí[70] but to life in general.

There are two poems in which Ó Ríordáin develops his notion of self from consisting of two parts to many, from right versus wrong to multiform. In 'Rian na gCos'/Footprints (*B* p. 11), the poet is divided into a plethora of selves dying and being replaced with each word or breath; not until he is dead will they all be united and his true essence be known. Indeed, it took a 'bunch' of selves to write the verses of the poem, the charm of which is that at first one believes the poet is missing some old friend, not fractions of himself. The theme is echoed in a second poem:

Catchollú

Is breá leis an gcat a corp,
Is aoibhinn léi é shearradh,
Nuair a shearr sí í féin anocht
Do tharla cait 'na gceathaimh.

Téann sí ó chat go cat
Á ndúiseacht as a ballaibh,
Fé mar nár chat í ach roth
De chait ag teacht is ag imeacht.

Í féin atá sí ag rá,
Is doirteann sí slua arb ea í
Nuair a shearrann an t-iomlán,
Á gcomhaireamh féin le gaisce.

Tá na fichidí catchollú
Feicthe agamsa anocht,
Ach ní fichidí ach milliúin
'Tá le searradh fós as a corp.

Incatation

The cat worships its body,
loves to unravel.
Tonight she stretched out
into many a catful.

She wakes from cat
to cat as if peeled,
spinning to life
from a cattering wheel.

She expresses herself,
sheds catalogues of skins;
at full stretch she counts
herself with a grin.

Tonight I've seen scores
of incatations,
and still to come:
not scores but millions.

(*B* p. 37)

These poems seem timeless and form a modern link in a chain which would include Metaphysical poets as well as the artful monk who gave us 'Pangur Bán'.

---

70 *ES* pp. 64–7 (p. 67).

As a whole, the poems of *Brosna*, Ó Ríordáin's second volume, are more consistent than his previous work: they display, for example, a satisfying *frasca*-like[71] fusion of form and content, focusing and building on atmosphere through concentration on a single scene, image, or word. 'Fiabhras'/Fever (*B* p. 26) brings the reader right into the 'ceantar bráillín'/sheet-country of the long-suffering patient, Ó Ríordáin, where the landscape and climatic conditions denote a region of illness, miles and miles from health. The poet-speaker's foothold on life diminishes as his fever burns and senses melt but the poem ends with a possible, though uncertain, sign of recovery. In this way, each stanza charts a stage on a journey which Ó Ríordáin knew only too well.

'Claustrophobia' (*B* p. 13) convincingly develops the common image of a candle in the dark, signifying the poet's life or hope. The atmosphere is eerie because the physical details of wine, candle, and a 'powerless' image of God are no more real in the poem than the abstract feeling of terror:

> In aice an fhíona   *Next to the wine*
> Tá coinneal is sceon [. . .]   *is a candle and terror [. . .]*

Night itself is a threatening, expansionist 'crowd' in the yard ready to leap into the poet's lungs and extinguish his 'republic of light'. Another poem, 'An Gealt'/The Insane (*B* p. 32), creates an atmosphere of heightening tension by punning on the verbs 'géaraigh' and 'maolaigh' (the first meaning to quicken or sharpen, and the second, to make blunt or calm) which act respectively on the mania of a distracted and distraught woman. The poem could be a six-line commentary on the same famous scene in Tennessee Williams' *A Streetcar Named Desire*.

Nevertheless, Ó Ríordáin, the valiant gladiator, begins in *Brosna* to feel the net of language growing heavier. Although the poems in the collection are more formally unified and more attention is paid to language as it is spoken and has been handed down, there is a certain linguistic and artistic self-consciousness which leads at times to a lack of passion *in* the poems, though there is much *behind* them. 'Reo'/Frozen (*B* p. 17), for example, knits together two images: a frozen handkerchief on a bush slipping from the poet's grasp; the poet's aunt stretched,

---

[71] The title *Brosna* could have been based on the wide-ranging Italian poetry form *frasca* (meaning, 'a little twig') which was characterized by conciseness of form and concentration of material. See Milosc, C., *The History of Polish Literature* (London: Macmillan, 1969), 64 and 412.

'reoite'/frozen, in her coffin. The risk in the poem—although, perhaps, also its interest—is that Ó Ríordáin makes the gap between the stitches part of the pattern:

Is siúd ag taighde mé fé m'intinn	*I went searching in my mind*
Go bhfuaireas macasamhail an ní seo.	*till I found this scene's equivalent.*

Significantly, it is when Ó Ríordáin shakes his (linguistic and personal) self-consciousness by becoming immersed once again in something outside himself that his imaginative soul flies free of all nets, as in this Rabelaisian *and* bardic satire of a contemporary:

An Lacha	*The Duck*
Maith is eol dúinn scéal na lachan,	*We know all about the duck:*
Éan nár gealladh riamh di	*a bird unblessed*
Leabhaireacht coisíochta:	*with litheness of limb,*
Dúchas di bheith tuisleach	*by nature a staggerer*
Is gluaiseach léi ainspianta	*with both feet left*
Anonn is anall gan rithim,	*wondering rhythmless,*
Is í ag marcaíocht ar a proimpe:	*her arse in the air,*
Ba dhóigh leat ar a misneach	*so haughty you'd think*
Gur seo chughat an dán díreach	*she walks in metre*
Nuair is léir do lucht na tuigse	*when those in the know*
Gur dícheall di vers libre.	*know it's more like vers libre.*

(*B* p. 30)

1.3 *LÍNTE LIOMBÓ* (1971)

Seán Ó Tuama claimed that Ó Ríordáin 'ceased to be a major creative force after the publication of his second book, *Brosna*, in 1964'.[72] It is true that the quality of Ó Ríordáin's four collections gradually declines, yet there are many poems of note in the later work and one can trace the development of some of his early and important themes. In particular, one can chart how the poet who described himself as 'someone without roots, torn between two languages',[73] between Corkery and Joycery, starts to conceive of himself as existing in a limbo-like area, living in what Robert Welch has called, in another context, 'two places at once and therefore nowhere'[74] and splintering into many parts under the strain.

72 Ó Tuama, S., 'Seán Ó Ríordáin, Modern Poet', *Repossessions* (Cork: Cork University Press, 1995), 10–34 (p. 33).   73 Ó Coileáin, *Seán Ó Ríordáin*, 301.
74 Welch, R., 'Language and Tradition in the Nineteenth Century', *Changing States: Transformations in Modern Irish Writing* (London: Routledge Press, 1993), 11–34 (p. 17).

In *Línte Liombó*, therefore, Ó Ríordáin is still concerned with the divided and isolated self or selves but, generally, separation—between selves, and between the self and others—is now accepted and becomes a focus of interest in itself:

Ní d'ionspioráid ar an saol domhsa, *No inspiration exists for me,*
Ach mise, *but me,*
Ná duitse, *nor for you,*
Ach tusa. *but you.* (*LL* p. 42)

Here, in 'Mise'/Me, the poet seems to be 'loitering' in the 'bottle' of himself, yet we are reminded that the speaker is only one part of a fractured self talking about another self:

Níl fáil air san áit a mbímse, *He's not available where I tend to be;*
Ná ní san áit a mbíonn sé, *And it's not where he tends to be,*
Ina aonar, *By himself,*
A bhímse [. . .] *That I be [. . .]* (*LL* p. 42)

As before in 'An Bás'/Death (*ES* p. 69) and 'Rian na gCos'/Footprints (*B* p. 11), Ó Ríordáin suggests that it is only in death that all the elements that make up the self will be rounded up and the whole be known. The elusive self is thus as indefinite and indistinct as the illustrated images (by Pól Funge) which pad out the reprinted collection of 1980. It is as if the poet tried to put his own existence under the lens of poetry out of what Mahon calls a 'wretched rage for order', for meaning and form but was always left wondering whether the lines that got away were the ones best equipped 'to put me/in what I had to say' (*LL* p. 9). Increasingly, Ó Ríordáin despairs about the difficulty of attempting in any language to mirror and contain the many skin-layers shed in the life of an individual.

The net of religion also weighs Ó Ríordáin down eventually. The poem 'Toil'/Will (*LL* p. 27) confirms that his attitude to self was negative and burdened by notions of guilt bound up in religion. This philosophical ramble is rich in wordplay, puns, and rhymes but where are the images that make poetry startling and memorable? Moreover, the poet's stark honesty in baring his soul discomforts the reader because of its accompanying self-loathing and self-pity:

Ó deineadh an botún *Since the mistake was made*
I ngairdín úd Pharthais, *in the Garden of Eden,*
Do leath an truailliú *the pollution spread*
Go dtarla mo shamhailse. *and the likes of me happen.*

Auden once wrote that to ask the hard question is simple, and Ó Ríordáin keeps doing this with great skill in condensing his major concerns into short quatrains:

> An rabhas-sa im ní riamh
> Gan tús liom ná deireadh?
> An mairfeadsa choíche
> Ag malartú seithe?

> *Beginningless, endless,*
> *was I ever a thing?*
> *Will all my days*
> *be the changing of skins?*

He suggests that the individual is merely a channel for a greater will, in lines that reflect his attitude to the creation of poetry or to any other action:

> Nuair a smaoinítear tríom,
> Is léi siúd an machnamh,
> Sé mo ghnó é thabhairt slán,
> Mar a saolófaí leanbh.

> *When I am thought through,*
> *the thought is Hers;*[75]
> *what I have to do*
> *is ensure a safe birth.*

> Níl ionam ach ball
> De chorp mo shinsir,
> Is mairfidh an corp
> Nuair a bheith an ball cloíte.

> *I'm only a limb*
> *on my people's tree.*
> *The body will grow*
> *long after me.*

The poet's sad conclusion of this reflection on his Original Sin-bearing self is that since he was willed, he should be tolerated, not faulted.

Ó Ríordáin is no exception to the rule that poets cannot choose their obsessions, yet increasingly one feels that he forgot his own advice that poetry and health meant 'No Loitering',[76] being transformed by things other than the self. Subjects like the flight from self in the Larkinesque 'Obair'/Work (*LL* p. 39) were covered more imaginatively in *Brosna*. Consequently, one begins to picture the trajectory of his artistic flight as Dedalus descending if not already caught in Corkery's nets of 'creideamh' and 'náisiúnachas' dragging him down to 'talamh'.[77]

Another early but revealing theme repeated in *Línte Liombó* is that of self in relation to others. Whereas in the early poem 'Saoirse'/Freedom (*ES* p. 100), Ó Ríordáin had sought the crowd for refuge from 'venom-liberty', later in 'Tionlacan na nÓinseach'/The Fool's Accompaniment (*LL* p. 17), he claims that it is the individual's lot to be alone wherever s/he is. The latter poem states that the only

---

[75] The 'she' and 'hers' in this poem refer to God's 'Will'.
[76] Ó Coileáin, *Seán Ó Ríordáin*, 156.
[77] 'Religion, nationality and land', respectively.

certainty in life is that each person will accompany themselves to the grave and that anything else makes for a false compromise of oneself:

Ba chuideachta tuargaint an eithigh   *Company was a lie resounding*
Ar bhóthar na fírinne id chluais.   *in your ear on the road of truth.*

Here, Ó Ríordáin touches on a dilemma similar to that often rehearsed in Philip Larkin poems such as 'Reasons for Attendance'.[78] While it is hard to be alone alone/'is deacair bheith id aonar id aonar' according to Ó Ríordáin's poem, to lose oneself in a crowd or relationship is merely a deception. Both 'less deceived' poets instead choose, or resign themselves to, solitude with the sweetener of Art. Larkin, for example, once said 'I see life more as an affair of solitude diversified by company, than an affair of company diversified by solitude.'[79] Ó Ríordáin would have agreed entirely, though he had less choice due to his life-long illness, tuberculosis.

Surprisingly, there are a number of similarities between the life and attitudes of Ó Ríordáin and those of his contemporary, Philip Larkin. The ideas and work of both were conditioned by solitariness or aloofness. Larkin once confessed that he moved from novels to poetry because 'novels are about other people and poems are *about yourself* [. . .] I didn't know enough about other people.'[80] Even in his poems, Larkin was accused of not knowing or showing enough of other people as the one-dimensional types in 'The Whitsun Weddings' illustrate.[81] Ó Ríordáin was also self-obsessed and his work displays even more difficulty in representing other people. In several poems in *Línte Liombó*, he seems curiously detached and bitterly isolated from his fellow human beings. This is because he radically refuses to 'buy in' to the lie, as he sees it, of shallow civility and meaningless, superficial talk.[82]

Some poems actually suggest that Ó Ríordáin preferred animals to people, even if he was only joking in 'Aistriú'/Metamorphosis:

Aistrigh a chló cait   *Change her cat-form*
Id aigne go bean,   *in your mind to a woman*

---

[78]   Larkin, P., *Collected Poems* (London: Marvell and Faber, 1988), 80.

[79]   Larkin, P., *Required Writing: Miscellaneous Pieces 1955–1982* (London: Faber and Faber, 1983), 47–56 (p. 54).

[80]   Ibid., 49.

[81]   Larkin, *Collected Poems*, 114–16.

[82]   See the 'slim woman' of 'Bean Chaol' (*LL* p. 23) and censured friends of 'Dom Chairde' (*LL* p. 41).

Agus chífidh tú	*and you'll find*
Go mba bhreá an bhean í	*a fine figure of a woman*
Dá mbeifeá id chat fireann.	*if you were a tom.*

(LL p. 24)

Certainly, the poems in this third collection featuring other people contrast sharply with the plain and touching sincerity of 'Tar Éis Dom É Chur Go Tigh Na nGadhar'/After Leading Him To The Slaughter House, a poem about the pet Ó Ríordáin had to have 'put down':

Bhí béasa gadhair tí agat,	*You'd the ways of a house-dog,*
Is támáilteacht gadhair fháin,	*the shyness of the free;*
Níl ded ghrá rothaig sa mbith anocht	*what's left of your love tonight*
Ach a bhfuil im chroí ded chrá.	*is the misery in me.* (*LL* p. 30)

The only human characters to be treated more affectionately in Ó Ríordáin's work are his mother and the brown-eyed girl of 'Súile Donna'/Brown Eyes (*LL* p. 10). Perhaps his true home or nation is to be found in the remembered dreamworld of 'Cúl an Tí'/The Back of the House (*ES* p. 61) with Englishless, Irishless four-footed folk walking the roads. Ó Ríordáin once wrote:

I have come to a contempt, no a horror, of flesh [. . .] When in black moments I remember that I am enclosed in the filthy stuff I would fain bray with disgust. There is something beautifully turn-your-back-on-everything about the braying of an ass. When in the universal presence of a good bray I feel independent of Picasso and the Pope and people I like too much. That seems to be my reason for straining deathwards—I can't bray [. . .] It is a dreadful thing to be caught in the trap of life when one is dead.[83]

Grounded in 'Limbo', Ó Ríordáin, who began his career saying poems as prayers, ends up praying in the chapel that his lost inspiration be returned to him: 'Sa Séipéil Dom'/In the Chapel (*LL* p. 18). In 'Ní Ceadmhach Neamhshuim'/Indifference Not Permitted (*LL* p. 40), he reminds himself and us of all the things that he and we ought to take an interest in but other than listing these people, places, and things, he merely insists that they are part of us and, therefore, our concern. It is as if he is desperately trying to urge himself out of himself to meet these things, to stop 'loitering'[84] in himself but is unable to do so. Meanwhile,

---

[83] Quoted by Ó Coileáin, *Seán Ó Ríordáin*, 105–6.

[84] ' "No Loitering!" Ní mór do dhuine bheith ag síorthaisteal ó mhise go mise./"No Loitering!" A person must always keep travelling from me to me [or self to self].' From Ó Ríordáin's Diary, 12 April 1949. See Ó Coileáin, *Seán Ó Ríordáin*, 155–6.

his earlier prescript, in 'Fan!'/Wait! (*ES* p. 84), to let his thoughts rest a while in his mind until they form a more natural, native, and pleasing shape is completely contradicted in the later poem 'Ná Fan'/Don't Wait, which advocates a seizing of the day:

Beir air anocht is doirt	*Tonight catch and spill*
Gach beag, gach mórmhothú	*every sensation, big or little [. . .]*
[. . .] Ná caill ar d'aigne,	*Don't cheat your mind,*
Fág í neadaithe	*nest it in words next to you*
I mbréithre in aice leat,	*—however bad or good,*
Dá fheabhas, dá ainnise,	*and name everything that goes*
Cuir ainm ar	*through your eyes, ears or mind.*
Gach ar ghaibh trí d'shúil, trí d'chluais anocht, trí d'aigne.	

(LL p. 43)

However, the more Ó Ríordáin writes about writing, the more one wishes that he would look beyond himself and show again the power of poetry to engineer the flight from self, to transform and become.

The poet's attempts, in *Línte Liombó*, to recreate verbally what he witnesses, for example, are less successful than before. In 'Solas'/ Light, Ó Ríordáin admits that his memory is reluctant to reshape the world of his room under dark: 'is leisc lem chuimhne é athchruthú'. His attention is more on the next world than on this:

> Fágfad domhan im dhiaidh 'na riocht,
> Ach fágfad é sa doircheacht.
>
> *I'll leave the world behind in one piece,*
> *but I'll be leaving it in darkness.*

(LL p. 35)

His recreation of the battle between light and dark in the moonlit sky of 'Oíche Ghealaí'/Moonlit Night (*LL* p. 32) similarly ends with the poet turning away, tired of the struggle between light and dark.

Increasingly, Ó Ríordáin's concerns become almost entirely philosophical and it is in the area of abstract thought that his voice retains authority:

Imímid as amharc	*We lose sight*
uainn féin gach re tamall,	*of ourselves each time*
ag tnúth lenár malairt inár gcló féin,	*we want a change of design,*
ach fillimid folamh	*but return empty*
i ndeireadh gach aistir,	*after each journey,*
is séala síoraí ár gcéad chló orainn.	*our eternal seal on our one body.*

('Cló'/Design, LL p. 31)

Tangled in a complex, metaphysical design argument, Ó Ríordáin sought certainty, purity, an absolute, the state of oneness, of fulfilment, of reaching, as Heaney noted, 'that universal, paradisiacal place where our conflicts will be resolved'[85] and which only possibly comes with death to which he next turned his attention.

1.4   *TAR ÉIS MO BHÁIS* (1978)

Ó Ríordáin's last volume, published one year after his death, consists of previously uncollected work taken from journals such as *Scríobh* and *Feasta*, and unpublished material selected from his papers. The poems are divided into two corresponding sections by the editor, Ó Ríordáin's biographer, Seán Ó Coileáin. The collection spans twenty-three years and includes poems which Ó Ríordáin left out of earlier volumes, some that he wanted to work on and some that he would probably never have published. Nevertheless, *Tar Éis Mo Bháis* provides valuable insights into Ó Ríordáin's character and concerns.

A life marked by illness, sanatoriums, and the early loss of family members gradually made Ó Ríordáin view death as another 'tionlacan na n-óinseach'/fool's escort[86] accompanying the individual throughout his/her days. One could say that he continually lived with and battled against death. In the same way that Larkin dreaded 'endless extinction',[87] Ó Ríordáin saw words as 'stones to throw at fate' and sentences as 'ways of fighting the death-sentence'.[88] In his earlier work, his attitude to death veered from curiosity (*ES* p. 31) to resignation (*ES* p. 42) to welcome (*ES* p. 69); in his last collection, as the title suggests, his own imminent death became a major theme. Developing his earlier concept of divided selves, Ó Ríordáin now produced some of his most startling poems such as 'An Gad Is Giorra Don Scornach'/The Noose Nearest the Neck:

> Chím an duine romham amach
> Agus pian mhór air, chím a bhás:
>
> Ach is fuirist dom é féin agus a phian agus a bhás
> A chur ar an méir fhada;

---

[85] Heaney, 'Forked Tongues', 116.
[86] A reapplication of the idea in the poem by that name, *LL* p. 17.
[87] Larkin, *Required Writing*, 55.
[88] Ó Coileáin, *Seán Ó Ríordáin*, 2.

Mura gcuirfinn
Ní mhairfinn;
Is leor liom pian an té
Atá faram i láthair na huaire:

Cé gur mise an duine romham amach,
Ní hé mé go fóill,
Agus is cuma liom cén íde a thabharfar air
Nuair ná caithfidh mise an lae inniu
Í fhulang:

Cé go n-aithníonn an fhuil a chéile
Ní trua liom mo mhise féinig—
Achar ó bhaile:

Tá gach mise tá caite dearmhadta, mílítheach,
Is iad súd tá le teacht, tá gach mise acu coimhthíoch:
Ní beag do gach mise
A chuid oilc féin.[89]

In this unnerving poem, Ó Ríordáin appears to *see* ghostly divisions of self about which he had previously only speculated philosophically.

In the title poem 'Tar Éis Mo Bháis'/After My Death (*TÉB* p. 32), the poet reports seeing his hands in a mirror as he would his body after death. It is as if the bodiless self is growing out of him. He seems to view life as a gradual transformation to death. Indeed, in the later poem 'Mo Bhás Féin'/My Own Death, Ó Ríordáin reflects on his own demise not as something that will happen but as something that happened long ago and was forgotten, although he still possesses and is possessed by it. His 'hoard' of death, what is more, makes the poet a 'rich man' even though

Ní féidir do bhás a chaitheamh	*you can't spend your death*
Go n-aibeodh sé;	*till it accumulates;*
Talamh nach féidir a dhíol	*death is land you can't sell,*
Nó airgead ceangailte síos	*money tied up for life.*
Is ea ár mbás i gcaitheamh ár saoil.	(*TÉB* p. 44)

Death is not the only theme in *Tar Éis Mo Bháis*, but it is the one which inspired Ó Ríordáin most consistently in his later work. Declan Kiberd writes that

reading Ó Ríordáin, we have the sense of every lyric as a little death, when something of himself is expressed and lost, in a kind of grim rehearsal for death.

---

[89] *TÉB* p. 28. Translation D in Appendix.

In 'Mise' he seems to suggest that his splintered selves will only be fully reintegrated 'on our deathbed'. In the meantime, the poem is as near as he can get, but it remains a marginal gloss on an unliveable, unknowable life. Ó Ríordáin's is a sensibility whose plight is to have lived through the consequences of its own extinction, even before it had a chance to know the self that died.[90]

I, too, see each of Ó Ríordáin's poems as 'something of himself [. . .] expressed and lost', messages in bottles sent out by a man marooned on the island of himself. One recalls Ó Coileáin's comment after the *Eireaball Spideoige* period: 'his subjects until now—youth, illness, the death of his mother, love and philosophy, his own scruples—were almost entirely used up [. . .] What had he now but himself, poorer than ever? If he'd learnt a lesson, he'd paid too dearly for it.'[91] It is sad and humbling to think that with himself as subject, 'poorer than ever', he shared even his death with us out of his loneliness, his sheer isolation/'méid a uaignis'.[92] Máire Mhac an tSaoi once wrote that love and death were the two great themes of Gaelic literature;[93] Ó Ríordáin certainly knew more of the latter and charted it as his main territory.

However, not all of Ó Ríordáin's final, posthumous volume is about death. For example, a strong anti-puritanical strain is revealed in poems such as 'Joyce', 'Préachán'/Crow, and 'Do Striapach'/To a Prostitute.[94] In the latter poem, Ó Ríordáin likens the prostitute to a saint for possessing the same virtue that he found in Yeats: the openness and honesty of 'hiding nothing'.[95] This later unconventional zig or zag on the graph of Ó Ríordáin's journey between the horizontal plane of Corkery and the vertical plane of Joyce is one where what Heaney would call the curve of Ó Ríordáin's feeling and the line of his argument coincide and tend more to the Joycean axis.

Some of Ó Ríordáin's latter-day views, however, are not so readily acceptable: his ironically stated belief in 'Banfhile'/Poetess (*TÉB* p. 45) that a woman cannot be a poet even though she may make poetry by masculine means is hardly redeemed by its bitterly satiric conclusion

---

90 Kiberd, *An Crann faoi Bhláth*, xxxviii.

91 Ó Coileáin, *Seán Ó Ríordáin*, 266.

92 *ES* p. 10.

93 Mhac an tSaoi, Introduction, *Nuala Ní Dhomhnaill: Rogha Dánta/Selected Poems* (Dublin: Raven Arts Press, 1991), 9–12 (p. 10).

94 See *TÉB* pp. 21–2, p. 19 and p. 50 respectively.

95 Ó Coileáin, *Seán Ó Ríordáin*, 69.

that a man can't be a poet either because a man is nothing/'neamhní'. Also, his generalizations in 'Suan na hÓige'/Youth-sleep (*TÉB* p. 41) and in 'Áthas is Buairt'/Happiness and Sorrow (*TÉB* p. 47) that youth is an untroubled snooze, merely remind the reader of his distance and isolation from other people. Nevertheless, the collection confirms that Ó Ríordáin's poetry, while still more at home in the cerebral and animal worlds, remains alive to the transformative, imaginative flight which art engineers:

> Eireablú
>
> Fuair sí í féin ina cat,
> Dar léi siúd nárbh ait,
> Mar bhí sí riamh ina cat—
> Ceathairchosach, ciúin,
> Eireaball as a tóin,
> Radharc san oíche, scrabhadh,
> Gomh lapa is mí-amha,
> Is í chomh soghluaiste leis an abhainn.
>
> Dá n-iompóinn féin im chat,
> Dar liom go mothóinn ait,
> Go mba dheacair dom an scrabhadh,
> An t-eireaball is an mí-amha,
> Do lánshamhlú lem shamhail.
>
> Ní bhraithim ait mo lámh,
> Táim inti iomlán,
> Ní coimhthíoch liom mo thóin,
> Tá sí de réir mo mheoin,
> Táim inti intleachtóil,
> Ach bheadh ríordánú catbhall
> Glan bunoscionn lem mheabhair—
> Ba chríocha aineoil im mhapa
> Eireaball nó lapa.
>
> Ní bheadh in eireaball ach éadach
> Mura bhfásfadh sí díscréideach,
> Ag gabháil tionlacain led éirim,
> Ribe ar ribe 'od athrú,
> Go n-eireablófaí tú catbhuan.[96]

---

[96] *TÉB* pp. 25–6. Translation E in Appendix.

CONCLUSION

Responses to Ó Ríordáin's 'prayers' of poetry reveal the critics' orientation in the on-going debate between traditionalism and modernism; how far they believe an Irish language poet should be grounded in nativeness with Corkery and/or fly their kite with Joyce. What is often highlighted is the lone voice of the isolated, dislocated, and divided individual in Ó Ríordáin's work as compared to the communal (if not national) public addresses of other writers, including Máirtín Ó Direáin; Ó Ríordáin's unconventional, versus their more traditional, use of the Irish language.

The American critic Frank O'Brien described the difference between Ó Ríordáin and his contemporaries as follows: 'if one sees Máire Mhac an tSaoi as the lyricist of love and Ó Direáin as a seer speaking of people's collective responsibility, it is clear that Ó Ríordáin is concerned with the feelings and conscience of the isolated individual.'[97] O'Brien's critical assessment of Ó Ríordáin is that while he introduced original metaphors and similes into his work, a lack of control caused him to 'often twist the normal meanings of words' too far away from the more natural language and music found in verse by Mhac an tSaoi and Ó Direáin who were, in this view, more consistent and kept their prosody closer to real speech and to the precedents of early Irish literature. However, O'Brien does concede that while, for example, Ó Ríordáin's unusual use of compound words[98] is 'closer in style to Hopkins than to traditional Irish verse', this in itself is not a bad thing.[99]

Ó Ríordáin himself was in awe of Ó Direáin whose mining of the rich linguistic ore of Aran tradition he envied, but was forever at loggerheads with Mhac an tSaoi both stylistically and personally. In his pamphlet, *Literature in Irish*, Proinsias MacCana describes the difference in their work as follows:

Whereas in her verse, emotional responses, however complex, tend to be outgoing and evolving, his are always ingoing and involute, his mind ever turning in upon itself in an anxious sometimes feverish search for reassurance about the purpose, and even the reality, of his existence in a world mocked by the thought of eternity.[100]

97 O'Brien, F., *Filíocht Ghaeilge na Linne Seo* (Dublin: An Clóchomhar Tta, 1968), 301.   98 See 'An Peaca'/The Sin, *ES* p. 41.
99 O'Brien, *Filíocht Ghaeilge na Linne Seo*, 326.
100 MacCana, P., *Literature in Irish* (Dublin: Dept. of Foreign Affairs, 1980), 60.

The two poets' differences of approach and of opinion were most pronounced on the subject of language itself. Reviewing Mhac an tSaoi's second volume of poetry,[101] Ó Ríordáin claimed that 'in the case of other writers, Irish is only a means of communication but in the case of Máire Mhac an tSaoi, it's almost as if Irish is all her poems have to offer'.[102] Elsewhere, he called her a 'real poet';[103] here, he was reaping revenge for Mhac an tSaoi's earlier attacks on his own ability to use Irish.

It is interesting to note, however, that Máire Mhac an tSaoi later changed her opinion of Ó Ríordáin's command of Irish. In 1970, Ó Ríordáin appeared on an RTE television programme called *Writer in Profile* during which Mhac an tSaoi phoned the station to say that she had 'never heard better Irish spoken than that by Seán Ó Ríordáin tonight'. Ó Ríordáin's reaction? 'My bowels moved with disdain.'[104] He had still not forgiven her for her earlier complaints which now sound like pedantic nit-picking when compared to the inventiveness brought to Irish by Ó Ríordáin in poems such as 'An Peaca'/The Sin (*ES* p. 41). The Russian critic Boris Tomashevsky has commented that

quarrels between new and old literary groups arise over artistic motivation. The old, tradition-oriented group generally denies the artistry of the new literary form. This is shown, for example, in poetic diction, where the use of individual words must be in accord with firmly established literary traditions.[105]

Similarly, the dispute between Mhac an tSaoi and Ó Ríordáin represents the classic struggle between the traditionalist whose aim is to conserve and the modernist who serves tradition by extending it.

Seán Ó Tuama, Ó Ríordáin's greatest advocate, singles him out from his generation for being the most innovative in his language and the most European in his concerns. In his view, Ó Ríordáin managed to mould and expand the language in order to communicate abstract thoughts and, sometimes, deep personal torment resulting from the widely felt instability of the post-war, 'post-Christian' world. Ó Tuama lauds the poet for being able to 'reveal fully and satisfactorily in images and metaphors every corner of his mind—from delight to disgust, from

---

[101] Mhac an tSaoi, M., *Codladh an Ghaiscigh* (Dublin: Sáirséal agus Dill, 1973).
[102] Ó Coileáin, *Seán Ó Ríordáin*, 370.
[103] Ibid., 369.   [104] Ibid., 367.
[105] Tomashevsky, Boris, from 'Thematics', in R. Rylance (ed.), *Debating Texts*, 57–65 (p. 63).

the physical to the metaphysical'[106] and to do so, in poems such as 'Reo'/Frozen (B p. 17), 'in an idiom and tone that an 18th century poet such as Aogán Ó Rathaille would have recognised' while yet remaining 'absolutely modern'.[107] In Ó Tuama's estimation, Ó Ríordáin successfully bridges the gulf between the opposing banks of native tradition and the modern world. I agree, but it is important to acknowledge that he did so by being stretched beyond limit and, like Yeats, 'hurt into poetry'.[108]

Other commentators, however, found Ó Ríordáin's scruples about death and morality, for example, rather ordinary and believed his Gaelicization of common continental concerns to be an insufficient source for a body of original work. Proinsias MacCana welcomes Ó Ríordáin's irony and humour, viewing him as a 'symbol of the renewal of Irish poetry' but wonders if his achievement has not been exaggerated by the novelty in Irish of familiar European themes, such as 'metaphysical *angoisse*'.[109] One answer, in the words of Stephen Patrick Morrissey, is that 'the story is old/but it goes on',[110] pursuing even Seamus Heaney to 'Station Island'[111] and beyond.

In *Gaelic Literature Surveyed*, Eoghan Ó hAnluain accounts for the high octane atmosphere, stay-fresh imagery and electric energy of Ó Ríordáin's poetry as follows:

with Seán Ó Ríordáin one is aware of being at a frontier both of language and sensibility. The interaction of these has produced poems, at times elusive and obscure but his extension of both language and sensibility marks one of the finer achievements in Irish writing over the past thirty years.[112]

Uniquely, Ó Ríordáin can be compared to the great Metaphysical poet John Donne in that he is characteristically at full stretch both in content (including passionate and powerful struggles with faith) and in technique (including extenuated and elaborate 'conceits').

---

[106] Ó Tuama, *Filí faoi Scéimhle*, 10.

[107] Ó Tuama, 'Seán Ó Ríordáin', in S. Mac Réamoinn (ed.), *The Pleasures of Gaelic Poetry*, 140.

[108] 'Mad Ireland hurt you into poetry.' See Auden, W. H., 'In Memory of W. B. Yeats', *Collected Shorter Poems: 1927–1957*, 2nd edn. (London: Faber and Faber, 1969), 141–3.

[109] MacCana, P., *Literature in Irish*, 60.

[110] The Smiths, 'Last Night I Dreamt', *Strangeways, Here We Come* (London: Rough Trade, 1987).

[111] Heaney, S., *Station Island* (London: Faber and Faber, 1984), 163–93.

[112] Ó hAnluain, E., 'The Twentieth Century: Prose and Verse', additional chapter in de Blacam, A., *Gaelic Literature Surveyed*, 387–405 (p. 391).

As for nativeness, his poems, like the shards of Ireland's cracked looking-glass itself, face in *many* directions: East and West; past and present; this world and the next. For me, his scattered, shattered vision and reflections make the poet, like his hero Joyce, all the more Irish. Yet, the diverse elements in his personal, linguistic, and literary make-up often made Ó Ríordáin feel (and appear to others) more like one of Paul Muldoon's 'Mules': 'neither one thing nor the other',[113] neither Gael nor Gall, his language a hybrid and his place a limbo, his status alien since he was—or, like the 'kitten' in 'Piscín' (*TÉB* p. 15), *seemed* to his 'co-Westerners' to be—not wholly integrated or fully present in, and expressive of, his 'native' self.

Yet, debates about the 'nativeness' of Ó Ríordáin seem rather ancient and irrelevant now compared to his achievement which was to show Irish to be (as it is) a thoroughly modern and world-embracing language, capable of stretching its shadow and shedding its light on abstract and concrete alike, and on Gaeltacht, semi-Gaeltacht and Galltacht experience alike.[114] If Ó Ríordáin's heritage was mixed, so too was that of the country, especially in what Louis MacNeice has called 'an impure age'.[115] Ó Ríordáin was surely impressed by the defiant Dedalus who declared that 'this race and this country and this life produced me [. . .] I shall express myself as I am.'[116] Therefore, if Ó Ríordáin, as an Irish language poet, did not always satisfy the hidebinding standards of some, it was because he had his own standards of truth to himself, the demands of experience (a respecter of no borders) and of his craft to spread Irish into some new and previously unexplored territories in an original way, refusing to serve or wait for 'the dictionary and grammar-makers'.[117] This is the source of Ó Ríordáin's modernist achievement which earned him recognition even from Kinsella as the 'one poet [writing in Irish at that time] who

---

[113] Muldoon, P., *Selected Poems 1968–83*, 5th edn. (London: Faber and Faber, 1986).

[114] For a more recent example, partly influenced by Ó Ríordáin, see Gearóid Mac Lochlainn, *Babylon Gaeilgeoir* (Belfast: An Clochán, 1997) and *Na Scéalaithe* (Dublin: Coiscéim, 1999).

[115] Muldoon, P. (ed.), *The Faber Book of Contemporary Irish Poetry* (London: Faber and Faber, 1986), 17.

[116] Joyce, J., *Portrait of the Artist as a Young Man*, in Levin, H. (ed.), *The Essential James Joyce*, 176–367 (p. 327).

[117] *transition*, no. 18 (November 1929) n.p., quoted by O'Brien, D., 'Piety and Modernism: Seamus Heaney's "Station Island" ', *James Joyce Quarterly*, Vol. 26, No. 1 (Fall 1988), 51–65 (p. 61).

had responded to the demands and opportunities of modern poetry'.[118]

However, for some, Ó Ríordáin could still be *too* traditional. Gabriel Rosenstock, a successor, described his and Michael Davitt's attitude to their predecessor's work as follows:

We both had a great respect for Seán Ó Ríordáin (and still do) except that I find lines like

'Maidin sheaca ghabhas amach
Is bhí seál póca romham ar sceach'

make me want to march. That's the danger with regular metre.[119]

Williams and Ní Mhuiríosa, joint authors of *Traidisiún Liteartha na nGael*, also record the poet's mixed reception on account of rhythm:

Normally he uses simple ordinary words but manages to bestow on them an unusual power and meaning [. . .] However, some commentators feel that some of his work is marred by childish meter and un-native rhythm.[120]

Undoubtedly, however, Ó Ríordáin's poetic testimony (whether it has been absorbed, adapted, translated or reacted against by writers including Máirtín Ó Direáin,[121] Alan Titley,[122] Michael Davitt,[123] John Montague,[124] Ciarán Carson[125] and Seamus Heaney[126]) is an invaluable asset to the literature of Ireland. What is more, it is not because the pond is small that Ó Ríordáin is a big fish. The more obviously international poet Cathal Ó Searcaigh views him as 'a major modern master' significant for having 'found a voice for the dislocated individual in

---

[118] Kinsella, T. (ed.), *The New Oxford Book of Irish Verse* (Oxford: Oxford University Press, 1986), xxviii.

[119] Ó Tuairisc, E. (ed.), *Rogha an Fhile*, 81. My translation.

[120] Williams, J. E. C., and Ní Mhuiríosa, M., *Traidisiún Liteartha na nGael* (Dublin: An Clóchomhar Tta, 1979), 382.

[121] Mac Giolla Léith, C., 'An Cloigeann Mícheart nó Ríodánú an Direánaigh', in C. Mac Giolla Léith (ed.), *Cime Mar Chách* (Dublin: Coiscéim, 1993), 73–83.

[122] Ó Ríordáin's influence is evident throughout Titley's prose and criticism.

[123] See Michael Davitt, 'Ragham Amú', in M. Ó Conghaile (ed.), *Sláinte: Deich mBliana de Chló Iar-Chonnachta* (Indreabhán: Cló Iar-Chonnachta, 1995), 78.

[124] See John Montague, 'The Two Seáns', *Smashing the Piano* (Loughcrew: Gallery Press, 1999), 58–9.

[125] See Ciarán Carson, 'Beagles, Horses, Bikes, Thighs, Boats, Grass, Bluebells, Rickshaws, Stockings', in N. Duffy and T. Dorgan (eds.), *Watching the River Flow: A Century in Irish Poetry* (Dublin: Poetry Ireland, 1999), 81–6 (p. 86).

[126] See Chapter 1 Section 2 above.

Irish', and likens Ó Ríordáin's 'philosophical, angst-ridden poetry' to that of 'Baudelaire, Eliot and Pound'.[127]

In my view, Ó Ríordáin can best be compared, or rather contrasted, with the Russian artist Marc Chagall who once asked: 'and weren't our artistic premonitions right—since we really are up in the air and suffer from one disease alone: the thirst for stability?'[128] The stability thirsted for here does not represent stasis, fixity, or inertia but reflects the desire for what Heaney calls 'a sense of belonging to a place' to *attend* one's 'sense of displacement';[129] the desperate need for a transcendental foothold on the quaking sod of home. This, I believe, is what makes Chagall's testimony valuable and increasingly referred to in relation to Irish poetry.[130]

Significantly, the arc of the Russian's artistic journey contrasts sharply with that of Ó Ríordáin. Whereas Chagall could say: 'I plunge into my thoughts. I fly above the world', Ó Ríordáin flew into his thoughts and plunged under the world.[131] Also, while Chagall portrayed his experience or sensation of life's transitions in visual metaphors of floating or flying through the air, at times thirsting for stability,[132] Ó Ríordáin characteristically felt as if he was flung down into the sea, drunk on instability.[133] 'O, to walk in the steps of Chagall!'— Mayakovski and Heaney recommend it[134] but it is not easy to stand back and remain in control as an individual or artist while one's life and country is transformed: 'Russia was covered with ice. Lenin turned her upside down the way I turn my pictures.'[135] In Ó Ríordáin's case, witnessing Ireland's apparent Anglicization, *he* was turned upside down. Nor is it easy to escape like Joyce or one of Chagall's goats (representing his wandering, Jewish, 'Bloom'-ing self) to create a home from

---

[127] From a conversation with Ó Searcaigh, writer-in-residence at the University of Belfast, 1993.

[128] Chagall, M., *My Life* (Oxford/New York: Oxford University Press, 1989), 171.

[129] Heaney, 'Forked Tongues', 114.

[130] See Longley, E., *The Living Stream: Literature and Revisionism in Ireland* (Newcastle-upon-Tyne: Bloodaxe Books, 1994), 212.

[131] See Chagall, *My Life*, 72, and Ó Ríordáin, 'An Dilettante', *ES* pp. 115–16.

[132] See, for example, Chagall's painting *Le temps n'a pas de rive* which resurfaces in Nuala Ní Dhomhnaill's poem 'Báidín Guagach'/A Rocky Boat, *Féar Suaithinseach* (Maynooth: An Sagart, 1984), 107.

[133] 'Cnoc Melleri', *ES* p. 67.

[134] For Mayakovski, see Chagall, *My Life*, 153; and for Heaney, see Longley, E., *The Living Stream*, 212.

[135] Chagall, *My Life*, 135.

home: 'Paris, you are my second Vitebsk.'[136] Ó Ríordáin's emblem would be one of his cats with many lives, trying to make one home for himself but finding that 'ní chuireann an Chinniúint a cos fúithi san Iarthar'/*Destiny [or Fate] doesn't get setting its foot down in the West.*[137]

[136] Ibid., 114.
[137] From 'Piscín'/Kitten, *TÉB* p. 15.

CHAPTER 2

Cathal Ó Searcaigh: Zig-zagging All Over Creation

Choose one set of tracks and track a hare
Until the prints stop, just like that, in snow.
End of the line. Smooth drifts. Where did she go?

Back on her tracks, of course, then took a spring
Yards off to the side; clean break; no scent or sign.
She landed in her form and ate the snow.

Consider too the ancient hieroglyph
Of 'hare and zig-zag', which meant 'to exist',
To be on the *qui vive*, weaving and dodging [. . .]

Seamus Heaney[1]

INTRODUCTION

Jacques Derrida, in his essay 'Structure, Sign and Play in the Discourse of the Human Sciences',[2] argues that an 'event' or 'rupture' has taken place in the history of the concept of structure. He ingeniously declares that up to now structure or its structurality was limited by the imposition of a 'centre', a point of reference or fixed origin whose function was to 'orient, balance and organize the structure' but also to limit the 'play' it could facilitate. If one thinks of Seán Ó Ríordáin's idea of 'oileán'/island,[3] or indeed soul, as the 'centre', and his view of self as the 'structure', a curious and revealing pattern is uncovered:

[1] Heaney, 'Squarings' Part 4, *xliii*, *Seeing Things* (London: Faber and Faber, 1991), 103.

[2] Derrida, J., 'Structure, Sign and Play in the Discourse of the Human Sciences', in R. Macksey and E. Donato (eds.), *The Structuralist Controversy: The Languages of Criticism and the Languages of Man* (Baltimore and London: Johns Hopkins University Press, 1970, 1972), 247–65.

[3] Ó Ríordáin, 'Oileán agus Oileán Eile', *ES*, pp. 80–3.

The concept of centered structure is in fact the concept of a freeplay based on a fundamental ground, a freeplay which is constituted upon a fundamental immobility and a reassuring certitude, which itself is beyond the reach of the freeplay. With this certitude anxiety can be mastered, for anxiety is invariably the result of a certain mode of being implicated in the game, of being caught by the game, of being as it were from the very beginning at stake in the game.[4]

If one feels 'at stake in the game', as Ó Ríordáin surely did, ideas about the nature of the 'centre' and its relative positioning become crucial to the individual. I would compare this to the gravity with which theologians through the centuries debated the nature of the 'soul', which animals had one and in what part of their anatomy it was located. How would such scholastic philosophers have received Derrida's thesis that even before the trinity of Nietzsche, Freud, and Heidegger, 'the centre [was] not the centre' and that after these three wise men it was 'necessary to begin thinking that there was no centre, that the centre could not be thought of in the form of a present-being, that the centre had no natural site, that it was not a fixed locus but a function, a sort of non locus in which an infinite number of sign-substitutions came into play'?[5]

For Derrida, this 'rupture' or decentring that caused the structurality of the structure to be re-thought, occurred when European culture 'had been *dislocated*, driven from its locus, and forced to stop considering itself as the culture of reference'.[6] I would like to open out and extend this argument like a matrioshka doll.

The continent of Europe has inside her many nations which had already been internally 'dislocated' in this sense by the colonialism of their neighbours. The shattered nation survives by creating a 'new structure' or 'original system' which, seen positively, is free of history and benefits from the play of 'chance and discontinuity'. Seen negatively, however, the new structure represents a 'catastrophe—an overturning of nature in nature, a natural interruption of the natural sequence, a setting aside *of* nature'.[7] The latter view which Derrida claims is taken

[4] Macksey and Donato, *The Structuralist Controversy*, 248.

[5] Derrida, J., 'Structure, Sign and Play in the Discourse of the Human Sciences', in R. Rylance (ed.), *Debating Texts: A Reader in Twentieth Century Literary Theory and Method* (Milton Keynes: Open University Press, 1987, 1990), 123–36 (p. 124). Where the translation is clearer, I shall quote from this version.

[6] Macksey and Donato, *The Structuralist Controversy*, 251.

[7] Ibid. 263.

by Lévi-Strauss and Rousseau (also, I would say, by Ó Direáin and, at times, Ó Ríordáin) assumes the impossibility of total repair and perfect continuity plus the unseemliness of any stitched wound and new growth. Yet, history and literature show that if there are enough survivors, such a rupture or catastrophe for the nation necessitates the building anew (it can't, strictly speaking, be called 'rebuilding') of that nation's identity for which it is then known, and so far conspicuously honoured, throughout the world: 'we find the most soaring imaginations, as a rule, in defeated or oppressed nations, like the Hebrew and the Celts'.[8]

Let's extract from the matrioshka doll of the nation that of the individual. Derrida detects in Lévi-Strauss's work 'an ethic of presence, an ethic of nostalgia for origins, an ethic of archaic and natural innocence, of a purity of presence and self-presence in speech—an ethic, a nostalgia, and even remorse'.[9] I have illustrated in Chapter 1 how this ethic operates in the poetry of Seán Ó Ríordáin but now, with Derrida's help, I want to activate an alternative view:

> Turned towards the lost or impossible presence of the absent origin, this structuralist thematic of broken immediacy is therefore the saddened, *negative*, nostalgic, guilty, Rousseauistic side of the thinking of play whose other side would be the Nietzschean *affirmation*, that is the joyous affirmation of the play of the world and of the innocence of becoming, the affirmation of a world of signs without fault, without truth, and without origin which is offered to an active interpretation. *This affirmation then determines the noncentre otherwise than as loss of the centre.* And it plays without security. For there is a *sure* play: that which is limited to the *substitution* of *given* and *existing*, *present*, pieces.[10]

These 'absolutely irreconcilable' views which, nevertheless, Derrida admits we live 'simultaneously', reveal the 'tension of freeplay with history [and] of freeplay with presence'.[11] For example, Ó Ríordáin's grasping for elusive straws of truth, certainty, continuity, and stability, engaged him in the play of his speculative and exploratory poetry. It was through imagination and linguistic play, after all, that Ó Ríordáin sought the essence of ideal self, actual self, and that beyond self. Yet, his play (and consequently his vision) was often limited to the disappointed viewpoint which

---

[8] Frye, N., 'The Imaginative and the Imaginary', *Fables of Identity: Studies in Poetic Mythology* (New York: Harcourt, Brace and World, Inc., 1963), 151–67 (p. 153).

[9] Macksey and Donato, *The Structuralist Controversy*, 264.

[10] Rylance, *Debating Texts*, 134–5.

[11] Macksey and Donato, *The Structuralist Controversy*, 263.

seeks to decipher, dreams of deciphering a truth or an origin which is free from freeplay and from the order of the sign, and lives like an exile the necessity of interpretation . . . [due to its insistent dream] of full presence, the reassuring foundation, the origin and the end of the game.[12]

Indeed, Roland Barthes's comments in 'The Utopia of Language' could well apply to Ó Ríordáin's work:

Like modern art in its entirety, literary writing carries at the same time the alienation of History and the dream of History . . . Feeling permanently guilty of its own solitude, it is none the less an imagination eagerly desiring a felicity of words, it hastens towards a dreamed-of language whose freshness, by a kind of ideal anticipation, might portray the perfection of some new Adamic world where language would no longer be alienated.[13]

Yet, this leads, as Paul De Man via William Empson has shown, to 'all the traps of *impatient* 'pastoral' thought: formalism, false historicism and utopianism'[14] [my italics] which one finds in a poem such as 'Fill Arís'/Return Again (*B* p. 41). All ideologies (including Ó Ríordáin's) can become 'impatient' because they contain, according to Robert Eccleshall's definition, a view of society as it is, as it should be and a programme to connect the actual society with the ideal.[15] The glamour of the ideal (whether it is modelled on the past or not) can, when over-emphasized, reflect badly on the present which it distorts into an even more negative light. So how does one walk the tight-rope between Barthes's 'alienation of History and the dream of History' taut with Derrida's 'tension between play and history [. . .] play and presence'?

By following Stephen Dedalus's advice in *A Portrait of the Artist As a Young Man* to encounter 'the reality of experience' and, in *Ulysses*, to 'hold to the here and now, the here through which all future plunges to the past'.[16] For the individual, this involves Lévi-Strauss's notion of 'bricolage', interpreted by Derrida as 'the necessity of borrowing one's

---

[12] Ibid. 264–5.
[13] Barthes, R., 'The Utopia of Language', *Writing Degree Zero* (New York: Hill and Wang, 1968), 84–8 (pp. 87–8).
[14] de Man, P., from 'The Dead-end of Formalist Criticism', in R. Rylance (ed.), *Debating Texts*, 101–9 (p. 108).
[15] See Eccleshall, R., *Political Ideologies: An Introduction* (London: Hutchinson, 1984), 7–35.
[16] See Welch, R., 'James Clarence Mangan: Apples from the Dead Sea Shore', *Irish Poetry from Moore to Yeats*, Irish Literary Studies, 5 (Buckinghamshire: Colin Smythe Ltd., 1980), 76–115 (p. 80).

concepts from the text of a heritage which is more or less coherent *or ruined* [my italics].[17] The literary *bricoleur* would, therefore, be someone who uses 'the instruments he finds at his disposition around him'[18] whatever they are and in any combination, someone like Cathal Ó Searcaigh, Nuala Ní Dhomhnaill or other poets of the *INNTI* generation.

My point is that after the event or rupture that decentred the structure of Gaelic civilization, Irish writers have had to go through crash-courses in a rebuilding or, as I prefer, building anew programme of literary construction. Literature, like architecture, develops slowly; its practitioners gradually mastering the control of diverse materials and methods from home and abroad. From the first picking up of the pieces, a whole tradition may be built up through, for example, the rickety renovation of ruins by Mangan to the piling of 'buildung supra buildung' by Joyce. In twentieth-century Irish language literature, the generation of Pearse, Mac Donagh, and Ó Conaire were the architects who drafted the *inter*nationalist plans and laid the foundations for future writing;[19] the generation of Ó Ríordáin, Ó Direáin, and Mhac an tSaoi were the labourers and craftspeople (*bricoleurs*) who gathered diverse and scattered material, mixed and set it to use, creating the first modern dwellings for new poetry in Irish. Now, in the generation of Ó Searcaigh and Ní Dhomhnaill, the literary estate or new Alhambra of the language is expanding and looking like it is lived in, much as Ciarán Carson described:

> Forget the corncrake's elegy. Rusty
> Iambics that escaped your discipline
> Of shorn lawns, it is sustained by nature.
> It does not grieve for you, nor for itself [. . .]
>
> A shiver now runs through the laurel hedge,
> And washing flutters like the swaying lines
> Of a new verse.[20]

[17] Macksey and Donato, *The Structuralist Controversy*, 255.   [18] Ibid.
[19] See Denvir, G., 'Litríocht agus Pobal: Nualitríocht na Gaeilge agus an Traidisiúin', *Litríocht agus Pobal* (Indreabhán: Cló Iar-Chonnachta, 1997), 21–59 (pp. 39–41). See also Ó hÁinle, C. G. ' "The Inalienable Right of Trifles": Tradition and Modernity in Gaelic Writing Since the Revival', in *Eire-Ireland*, Vol. XIX (Winter 1984), 59–77 (pp. 60–8).
[20] Carson, C., 'The New Estate', *The New Estate: and Other Poems* (Oldcastle: Gallery, 1988), 69.

2.1 *SÚILE SHUIBHNE/SWEENEY'S EYES* (1983)

I rely often on this ordinary thought:
near Lake Baikal my own town waiting for me.[21]

It is a long way from Caiseal na gCorr Station[22] to Yevtushenko's Zimá Station. As Ó Searcaigh tries to put them on the same literary map, the best way first to encounter the Donegal poet's work is to look into *Súile Shuibhne*/Sweeney's Eyes (1983), his second full collection.[23] Illustrated with black-and-white photographs by Rachel Giese, this volume shows a growing concentration on the poet's experiences of his home ground around Mín a' Leá at the foot of Mount Errigal in Co. Donegal. The map of Ó Searcaigh's poetic territory, its main themes, his own voice and language emerge and are identifiable from this volume onwards.

There is a formal unity in the order of poems. The collection begins with 'Cor Úr', which calls upon the land to give the gift of 'A Fresh Dimension' (*ABB* p. 86) to the poet and his work, and ends with the manifesto-like poem 'An Tobar/The Well' which concludes: 'caithfear pilleadh arís ar na fóinsí'.[24] Going back to sources is, indeed, the key to Ó Searcaigh's practice in *Súile Shuibhne*.[25] He returns to his native area and utilizes the local place-names and, importantly, dialect. Surprisingly, Ó Searcaigh's first volume had borrowed from Ó Ríordáin's Munster Irish; from the second volume on, the poet realizes the necessity and potential of drawing from the living speech of his own area which turns out to be an enviable resource. See, for example, 'Portráid den Ghabha Mar Ealaíontóir Óg/A Portrait of the Blacksmith

---

[21] Yevtushenko, from 'Zimá Station', *Yevgeny Yevtushenko: Selected Poems*, ed. by R. Milner-Gulland and P. Levi, S.J. (Middlesex: Penguin Books, 1962, repr. 1964), 19–51 (p. 19).

[22] An old disused local railway station near Ó Searcaigh's home in Donegal, also the setting for a poem central to his oeuvre: 'Anseo ag Staisiún Chaiseal na gCorr/Here at Caiseal na gCorr Station', in *An Bealach 'na Bhaile/Homecoming*, 94–7. The poet was born in 1956 and grew up in the Gaeltacht area of Gort a' Choirce. Further autobiographical details are given in the poems.

[23] Two collections appeared earlier: *Miontraigéide Cathrach* (1975) and *tuirlingt* (1978). Both of these collections, however, were published prematurely, are now out of print, and no longer representative of the poet's work.

[24] 'There will have to be a going back to sources.' From 'An Tobar/The Well', *ABB* pp. 42–5.

[25] See also Longley, M., 'A going back to sources', *Poetry Ireland Review*, 39 (Autumn 1993), 92–6. This is a review of *An Bealach 'na Bhaile* (containing many of the poems from *Súile Shuibhne*).

as a Young Artist' (*ABB* p. 84) and also 'An Tobar/The Well' in which
Old Bríd's advice to 'aimsigh do thobar féin'/find your own well is on a
par with that of MacLaverty to Heaney in 'Fosterage'[26] or with that of
Auden's philosophical mentors: 'I have drawn from the well of language
many a thought which I did not have and could not put into words'.[27]
Is Ó Searcaigh's Gort a' Choirce, then, yet another example of an Irish
poet's 'parish'?

Kavanagh wrote that 'parochialism is universal; it deals with the
fundamentals'.[28] There are great differences in 'blas' or taste, in Ó
Ríordáin's sense, between Heaney's bog and place-name poems,
'Anahorish' or 'Broagh'[29] and Muldoon's use of the Moy area of
Armagh, Carson's 'Belfast confetti', Mahon's lonely bird-like scaveng-
ings and Longley's Mayo discoveries, but one can see that they all give
voice to varying senses of place and displacement. Ó Searcaigh's contri-
bution to post-modern dinnseanchas/place-lore seems much more
traditional but is also deeply philosophical. His engagement with place
is akin to that with all acutely observed sensibilia: a two-way process of
perception and reflection of the kind John Gordon has noted in the
work of Joyce:

Perception, by itself and in its extreme manifestation hallucination, is always in
Joyce projection to some extent; to 'encounter the reality of experience' is
always, to some extent, to encounter oneself. Joyce could have had this observation confirmed by, among others, Giambattista Vico, who observed the way
that men named the landscape after themselves—as in foothill and cavemouth—and concluded that the story of Ulysses' encounter with Proteus,
interpreted as 'first matter', was really the story of Narcissus, Man's encounter
with his own image.[30]

Similarly, Ralph Waldo Emerson commented on humankind's life-
long interrelationship with the objects of nature as follows:

And neither can man be understood without these objects, nor these objects
without man. All the facts in natural history taken by themselves have no value,

---

[26]   Heaney, *New Selected Poems*, 89.
[27]   Lichtenberg quoted by Auden, W. H., *Secondary Worlds* (London: Faber and Faber,
1968), 122.
[28]   Kavanagh, P., 'The Parish and the Universe', *Collected Prose*, 2nd edn. (London:
Martin Brian and O'Keefe, 1973), 281–3 (p. 283).
[29]   Heaney, *New Selected Poems*, 21 and 25.
[30]   Gordon, J., *James Joyce's Metamorphoses* (London: Gill and MacMillan, 1981), 2–3.

but are barren like a single sex. But marry it to human history and it is full of life.[31]

W. H. Auden in turn realized that humankind's interaction with the objects of nature had implications for not only the image-seeking artist but also for the reader's encounter with the poem-object:

Not only is every poem unique, but its significance is unique for each person who responds to it. In so far as one can speak of poetry as conveying knowledge, it is the kind of knowledge implied by the Biblical phrase—*Then Adam knew Eve his wife*—knowing is inseparable from being known.[32]

Ideas such as those above, based on his readings from the prose of Auden and Emerson, inform Ó Searcaigh's developing aesthetic. As a consequence, two main motifs or characteristics emerge in his work. Firstly, the poet-speaker completely identifies or expresses himself in terms of his environment and its objects as, for example, in 'Maidin i Mín a' Leágha'/Morning In Mín a' Leá (*SS* p. 32) or 'Bó Bhrádach/A Braddy Cow' (*ABB* p. 126). Secondly, he sexualizes his environment, nature, and its objects, into a feminine muse-figure through whom the Adamic poet-speaker can 'know' and be 'known', as in 'Súile Shuibhne/Sweeney's Eyes' (*ABB* p. 180). Incidentally, Ó Searcaigh's meeting or mating of the 'sexes'—Self with Notself, male poet with feminine landscape and/or Muse—continues a chain of *artistic* productivity:

[. . .] nach síolrófaí de chlann	*the only children to spring*
do mo leithéidse choíche	*from the likes of me ever*
ach cibé clann bheag bhéarsaí	*would be a family of verse*
a shaolófaí domh san oíche	*born to me in the night*
as broinn mhéith na Béithe [. . .]	*from the juicy womb of the Muse [. . .]*

Such, we are told, is the 'bond' placed on the poet by 'Poetry' in 'Geasa'/The Bond, or Taboo (*OO* p. 78). Yet what is crucial and significant in terms of Ó Searcaigh's aesthetics is that, in almost all of his poems referring to nature and the natural world, he is pursuing Joyce's objective: 'our object is to create a new fusion between the exterior world and our contemporary selves [. . .] Sensation is our object, heightened even to the point of hallucination'.[33]

---

[31] See Auden, *Secondary Worlds*, 130–1.
[32] Ibid. 131.
[33] James Joyce, speaking to Arthur Power, quoted in Gordon, J., *James Joyce's Metamorphoses*, 1.

In this regard, one of the most interesting poems in *Súile Shuibhne* is the title poem:

> Tá mé ag tarraingt ar bharr na Bealtaine
> go dúchroíoch i ndorchacht na hoíche
> ag ardú malacha i m'aistear is i m'aigne
> ag cur in aghaidh bristeacha borba gaoithe.
>
> B'ise mo mhaoinín, b'ise mo Ghort a' Choirce,
> mise a thug a cuid fiántais chun míntíreachais
> ach tá a claonta dúchais ag teacht ar ais arís
> anocht bhí súile buí i ngort na seirce.
>
> Tchím Véineas ansiúd os cionn Dhún Lúiche
> ag caochadh anuas lena súile striapaí
> agus ar ucht na Mucaise siúd cíoch na gealaí
> ag gobadh as gúna dubh na hoíche.
>
> Idir dólás agus dóchas, dhá thine Bhealtaine,
> caolaím d'aon rúid bhuile mar leathdhuine.
> Tá soilse an ghleanna ag crith os mo choinne—
> faoi mhalaí na gcnoc sin iad súile Shuibhne.[34]

This poem brings the reader into the centre of Ó Searcaigh's geographical and linguistic 'parish', a strongly feminine and apparently capricious combination of landscape, language, and Muse, in Irish—dúiche, Gaeilge and Bé na filíochta, all feminine nouns. While for Kavanagh, 'the love-act and its pledge' was 'naming things';[35] here, as often for Ó Searcaigh, it is place-naming. A litany of local townlands and landmarks is recited with loving familiarity, with—and also *for*—a reassuring sense of intimacy, of 'knowing' and 'being known', of being at home or at one with, and in, the language as much as the place. A difficulty arises, therefore, for any subsequent translator of his work, as Dúghlas Sealy noted: 'a chain of local placenames keep the poet's soul from straying but in English these are just meaningless names for places. The well, the water, the rock, the mountain hollow, the muck, the enclosures, all lose their meaning in English.'[36] In 'Súile Shuibhne'/Sweeney's Eyes, for example, Gort a' Choirce should appear literally as a golden 'field of oats' and flash upon the reader's inward eye as brightly as Wordsworth's daffodils.

---

[34] 'Súile Shuibhne'. Translation F in Appendix. See also *OO* pp. 50–1.
[35] Kavanagh, 'The Hospital', in P. Muldoon (ed.), *The Faber Book of Contemporary Irish Poetry* (London: Faber and Faber, 1986), 76–7.
[36] Sealy, D., Review of *An Bealach 'na Bhaile*, in *Comhar* (July 1993), 21–2. [My trans.]

Of course, the successful transmission of all poetry depends upon a belief that its terms of reference, if not shared, are at least understood by its readers. Readers with a knowledge of Irish would probably appreciate more readily allusions such as that to Bealtaine which, in modern Irish, denotes the month of May but originates in the Celtic festival celebrating the beginning of summer with the lighting of bonfires. Bealtaine, literally meaning 'bright fire' or 'goodly fire' (name also of the mountain in Donegal where the poet lives), welcomes the sun and usually heralds change.[37]

It is characteristically paradoxical that the god being worshipped, Bel, is god both of life and death. Knowing this makes the sense of crisis in the poem more acute. Poet and poem, caught between despair and hope, light and dark, must pass through the flames of Bealtaine to live and (be) regenerate(d). Passage through the flames promises both purgation and fertility. There is, after all, a combination of traditionally masculine and feminine forces at work in the poem. These suggest that a successful negotiation of the meeting point or flash-point of light and dark, the will and the wild, should prove productive. Thus poem and poet travel from darkness and apparent loss to the vision at the end of the poem where, finally, the poet-speaker is brought face to face with the archetypal Sweeney; the bird-man in whom, of course, nature and art are combined. It is easy to imagine the poet, at this point, 'down on all fours' like Thomas Hardy in Heaney's 'Lightenings',[38] knowing and known 'even to the point of hallucination',[39] finding himself and his psychological, emotional journey mirrored back through his physical tracks and the word-tracks of the poem.

Gréagóir Ó Dúill claims that Ó Searcaigh's landscape poems 'do not only celebrate the place [. . .] but use placenames and describe areas in order to refer to people, a community and his relationship with it'.[40] Equally, however, Ó Searcaigh refers to the landscape in *human* terms in order to explore his relationship with that landscape. His passion for his locale can take on a sexual intensity and is encouraged to do so by his observation (made also by Vico and Joyce among others) of 'the way

---

[37] See Berresford Ellis, P., *A Dictionary of Irish Mythology* (London: Constable and Co. Ltd., 1987), 41–2.

[38] Heaney, 'Lightenings' Part VII, *Seeing Things*, 61.

[39] Gordon, *James Joyce's Metamorphoses*, 2–3.

[40] Ó Dúill, G., 'Filíocht Chathail Uí Shearcaigh: i dtreo anailíse téamúla', *An tUltach* (January 1993), 12–19 (p. 14).

that men named the landscape after themselves—as in foothill and cavemouth . . .'[41] Therefore, it is the linguistic as well as the physical nature of his surrounding area which invite the poet to set his language 'inclining towards things, as things incline towards language',[42] to let his linguistic 'gesture'[43] mimic that of the piece of the universe known to him:

> Ciúnaíonn tú chugam as ceo na maidine
> mus na raideoige ar d'fhallaing fraoigh,
> do ghéaga ina srutháin gheala ag sní
> thart orm go lúchaireach, géaga
> a fháiltíonn romham le fuiseoga.

> *Like silence you come from the morning mist,*
> *musk of bog-myrtle on your heather cloak,*
> *your limbs—bright streams lapping joyfully*
> *around me, limbs*
> *that welcome me with skylarks.*[44]

Ó Dúill strays slightly when he tries to work out which stanzas of the poem refer to topographical flesh and which to human. The strength of the poem is embedded in its imaginative play between these two possibilities which the placenames in stanza four tease out: the hollow of the back of the sun, the elbowed hillock, the red brows, the smooth or level breast.[45] The poem works its way down to a climax between 'cabhsaí geala do chos'/the bright causeway of your [the place's] legs, culminating in the suggestion of the impregnation of the poet's future or fate[46] with a new life or vitality, a 'cor úr' or 'fresh dimension'—including, by implication, off-spring: this and subsequent poems.

It is worth remembering Ó Searcaigh's comment 'gurb é atá i bhfilíocht ná sraith de chodarsnachta a bhfuil gaol gairid eatarthu agus a fhreagraíonn dá chéile ar bhealach a dheimhníonn teorainn an

---

[41] Gordon, *James Joyce's Metamorphoses*, 2.

[42] Welch, R., 'The Loutishness of Learning: the Presence of Writing', in E. A. Markham (ed.), *Writing Ulster*, Nos 2–3, 1991–2 (Dept. of English, Media and Theatre Studies, University of Ulster at Coleraine), 58–71 (p. 69).

[43] See Gordon, *James Joyce's Metamorphoses*, 5.

[44] 'Cor Úr/Fresh Dimension', *ABB* pp. 86–7.

[45] 'Ó Log Dhroim na Gréine go hAlt na hUilline/ón Mhalaidh Rua go Mín na hUchta'. See *ABB* p. 86.

[46] Ó Searcaigh often uses the one Irish word 'dán' to combine its various intertwined meanings in Irish: i.e. fate or lot, future, or destiny, but also poem, restriction, binding thread, or rope.

limistéir ag a dtarlaíonn gníomh diamhair amhail Apacailiops ag a cheartlár éiginnte.'[47] His notion of 'Apocalypse' borders on that of orgasm and vice versa. For example, love, passion, and reproduction—sexual and poetic—are usually seen in his work in terms and images of consuming flames which recall both the Apocalypse and the mythical Phoenix: the fiery purgation of 'Súile Shuibhne'/Sweeney's Eyes (*ABB* p. 180), the cosmic fire and rain of 'Dídean/Shelter' (*ABB* p. 154) and, most obviously, the poem 'Dúil/Desire':

> B'fhearr liomsa buachaill thí an leanna
> a bhfuil a chroí lán de theas ceana
>
> Is a labhrann i laomanna lasánta
> faoina dhuáilcí is faoina dhánta
>
> Is a dhéanann gáire chomh gríosaitheach
> le craos de mhóin chipíneach
>
> Is a chaitheann spréachta óna shúile
> a lasann tinidh mo dhúile
>
> Ná Nefertítí í féin i mo leabaidh
> is iontaisí na bhFaróanna ar fud an tí.[48]

Hot on the heels of *Súile Shuibhne*'s opening invocation for the Donegal landscape to bestow on the poet a new movement or theme, life or dimension, comes a series of poems of exile. These city poems reveal a growing self-awareness on the part of Ó Searcaigh. He realizes that his true subject is not the city itself[49] but his own feelings towards it, and the perspective it gives him on home, as well as that which home gives him on the city.

The poem 'Londain'/London (*OO* p. 148), is a synthesis of 'Miontraigéide Cathrach'/A Minor City-tragedy No. 2 (in which the city was actually Dublin) and 'Stoite'/Uprooted.[50] Its extended metaphor of workers spilling out of a 'carn lofa d'oifigí gnó/stinking pile of office blocks' like 'pláigh chuileog/a plague of flies' reminds one of Kafka; the alienation of the individual with only his or her precious

---

[47] 'In poetry you get a series of contrasts that are closely related and mirror each other in a way that affirms the sphere where a mysterious act like an Apocalypse happens at its uncertain centre . . .'. See *MC* p. 9.

[48] *OO* p. 96. Translation G in Appendix.

[49] He tried and failed, for example, to encompass the city in his first (and premature) collection *Miontraigéide Cathrach*.

[50] See *MC* pp. 19–21 and pp. 23–4, respectively.

time or body to sell is Marxist; while the one-dimensional hollow men and women of the office blend Marcuse with Eliot; also, the dark humour, particularly of names like 'Dodo' or 'Boremann', recalls Gogol. The conclusion, however, is pure Ó Searcaigh:

> . . . Amárach
> pillfidh mé ar Ghleann an Átha, áit a nglanfar sileadh an anró
> as m'aigne, áit a gcuirfear in iúl domh go carthanach
> go gcneasaíonn goin ach nach bhfásann fionnadh ar an cholm.

> . . . *Tomorrow, I'm back*
> *in Glenford where I'll be purged of this poison*
> *and learning the all-too-familiar lesson*
> *that a wound heals but hair doesn't grow on the scar.*

His solution is traditional sanctuary, 'man to the hills'. Yet, grafting himself back to the body of his homeland will not be without pains or complications as indicated by that powerful and suggestive image of the scar, all the more potent because it is not reduced by explanation.

What is remarkable about the poem 'Gladstone Park' (*OO* p. 150) is how the desolate scene of inner-city decay, both social and environmental, does not disillusion or depress the poet but instead reassures him, by way of contrast, of his own personal youth, virility, and individuality:

> Mar d'ainneoin na déistine, braithim bród i mo chroí;
> mar bhuachaill ar fheiceáil a chéad ribí fionnaidh,
> bród go bhfuilim anois in aois fir is gur tús fáis
> mo dhaonnachta an bháidh seo le lucht an dóláis.

> *apart from my disdain, I'm proud as a boy*
> *discovering his first hairs, proud*
> *to become a man whose humanity begins*
> *plumbing these depths with the woebegone.*

Moreover, the poet does not only feel disdain towards

> daoine dubhacha na cathrach,
> na seanphinsinéirí a bhíonn ina suí leo féin ar bhinsí,
> a gcnámha ag scamhadh, iad goncach le slaghdán,
> na bacaigh chromshlinneánacha ag rúscadh i gcannaí [. . .]

> *the blighted city folk:*
> *old-age pensioners sitting snot-*
> *nosed on lonely benches, failing,*
> *hunched-up tramps hoking in tins [. . .]*

but feels 'a mbuairt mar bheadh sconnóg chársánach fola/i bhfostú i mo sceadamán'[51] and marvels at their suffering: ' 'Dhia, a leithéid de phionós./God, what punishment!' His response could hardly differ more from that expressed by Philip Larkin's persona in 'Toads Revisited' who finds the habitués of *his* pack to be

> Palsied old step-takers,
> Hare-eyed clerks with the jitters,
>
> Waxed-fleshed out-patients
> Still vague from accidents,
> And characters in long coats
> Deep in the litter-baskets—
>
> All dodging the toad work
> By being stupid or weak.[52]

The middle-aged Larkin's ironic conclusion is not renewed faith in his own (temporary) strength and health but a comically hasty retreat back to the distraction of work at the office: 'What else can I answer . . ?'

For Ó Searcaigh, Gladstone Park has the virtue of being 'out in the open' air. Inside his dungeon-like bedsit, even *his* immunity to the city etiolates with the absence of light in 'Aon Séasúr den Bhliain/Any Season of the Year':

Is anseo i saol seargtha	*And here in the withered world*
an bhrocsholais, tá sé ina Shamhain	*of this foul light, it is November*
ag plandaí is ag leannáin.	*for plants and lovers.*
	(*ABB* p. 82)

'Samhain' (November) also denotes the period opposite to that of Bealtaine. Samhain marked the passing of summer and the beginning of winter, when livestock were rounded up, some for slaughter, others for breeding. It was a time of ritual mourning at the death of summer, a suspended time of danger and vulnerability, falling between the two halves of the Celtic year. During Samhain, between the thirty-first of October and the first of November, this and the other world, it was believed, interpenetrated as 'the worlds of life and death were inextricably intertwined'.[53]

It is characteristic of Ó Searcaigh to unite the plight of the lovers in

---

[51] 'Their sorrow, like blood, clot/the back of my throat'.

[52] Larkin, P., *Collected Poems* (London: Faber and Faber, 1988), 147–8.

[53] Greene, M. J., *Dictionary of Celtic Myth and Legend* (London: Thames and Hudson Ltd., 1992), 186.

this poem with that of the plants. His technique here and in
'Cíoradh'/Combing (*SS* p. 12) is the opposite of personification which
endows 'inanimate objects or abstract ideas [. . .] with human qualities
or action'.[54] On the contrary, Ó Searcaigh most often endows humans
with the qualities of 'inanimate' objects taken (usually) from nature. In
this way, he escapes the weakness which Ruskin detected in 'Pathetic
Fallacy' which was that it distorts nature, produces 'a falseness in all our
impressions of external things.'[55] However, in all poems there are varying degrees of tension between outer and inner reality, varying degrees
of attachment and detachment, of inclination between language and
the thing,[56] the thing and language.[57] Occasionally, therefore, in Ó
Searcaigh's work, one sees Ruskin's ideal (of a perfect balance in the
imagery linking the human world and nature) break down. In such
cases, it is humanity and the creations of humanity, not nature, that the
Donegal poet 'distorts', neglecting perhaps the 'otherness' of very different things that still may form part of a total world unity:

> Is dá dtiocfá liom, a ghrá,
> bheadh briathra ag bláthú ar ghas mo ghutha
> mar shiolastrach Ghleann an Átha [. . .]
>
> Ach b'fhearr leatsa i bhfad
> brúchtbhaile balscóideach i mBaile Átha Cliath
> lena ghleo tráchta gan stad [. . .]
>
> *. . . and if you would come with me, love,*
> *words would flower on the stem of my voice*
> *like yellow-flag in Gleann an Átha . . .*
>
> *But you'd much prefer*
> *a smutty [literally, poxy and spewed-out] suburb in Dublin*
> *with the incessant din of traffic . . .*
>   (from 'Níl Aon Ní/There's Nothing', *ABB* p. 89)

If Ó Searcaigh's vision of humans is blurred—or conveyed, depending

---

[54] Beckson, K. and Ganz, A., *Literary Terms: A Dictionary*, 3rd edn. (London: André
Deutsch Ltd, 1990), 198.
[55] Ibid. 195.
[56] See Douglas, 'Words', in D. Graham (ed.), *Keith Douglas: Complete Poems* (Oxford:
Oxford University Press, 1990 edn.), 101; and Welch, 'The Loutishness of Learning', 69.
[57] Northrop Frye wrote that poets and painters operate in 'the flux between the thing
as idea and the idea as thing'; also, he quotes Wallace Stevens' statement that 'there is
always an analogy between nature and the imagination, and possibly poetry is merely the
strange rhetoric of that parallel.' See Frye, *Fables of Identity*, 295 and 248.

on your view—with foliage, his vision of the city is also blinkered or, in this case, distorted by his perception of cities as eye-sores, his identification of the urban landscape with blots, blemishes, and boils: 'brúchtbhaile balscóideach i mBaile Átha Cliath', an ill-sounding account of Dublin's 'fair' City.

As in 'Gladstone Park', where the poet was contrasted with, but strangely drawn towards, the local 'odd-birds and invalids', there are throughout Ó Searcaigh's work examples of poems in which he is attracted and fascinated by characters who seem polar opposites of the persona which the poetry would normally have us associate with its author. If he is characteristically 'on the side of light, and of life',[58] these characters who fascinate him have either been consumed by some darkness or have surrendered to it.

Muiris, in 'An Croí ba Shú Talún/The Strawberry Heart' (*ABB* p. 192), was a friend of Ó Searcaigh's who lost his family tragically in a fire and died broken-hearted afterwards. This man's grief not only moved the poet as a human being but fascinated a part of his imagination which appears to be attracted to the morbid. However, he sees death and decay as part of life and nature, responding with awe to those who embrace the dark, as well as the light, just as long as they do so passionately. Ó Searcaigh has inherited Kerouac's sixties-style preference for people who are 'mad to live' and 'burn like fabulous roman candles' (*ABB* p. 188) but accepts that, as a consequence, they are destined to die young, to quickly burn out. It is not altogether a coincidence, then, that the person celebrated in 'Na Píopaí Créafóige/The Clay-Pipes' (*ABB* p. 198) is Ted Holmes, a poet of the Beat generation, whose experiential quest ended in a desire to taste death 'fully and completely'. Ó Searcaigh's poem recalls not only the sixties and the Beat generation but also Blake in its association of excess with learning, and danger with truth. What Muiris and Ted Holmes have in common is *passion*, a key-word and criterion in Ó Searcaigh's verse.

'Fiacha an tsolais'/The [Electric] Light Bill (*ABB* p. 120) examines the fate of a young man who drained himself of life by drinking himself to death. The Electricity Service Board man quoted at the end of the poem concludes:

> '. . . Ach an té a dhéanann faillí i bhfiacha an tsolais
> a thiarcais, nach é féin cúis a dhorchadais.'

---

[58] 'Ar thaobh an tSolais, fosta ar thaobh na Beatha'. From 'Do Isaac Rosenberg', *OO* pp. 240–3 (p. 242).

'. . . but he who fails to pay his dues to the light
—sure, doesn't he leave himself in the dark?'

Ó Searcaigh's outlook is stoical. Like Han Shan, he has faced the cold
mountain of his local terrain for years and gained 'the virtue of an art
that knows its mind'[59] and also of an art that knows something of
nature on which all traditions and mythologies are based. If there is a
message in his work, it is to embrace the light, the fires of Bealtaine, of
life, in the full knowledge that Samhain and death will come. In any
case, he makes it clear that even if the 'rothaí móra na bliana/big wheels
of the year' *were* somehow to stand still, this would only cause increased
stagnation and decay, as in 'Aon Séasúr den Bhliain/Any Season of the
Year' (*ABB* p. 82).

Perhaps Ó Searcaigh's most interesting and revealing poem on the
movement from life towards death is his most recent, 'An
Duibheagán/The Deep', which explores some of his own preoccupation
with the subject via the metaphor of death as a sea swelling gradually
within each of us. The death-pull is felt more strongly when the tide of
mortality suddenly comes closer to our own position on the shore when
we witness, say, an accident or suicide:

Tá 'n duibheagán ag drannadh leis, an scaifte ar fad
    ag feitheamh leis.
Níl le déanamh aige ach an cinneadh, a sciatháin
    a leathnú, léim
a thabhairt, snámh sa ghaoth, imeacht i bhfeachtaí
    fiala an aeir
thar Alltar. Tá an lá caoin le cách, ceo teasa ag éirí
    ó dhíonta agus ó linnte,
borradh i ngach beo. Chan tráth báis é seo, mheasfá, ach
    a mhalairt, tráth fáis.
Stánann siad in airde, slua de choimhthígh agus de chairde,
    téad teann tuisceana
á dteannadh i bpáirtíocht na péine, á mbrú gan trócaire
    i mbuairt na díomuaine . . .
Tá siad ar fad ina n-aonaráin, lom lag ina láthair féin:
    Ag stanadh airsean
ansiúd ar an airdeacht, tá siad ag stánadh ar an duibheagán
    atá thíos iontu féin;

---

[59] Heaney, 'Squarings', *Seeing Things*, 97.

An duibheagán atá ag drannadh leo aníos as na híochtair
   go diabhlaí dúshlánach
is a gcur as a meabhair. Tá mearbhlán ag teacht ar an iomlán,
   gafa i ngad a gcinniúna,
níl i gcaint, i ngeáitsí, i ngoithe reatha, i mbrealsúnacht
   bhocht a mbeatha
ach scáth cosanta agus gleo. Tá 'n duibheagán ag drannadh leo.[60]

Another important and recurring theme in *Súile Shuibhne* is religion. Poem-titles such as 'Transubstaintiú'/Transubstantiation and 'An tAngelus'/The Angelus[61] remind us that Ó Searcaigh was brought up in the Irish Catholic tradition. It is clear, however, that the poet's faith does not conform to orthodox Christianity but is closer to what Peter Berresford Ellis calls 'the Celtic' rather than the Catholic Church.[62] The 'transubstaintiú' to which Ó Searcaigh refers is the Joycean one of thought into word, and his Angelus has a ring of Celtic and/or Romantic pantheism:

> nuair a bhuail aingeal ón tséipéal anall
> slánaíodh an síol i ngach ball.
>
> *when the angel strikes from the chapel beyond,*
> *the seed is everywhere made safe and sound.*
>
> (*OO* p. 52)

This pantheistic strand in Ó Searcaigh's work ought not to be overlooked. Ó Dúill, for example, over-simplifies the poet's criticisms of the limitations of orthodox Christianity by attributing these to his sexuality alone: 'this leaning [homosexuality] made the poet feel he had to oppose the authorities and bureaucracies of his youth and that is why some of his references to the church and to formal religion are bitter and disrespectful; nevertheless, he did not think he had to reject the traditional values of his neighbourhood.'[63] By bitter and disrespectful, I assume that Ó Dúill refers to poems such as 'Briathra agus Bráithre/Brotherly Words':

'Is bráithre muid go léir,'   *'We're all brothers'*
arsa an manach le m'athair   *said the monk to my father*
ach nuair a thrasnaíos   *but when I cut through*

---

60 From 'An Duibheagán/The Deep', *OO* pp. 228–31. Translation H in Appendix.
61 See *ABB* pp. 184–5 and *OO* pp. 52–3, respectively.
62 Berresford Ellis, P., *Celtic Inheritance* (London: Frederick Muller, 1985).
63 Ó Dúill, 'Filíocht Chathail Uí Shearcaigh', 12–19 (p. 17). My translation.

an cur i gcéill go groí
le 'macasamhail Cháin is Aibéil'
chreathnaíos. Bhí miodóga
fionaíolacha na súl
sáite ionam go croí.

his bull with 'Yeah,
like Cain and Abel',
I near shit. The hook
in his eyes cut me
to the quick.

(*OO* p. 36)

However, it is not only Ó Searcaigh's sexual orientation—more apparent as he gradually comes out and speaks out—that sets him at odds with Christian orthodoxies but the very 'traditional values' to which Ó Dúill refers: for example, the Celtic animism of 'An tAngelus' (*OO* p. 38) and the zoomorphic imagery of 'Trasnú/Crossing' (*SS* p. 18) do not refute Christianity but adapt it to an older tradition.

Notably, Ó Dúill has recently accepted that Ó Searcaigh's occasional challenges to authority, in part, stem from his people's traditionally unruly attitude to bossmanship,[64] as evidenced in 'Bean an tSléibhe/Mountain Woman' (*OO* p. 22) and 'Agallamh na Seanorach/The Colloquy of the Ancients (*ABB* p. 134). Yet, Ó Searcaigh's own unruliness does not cause him to dismiss formal religion—despite its own exclusivity—rather, he regrets those limitations that not only place some kinds of love 'ar an taobh thuathal den tsoiscéal/on the wrong side of the Gospel' (*OO* p. 112) but generally confine worship to the temple and to one image of God. Thus it is not simply his sexual but also his cultural identification which drive the poet to challenge and breach the bounds of set religion. This places him in good company: Miranda J. Greene writes that 'the free Celtic traditions of open-air worship and aniconic perceptions of the gods [. . .] allowed the Celtic king, Brennus to scoff at anthropomorphic representations of Greek deities at Delphi.' The period to which Greene refers is that before 'Roman cults were accepted and absorbed into the Celtic religious system'. Even afterwards, she tells us 'Celtic perceptions of the divine world remained fundamentally the same',[65] that is, nature-based and topographical as in Ó Searcaigh's poem, 'Tearmann/Sanctuary':

Istigh anseo in ísleán an tsléibhe
tá sé níos suaimhní ná séipéal tuaithe.
Siúlaim, bearád i bpóca, go tostach
síos cairpéad caonaigh na pasáide,

---

[64] Ó Dúill, 'Cathal Ó Searcaigh: A Negotiation with Place, Community and Tradition', *Poetry Ireland Review*, 48 (Winter 1995), 14–18 (p. 16).
[65] Greene, M. J., *Dictionary of Celtic Myth and Legend*, 22.

síos idir na piúnna tortógacha,
is ag ardán na haltóra, seasaim bomaite,
is beochán beag gaoithe—an cléireach—
ag croitheadh tuise fraoigh ar fud na háite.

Here in the hollow of the mountains
it is more peaceful than a country chapel.
I walk, cap in pocket, silently
down the mossy carpet of the aisle,
down between the grass-clump pews,
and at the altar-height, stand a moment,
while a faint breeze—the altar-boy—
dispenses heather incense everywhere . . .

(*ABB* pp. 46–7)

What changes, over time, is not so much God, Ó Searcaigh infers in
'Cinniúint/Fate', as people's perceptions of God and our modes of
worship:

Is é cinniúint Dé
anois le déanaí
cinniúint na gréine is na gealaí
na gcrann is na gcarraigeacha
is iadsan uile ar tréigeadh a n-adhradh go brách
nuair a tugadh an creideamh Dósan tráth.

For a while now,
God has shared the same fate
as the sun and moon,
the trees, the rocks
and all the others whose worship
was abandoned once and for all
when faith was placed in Him. (*SS* p. 41)

Most controversial about Ó Searcaigh's poetry is his practice of
making a religion of love. He celebrates not just the 'brotherly' love of
the Hippies in 'If You're Going to San Falcarragh . . .' (*SS* p. 28), but the
free-wheeling sexual love of the 60s Beat poets whose teaching, he
claims in 'Do Jack Kerouac/For Jack Kerouac', was to make 'an
Orpheus of every orifice' (*ABB* p. 190). Joyce and Ó Ríordáin also
found in religion a language for art. Ó Searcaigh applies that language
with catholicity to all the 'things' of the universe which life permits the
sensitive observer or participant to encounter and experience:

Ar altóir na leapa
ceiliúraim do chorpsa anocht, a ghile,

le deasghnátha mo dhúile [. . .]
Is de réir mar a théann
an searmanas i ndéine is i ndlúthpháirtíocht
tá mo bhall bheatha ar crith
ag fanacht le míorúilt mhacnais
is tiocfaidh, tiocfaidh go fras
nuair a bhlaisfead diamhrachtaí do ghnéis—
cailís an mhiangais
tiocfaidh áthas na n-áthas
ina shacraimint, ina thabhartas,
ina theangacha tine an eolais.
Tiocfaidh
réamhaisnéis na bhflaitheas.

On the altar of the bed
I celebrate your body tonight, my love,
with the rites of my desire [. . .]
And as the ceremony intensifies
in solidarity
my body trembles
expecting the miracle
which will come voluptuously
when I taste the mystery of your sex—
the chalice of desire.
It will come, joy of joys,
a sacrament, a gift,
the fiery tongues of knowledge
and I will have
intimations of heaven.

(from 'Searmanas/Ceremony', *ABB* pp. 156–7)

This poem is a companion piece to 'Cor úr/A Fresh Dimension' (*ABB* p. 86) in which the land—through sexual intensity—is addressed, metaphorically, as a lover; here, in 'Searmanas/Ceremony', loving—through religious intensity—turns to veneration. All this was either too much sex, worship, or both for Dúghlas Sealy who described the poem as 'a nauseating mixture of lust and sentimentality.'[66] Too many reviewers want poets to be tame beasts, when they rarely are: Auden once noted that 'scepticism, said Santayana, is the chastity of the intellect. Precisely. But a chastity which is not founded upon a deep reverence for

---

[66] Sealy, Review of *An Bealach 'na Bhaile*, 22.

sex is nothing but tight-arsed old maidery';[67] and Ó Ríordáin once remarked (in English), in a letter which Ó Searcaigh likes to quote, that he would like to experience

> the Vatican and V. D. in juxtaposition. Pope Alexander the 6th was the great-est man [. . .] that ever lived, because, whoremonger that he was, he was not too uppish to take the job of Pope. Here in Ireland rosaries are said listlessly and lustlessly. When I hear them pray around me I feel that I have eaten wet towels [. . .] Fellows here read *The News of the World* between rosaries and x-rays. The words 'intimacy took place' are repeated about fifty times. This is totally disgusting. Latin Europe would never do that, I think. They understand ritu-alistic sin in Europe as Byron did. The ritual is half the secret. The other half is that a man should be in love with a woman, no matter how transiently, before he makes a human lodgement. Otherwise his progeny is bound to be unin-spired. Such offspring approach religion without sexual excitement and approach sin without religious feeling or ritual.[68]

So, to say that, in *Súile Shuibhne*, Ó Searcaigh advocates and performs a 'going back to sources' (poetic *and* national), does not imply a conservativism on his part, a desire to conform to narrow doctrines; on the contrary, his 'source' is generally wild and unpredictable (some-times even to his own dismay) like the unruly field of oats in 'Súile Shuibhne/Sweeney's Eyes', or the goddess of nature/poetry/love who blows away the 'ballaí dochta an tsearbhadais/staunch thick walls of bitterness' in 'Jericho' (*OO* p. 54). Ó Searcaigh's approach to conservat-ion or -ism, consciously and unconsciously, is the kind that wants to take the clear cold water from the traditional 'tobar an fhíoruisce/well of true water' (*ABB* p. 42) and throw it on the more militant, right-wing type of 'conservatives' who would shoot a corncrake (*ABB* p. 132), denounce or pounce on a hippie (*SS* p. 28), discriminate on the grounds of class, gender, sexuality, race, or species, and draw strict border-lines like 'The Pencil' in 'An Peann Luaidhe':

Ní bheidh a thaibhrithe choíche	*No sign of him dreaming*
ar chasadh gruaige ná ar thonnta.	*of curls or waves,*
Ar shaighdiúirí ina seasamh ar aire	*just stiff-backed soldiers*
a bhéas siad ná ar chónraí.	*standing to attention, or graves.*
Na nithe a bhfuil comhbhá aige leo	*He knows where to draw the line*
tá siad díreach.	*and rubs shoulders*
Na nithe nach bhfuil tá siad cam [. . .]	*only with the straight.* (*SS* p. 42)

---

[67] Auden, *Secondary Worlds*, 126.   [68] Ó Coileáin, *Seán Ó Ríordáin*, 106.

The poems of *Súile Shuibhne* are placed vis à vis photographs of Ó Searcaigh's local terrain taken by Rachel Giese which depict scenes where human life has intervened in the natural world and vice versa. Whether it is the road that has to bend like a nearby tree in the wind or the sheep sheltering in the shell of a Ford transit, these photographs take a wry look at objects from a perspective which spans time and highlights erosion but also implies a tenacious endurance.

On page forty-four, there is a photograph of a ruined house or small building with only one wall remaining.[69] In the centre, there is a perfect rectangular space where a window once was. Meeting this old ruin is like meeting the elderly woman of Heaney's 'Field of Vision' who is restricted to a wheel-chair and one window. Heaney writes of this 'steadfast' lady that

> Face to face with her was an education
> Of the sort you got across a well-braced gate—
> One of those lean, clean, iron, roadside ones
> Between two whitewashed pillars, where you could see
>
> Deeper into the country than you expected
> And discovered that the field behind the hedge
> Grew more distinctly strange as you kept standing
> Focused and drawn in by what barred the way.[70]

That gate to a field stands like form to the content, technique to the meaning of a poem; and one characteristic of the *Súile Shuibhne*/Sweeney's Eyes volume is its movement towards more formal versification, including regulated stanza length, rhyme, and regular metre. This more formal method is applied not just to new poems but to the revised versions of earlier efforts which appear, such as 'If You're Going to San Falcarragh . . .' (*SS* p. 28), a poem much improved from its sprawling free verse original: 'Teachtairí na mBláth'/Flower People (*MC* p. 60).

Ó Searcaigh attempts and explores a variety of forms from *Súile Shuibhne* on, a collection which ranges from the strict sonnet form of 'Fiacha an tSolais'/Debts to the Light (*ABB* p. 120) to the strong-arm, free-versing bellows of 'Portráid den Ghabha mar Ealaíontóir Og/A

---

[69] 'The power of the visible/is the invisible.' Marianne Moore quoted by Charles Simic, 'Secret Maps: Holly Wright's Photographs of Hands', *The Yale Review*, Vol. 84 No. 4, (October 1996), 26–36 (p. 26).

[70] Heaney, 'Field of Vision', *Seeing Things*, 22.

Portrait of the Blacksmith as a Young Artist' (*ABB* p. 84), a poem which draws from 'Miontráigéide Cathrach 2'/A Minor City-tragedy 2 (*MC* p. 19), the 'smithy' of Joyce's soul, and the 'forge' of Heaney's *Door into the Dark*.[71]

2.2 *SUIBHNE* (1987)

Suibhne/Sweeney is a large and generous collection, running to over one hundred and fifty pages. However, of the forty poems in *Súile Shuibhne*/Sweeney's Eyes (1983), all but one appear again in *Suibhne*. Moreover, among the new poems, a number are culled from earlier drafts in *Miontráigéide Cathrach*/A Minor City-Tragedy. Some like 'Maigdiléana'/Magdalen (*ABB* p. 66) and 'Londain'/London (*S* p. 22) are improved, with sharper imagery, more selective diction, and better use of rhyme together with regulated stanza length, including Ó Searcaigh's repeated device of an additional single final line to empower the endings of certain poems. Others, however, read like poetic exercises in rhyme and stanza formation: 'Uamhan/Dread' (*S* p. 10), for example, remains weak and desultory; while 'Charm' (*S* p. 12), in tightening up the rhymes of 'Do m'Athair'/For My Father (*MC* p. 30), loosens and loses the grip of the latter with obvious line-fillers (such as 'is an saol ag goillstean orm go cráite'/and life bitterly galling me) which cancel out any gain in the newer version's more optimistic conclusion.

Yet, this is not to suggest that Ó Searcaigh's poetry was in regression. Rather, the poet was 'on the road' as the first poem in the collection, 'Ma Bohème', makes clear. He was out encountering the reality of experience and of himself:

> Ag síobshiúl ó mhaidin ar an bhóthar go Londain
> mothaím sú an tsamhraidh ag cuisliú i ngach ní.
>
> *Hitch-hiking all morning on the road to London*
> *I feel summer juices pulsing in every thing.*
>
> (*ABB* p. 62)

Ó Searcaigh traces his wanderlust back to his reading from the Beat generation of whom he has written that 'Kerouac made me a rucksack romantic. *On the Road* became my travelogue for inner-space travel' (*ABB* p. 210). Making his own of Kerouac's influence, Ó Searcaigh travels inward to see the familiar outside world from a new and exciting

---

[71] Heaney, *Door into the Dark* (London: Faber and Faber, 1969, 1991), 7.

angle in almost the same way that Heaney does when he takes on board 'the stranger' in 'Making Strange'.[72] However, Ó Searcaigh's version is like Heaney on speed:

Tá do leabhar ina luí druidte ar m'ucht ach faoi chraiceann an chlúdaigh
    tá do chroí ag preabadaigh i bhféitheog gach focail.
Oh man mothaím arís na *higheanna* adaí ar Himiléithe na hóige:
Ó chósta go cósta thriall muid le chéile, saonta, spleodrach, místiúrtha;
Oilithreacht ordóige ó Nua-Eabhrach go Frisco agus as sin go
    Cathair Mheicsiceo;
Beat buile inár mbeatha. Spreagtha. Ag bladhmadh síos bóithre i
    gCadillacs ghasta ag sciorradh thar íor na céille ar eiteoga na m*bennies*.
Thrasnaíagh muid teorainneacha agus thrasnaigh muid taibhrithe.
Cheiliúraigh muid gach casadh ar bhealach ár mbeatha, *binge*anna agus
    bráithreachas ó Bhrooklyn go Berkeley, *booze, bop* agus Búdachas; Éigse
    na hÁise; sreangscéalta as an tsíoraíocht ar na Sierras; marijuana agus
    misteachas i Meicsiceo; brionglóidí buile i mBixby Canyon.
Rinne muid Oirféas as gach *orifice.*

Your book close-tight on my chest, heartens
me; each word the loosed garment
of a lover. Oh man, I still feel the high
Himalayas of youth as we coasted the coasts,
zigging and zagging together, innocents
abroad, desperate to be one of the boisterous,
thumbing from the Apple to San Fran and on
to the sex of the Mex, a path unbeaten;
hot-wired, Cadillexcelerating down roads,
skidding out of our brains on bennies,
borders passed like dreams as we tuned
in and turned on to life's freeway,
bingeing and buddying from Brooklyn to Berkeley
on booze, bop and Buddha, the Wisdom
of the East, news from the nebulae; then way
down in Bixby canyon, our dreambats
high on Mexticism, we made
an Orpheus of every orifice. (*OO* pp. 180–3)

On land, Emerson said, 'every thing good is on the highway'; and on sea, 'the voyage of the best ship is a zigzag line of a hundred tracks';[73]

---

[72] Heaney, *New Selected Poems*, 154–5.
[73] Tanner, T. (ed.), *Ralph Waldo Emerson: Essays and Poems* (London: J. M. Dent

'life', Wallace Stevens noted, 'is motion';[74] and Heaney has observed and absorbed 'the zig-zag hieroglyph for life itself' in the criss-crossing tracks of a hare on the hop.[75] Naturally, therefore, after zigging inward, 'Californ-icating Cill Ulta' and 'Friscying Falcarragh' (as above), Ó Searcaigh zags outward again and goes 'beyond what's reliable/in all that keeps pleading and pleading.'[76] This movement, this 'pushing away from the known point' (as Tynyanov describes it[77]) is as necessary for development in literature as it is in life; it is certainly essential for the life-blood of a poet's imagination to keep flowing. Therefore, having used his imagination to see the familiar in a strange way, Ó Searcaigh now had to take off in a new direction and familiarize himself with 'strange' territory. 'No loitering', Ó Ríordáin instructed,[78] and it is interesting to catch up with Ó Searcaigh for the second time in London, reflecting on his loneliness and exile.

The difference between a mid-career poem by Ó Searcaigh which deals with the city, such as 'Piccadilly: Teacht na hOíche/Piccadilly: Nightfall' (*ABB* p. 68), and the earlier blanket condemnation of urban life in *Miontraigéide Cathrach*/A Minor City-Tragedy (1975), is a greater self-awareness on the part of the poet. The experience of city-life presented in the Piccadilly poem, for example, is even more manifestly a personal one. The 'I' of the poem is not only identifiable with Ó Searcaigh, as is generally the case, but the speaking voice is also fore-grounded as that of a *poet* alone or keeping himself company 'lena chuid focla/with his words': for example, the speaker compares his sufferings to those of Berryman and Celan; and also his reference to Botticelli has the same effect—suggesting, self-consciously, a measure of artistic sophistication—as Heaney's allusion to the 'Field at Boaz' in 'Making Strange'.[79] Most significantly, however, it is now made clearer than ever that Ó Searcaigh's true subject is not the city itself but his personal sense of alienation *from* the city, its people, and *modus vivendi* which he continues to compare negatively to his own preferred sense of stability and rootedness in the native soil and tradition of home:

Ltd./Everyman's Library, 1992). See 'Experience', 202–22 (p. 211); and 'Self-reliance', 23–46 (p. 30).

74 Stevens, W., *The Collected Poems of Wallace Stevens* (New York: Alfred A. Knopf, 1957), 83.   75 Heaney, 'Squarings' Part 4, *xliii, Seeing Things*, 103.

76 Heaney, 'Making Strange', *New Selected Poems*, 154–5.

77 Rylance, *Debating Texts*, 35.   78 Ó Coileáin, *Seán Ó Ríordáin*, 154.

79 Heaney, *New Selected Poems*, 154–5.

> tuigim anois agus choíche
> cumhaidh agus crá croí an aonaráin
> is mé imithe chun seachráin
> ar an fhóidín mearaí seo i bPiccadilly [. . .]
>
> *I understand now and forever*
> *the homesickness and heartache of the solitary*
> *since I have strayed out*
> *onto this 'fóidín mearaí' in Piccadilly* [. . .]

'Fóidín mearaí' is a Connacht term which Dinneen's dictionary defines as 'a little sod [of earth] on which if one tread he is led away and has to keep walking aimlessly till moonrise unless he turn his coat inside out, a cause of confusion or error like will o' the wisp.'[80] Significantly, the evil enchantment of Piccadilly hinted at in the poem tempts the poet to become a turncoat, to perhaps give in to the temptations of prostitutes, drug-abuse, and depression, cutting himself off from his native heritage/'dúchas' deprived of which he could be left like the sullen city-dwellers/'daoine dúrúnta' in the poem. Such a step could also mean cutting himself off from the language of *his* people, from communication—graphically symbolized by the 'guthán ag ringeáil/i mbosca folamh an choirnéil'[81]—or even from life itself.

However, by this stage relatively assured of his status as a poet, Ó Searcaigh appears to acknowledge that, having set foot on a Piccadilly fóidín mearaí, he may just have to 'keep walking aimlessly till moonrise'. For the moment, he chooses to wait at the ready for 'somebody'—lover or Muse; to wait 'mar bheadh an damhán alla/cuachta i ngréasán ar an bhalla', like the spider crouched in a web on the wall whose mirror image is, of course, that of the poet waiting for his words 'an file [ag fanacht] lena chuid focla'.

The *Suibhne*/Sweeney volume continues to chart a 'going back to sources', beginning with invocation, and then a tentative process of identification with the author's homeland. In 'Abhann an Átha'/Ford River (*S* p. 33), Ó Searcaigh asks the polluted river if it dreams, as he does, of the source from which it has sprung. Poems in the section 'Garbhchríocha mo Chinéal'/The Hard Lands of My People invoke the

---

[80] Dinneen, P. S. (ed.), *Foclóir Gaedhilge agus Béarla/An Irish-English Dictionary* (Dublin: Irish Texts Society/Educational Company of Ireland 1927, 1965), 469–70.

[81] 'The phone ringing/in the empty box in the corner.' See 'Piccadilly: teacht na hoíche/Piccadilly: nightfall', *ABB* pp. 68–77 (p. 75).

land as a lover, as an attraction for a lover and, in the poem 'Idir Mám an tSeantí agus Loch na mBreac Beadaí/Between Mám an tSeantí and Loch na mBreac Beadaí' (*ABB* p. 100), as a womb-like burial mound in which the poet foresees rebirth. The land is beseeched like a pagan God to nurture poem and poet alike in the Eastern atmospheric, almost Buddhist, poem 'Ciúnas/Silence':

> Na portaigh seo i mo thimpeall, thuaidh agus theas
> ón tSeascann Mhór amach go hAltán,
> bíodh an tionchar céanna acu ar mo dhán
> agus atá acu ar an bhácrán—
> tugadh siad chun cineáil é le ciúnas. (*ABB* p. 90)

> *These bogs surrounding me, north and south*
> *from Seascann Mór and out to Altán,*
> *may they have the same influence on my poem [fate/destiny]*
> *as they have on the bog-bean—*
> *nurture it with silence.*

No clearer indicator is needed of the essential unity of man and poet in Ó Searcaigh's case than his repeated double entendre of the word 'dán' (as above) to suggest that his poem and destiny are simultaneously at stake, and that they share the same horizon or scope.[82]

Kavanagh once wrote that

> Lot's wife would not be salt if she had been
> Incurious as my black hills . . .[83]

Ó Searcaigh at one point fears that *his* clay-footed visions will never be able to stretch and see further than can the surrounding earthbound hills 'lifting their heads' in 'Ag Síneadh a gCinn' (*S* p. 41). Yet, like Lot's wife, Kavanagh, Akhmatova, or any poet, he is compelled to share a curiosity and a *hunger* deeper than that of the hills:

> [. . .] 'Who owns them hungry hills
> That the water-hen and snipe must have forsaken?
> A poet? Then by heavens he must be poor.'
> I hear and is my heart not badly shaken?[84]

---

[82] A similar poetic stance to that of Kavanagh in his early work according to Heaney. See Heaney, 'The Placeless Heaven: Another Look at Kavanagh', *The Government of the Tongue* (London: Faber and Faber, 1988, 1989), 3–14 (pp. 4–5).

[83] Kavanagh, 'Shancoduff', *Collected Poems* (London: MacGibbon and Kee, 1964), 30.

[84] Ibid.

Not shaken, Ó Searcaigh is stirred and fortified by the encouraging view of his surrounding hills as the care and treasure of his hard-working people, as the manuscript upon which he too must stamp the imprint of his fate, destiny, or poem:

> Foilseoidh an fómhar do shaothar go hiomlán.
> Beidh gach gort ina dhán.
> *The harvest will publish your collected works.*
> *Every field will be a poem.*
>   (from 'Umhlaigh'/Submit, *OO* p. 56)

As a rallying cry to harness self to tradition, this poem is as remarkable for its similarities as it is for its differences to Ó Ríordáin's 'Fill Arís'/Return Again.[85] Avoiding the latter's overt political and cultural nationalism—emphasizing separatism—Ó Searcaigh's own poetic manifesto is more naturalistic, 'parochial' and personal but, ironically—though not at all surprisingly—it is thus more *inter*nationalist and universal.

The theme of following in one's father's fathers' footsteps continues in 'Anseo ag Staisiún Chaiseal na gCorr/Here at Caiseal na gCorr Station' (*ABB* p. 94). If Heaney contracts the spade of his fathers in 'Digging' to the poet's pen,[86] Ó Searcaigh contracts the field to the page:

> Seo duanaire mo mhuintire;
> an lámhscríbhinn a shaothraigh siad go teann
> le dúch a gcuid allais.
> Anseo tá achan chuibhreann mar bheadh rann ann
> i mórdhán an mhíntíreachais.
> Léim anois eipic seo na díograise
> i gcanúint ghlas na ngabháltas
> is tuigim nach bhfuilim ach ag comhlíonadh dualgais
> is mé ag tabhairt dhúshlán an Fholúis
> go díreach mar a thug mo dhaoine dúshlán an fhiántais
> le dícheall agus le dúthracht
> gur thuill siad an duais.
>
> *This is the poem-book of my people,*
> *the manuscript they toiled at*
> *with the ink of their sweat.*

---

[85] Ó Ríordáin, *Brosna*, 41.
[86] Heaney, *New Selected Poems*, 1–2.

Here every enclosed field is like a verse
in the great poem of land reclamation.
I now read this epic of diligence
in the green dialect of the holdings,
understand that I am only fulfilling my duty
when I challenge the void
exactly as my people challenged the wilderness
with diligence and devotion
till they earned their prize. (*ABB* pp. 94–7)

This assured and powerful poem would surprise modern readers who have become entirely unused to such proclamations of at-one-ness with his or her place and people on the part of a contemporary poet. However, the tone and pointedly personal vision of this poem are convincing:

Anseo ag Stáisiún Chaiseal na gCorr
d'aimsigh <u>mise</u> <u>m</u>'oileán rúin
<u>mo</u> thearmann is <u>mo</u> shanctóir.
Anseo braith<u>im</u> i dtiúin
le <u>mo</u> chinniúint <u>féin</u> is le <u>mo</u> thimpeallacht.

Here at Caiseal na gCorr Station
<u>I</u> discovered <u>my</u> hidden island,
<u>my</u> refuge, <u>my</u> sanctuary.
Here <u>I</u> find <u>myself</u> in tune
with <u>my</u> fate and environment.

'In tune' suggests a harmony of related but different notes. For example, Ó Searcaigh distinguishes between 'folús' and 'fiantás', the void and the wilderness. The void challenged by the poet is not literally the same as the wilderness with which the people struggle. Theirs is particular while his must also be universal. Yet, they provide him with the tools, method, and language of reclamation, preservation, and cultivation which is the function of a poet. It is in performing this task that Ó Searcaigh feels himself to be 'ag feidhmiú mar chuisle de chroí mo chine/beating like the pulse of my people's heart'. However, is it necessary for a poet to believe or to assert that s/he is so 'in tune' with, or useful to, her/his society?

Ó Searcaigh is certainly not the only poet to feel justified and vindicated by his striving through the medium of art to locate and celebrate the essence, the 'truth' of his homeland and people. In his *Precocious Autobiography*, Yevtushenko—Ó Searcaigh's early mentor—shares the most important piece of advice which he claimed to have ever received, and which came from an old factory worker, a Soviet version of 'old Bríd' (*OO* p. 22): 'find the truth in yourself and give it to others, and find it in others and store it up in yourself'.[87] Consequently, just as Ó Searcaigh, in his role as poet, feels reassured of his own 'efficacy and importance as a person', Yevtushenko is made to feel proud: 'it makes me proud not to be just an onlooker but to be taking part in my people's heroic struggle for the future.'[88] And what is the role of the poet? How does s/he earn this pride, efficacy, or importance as a person?

Yevtushenko recounts a lesson that he learnt from experience but, firstly, from Kirsánov: 'a poet has only one indispensable quality: whether he is simple or complicated, people must need him. Poetry, if it's genuine, is not a racing car rushing senselessly round and round a closed track, it is an ambulance rushing to someone's aid.'[89] For Yevtushenko, this 'aid' takes the form of restoring people's 'faith in life', in their own, and their country's, worth. He shares and, no doubt, encouraged Ó Searcaigh's view that poet and people are mutually dependent; that the poet is not only a microcosm of the people but an essential element of the larger organism. Yevtushenko asks:

do I seem to contradict myself by first speaking of the poet's irreplaceable 'I' and then of the poet as the mouthpiece of others? I don't think so. It seems to me that only in a sharply outlined individual can that which is common to many be combined and fused.

I should be very happy to spend all my life expressing the as yet unexpressed ideas of others while remaining myself. I know that if I ceased to be myself I would not be able to express them.[90]

From such certainties, Ó Searcaigh writes, come 'suaimhneas aigne/peace of mind':

Ceansaítear mo mhianta, séimhítear mo smaointe,
cealaítear contrárthachtaí ar an phointe.

My desires are tamed, my thoughts mellow,
contradictions are cancelled on the spot. (*ABB* p. 97)

---

[87] Yevtushenko, *A Precocious Autobiography*, translated by A. R. MacAndrew (Harmondsworth: Penguin Books Ltd., 1965), 124.

[88] Ibid. 137.

[89] Ibid. 74. Semyón Isaákovich Kirsánov was a poet born in Odessa in 1906. He was Jewish, a member of the Left Front in literature—a Futurist movement; and was close to Mayakovski.

[90] Yevtushenko, *A Precocious Autobiography*, 8 and 10.

Blake, however, warned in 'The Marriage of Heaven and Hell' that 'without contraries [there] is no progression'.[91] What is to stop the tame, mellow, conflict-free poet from becoming a stick-in-the-mud whose imagination ends with the fields, 'the horizons of consciousness' disappearing into those of the place,[92] a fault Heaney found with some of Kavanagh's early poetry?

What saves this—and any—poet is that he is 'on the road' that zig-zags 'all over creation' (*OO* p. 182) like the 'hieroglyph for life itself'[93] which alternately draws the individual in one direction and then another: for example, between Yevtushenko's 'city of yes and the city of no' or—just as paradoxically—the city of self and of community. Ó Ríordáin accepted this tripping and tension as part of the human condition:

> Is mar sin a bhíonn an duine; anonn is anall ag leanúint a phearsantacht féin scaitheamh, agus scaitheamh eile ag leanúint an traidisiún. Pé ceann a leanann sé bíonn an ceann eile á thionlacan chomh maith. 'Sé tionlacan na n-óinseach é.[94]

'Odi atque amo' was Louis MacNeice's judgement on his native land, with perhaps more hate than love at times;[95] Ó Searcaigh has a less, but still somewhat complicated relationship with his home territory. While loving the place undoubtedly, Ó Searcaigh returned in order to learn 'what is meant by home',[96] inspired partly by Mahon and Yeats to cast if not a cold eye, at least a wide open one on the reality of experience there, good and bad.

He found that while the city, for example, is prone to Kafkaesque flies, the flies that plague the country house are not so easily driven away either (*S* p. 53). The 'braddy cow' of 'Bó Bhradach' could use his tail to swish away the flies of loneliness, boredom, poverty, and narrow-mindedness

---

[91] William Blake, 'The Marriage of Heaven and Hell'. See Keynes, G. (ed.), *Blake: Complete Writings* (London: Oxford University Press, 1966), 148–60 (p. 149).

[92] Heaney, *The Government of the Tongue*, 3–14 (p. 4).

[93] Heaney, *Seeing Things*, 103.

[94] 'That's how people are; this way and that, following their own personality sometimes, and other·times following the tradition. Whichever they follow, the other comes too.' Ó Coileáin, *Seán Ó Ríordáin*, 212.

[95] Louis MacNeice, see 'Autumn Journal XVI', in P. Muldoon (ed.), *The Faber Book of Contemporary Irish Poetry*, 99–103 (p. 103).

[96] Derek Mahon, 'Afterlives', *The Snow Party* (London: Oxford University Press, 1975), 1–2. Living in London about this time, Ó Searcaigh read Mahon's work and was influenced by this poem in particular to learn 'what was meant by home'—in his case, the Donegal Gaeltacht.

for so long; eventually he had to 'hightail it' right out of there (*ABB* p. 126). However, for the most part, the spirit and humour of the poet in dealing with these subjects is likewise a reflection of his people's attitude. The 'Herring Women' of 'Cailíní na Scadán' (*S* p. 58) maintain their sense of fun, their femininity, pride, and identity despite extremely difficult economic and cultural working conditions. The first thing the reader hears of them is their mermaid-like laughter, and the last thing—their humanity and motherliness. These factors, together with its relevance to a generation of seasonal workers from Donegal including his own mother, are what drew Ó Searcaigh to translate the poem from the Scots Gaelic of Ruaraidh Mac Thòmais.

There is an Irish proverb which states that 'ar scáth a chéile a mhaireas na daoine/people live in the shadow of each other'. Ó Searcaigh's poetry helps to remind us that people live in the light of each other, too. Take, for example, the 'Mountain Woman' of 'Bean an tSléibhe' (*ABB* p. 116) who was never 'gruama nó grusach linn/gruff or gloomy with us' and whom the poet compares to an apple-tree of knowledge: 'mar shíolta thitfeadh a briathra in úir mhéith m'aigne/her words fell like seeds into the welcoming earth of my mind'. Her words quoted in the poem do, indeed, have an ancient ring of poetic, earthy, and proverbial wisdom: 'sa tír seo tugtar na crusts is cruaidhe don té atá mantach/in this country the hardest crusts are given to those with least teeth.' In commemorating this old woman, her ways and expressions, Ó Searcaigh carries out the Soviet worker's advice to Yevtushenko: 'find the truth in yourself and give it to others, and find it in others and store it up in yourself.'[97] A kind of eternity is achieved through which the present can be illumined by the light of knowing something of or from the past. This knowledge can be passed on again quietly and respectfully in poems: 'is fearr cogar sa chúirt ná scread ar an tsliabh'/a whisper in the court is better than a roar on the moor.

Significantly, Ó Searcaigh does not approach these people or their language like the 'anthropologist or alien invader' or even as the 'remembering exile' of, say, recent 'British' poetry[98]—certainly not since he moved back to have a permanent base among them. Rather,

---

[97] Yevtushenko, *A Precocious Autobiography*, 124.

[98] Morrison, B. and Motion, A. (eds.), *The Penguin Book of Contemporary British Poetry* (London: Penguin, 1982), 12.

his relationship with them is always personal. The poems make clear that he himself has savoured and stored, for example, the warmth of local characters before he allows or redirects that warmth to radiate out to readers. In 'Oícheanta Geimhridh', Ó Searcaigh illumines his current 'Winter Nights' by re-calling former heartening times in the company of Neddie Eoin, a local seanchaí/storyteller:

Tá sé corradh le fiche bliain anois
ó chuaigh a thinidh as, i mbarr na Míne Buí
ach istigh anseo i gcoigilt mo chuimhne
drithlíonn beo nó dhó den tinidh adaí
is leáfaidh na drithleoga sin an dubhacht
a mhothaím anocht i bhféitheoga an chroí.

His fire is out these twenty years
or more at the top of Mín Bhuí
but here in the banked hearth of my memory
a live coal or two from that fire sparkles,
and those sparks will dissolve the gloom
I feel in my heart tonight. (*ABB* p. 115)

By convincing the reader that the fiery spell of Neddie Eoin's talk, alive and glowing with songs by Burns and lays of the Fianna, has heartened him as an individual—the artist himself 'as a young man'—Ó Searcaigh proves the value of such things for one and all: 'only in a sharply outlined individual can that which is common to many be combined and fused.'[99]

Part of the thrill of reading Ó Searcaigh's poetry comes from following around the wide-eyed and open-eared poet as he stores in the 'album of memory' the essence of experiences with world and word. Indeed, Ó Searcaigh is one who tries to live out Krisnamurti's advice to 'have the capacity of meeting everything anew from moment to moment without the conditioning reaction of the past' (*S* p. 150). Increasingly, his poetry completely surrenders to the moment, the encounter, the sensation, the artistic satisfaction when objective co-relatives can be not just imagined but recognized, recreated, or relived in poems such as 'Attic' (*S* p. 25), 'Sneachta/Snow' (*ABB* p. 58) and in love poems like 'Fios/Knowledge' (*ABB* p. 158) and 'Searmanas/Ceremony' (*ABB* p. 156).

---

[99] Yevtushenko, *A Precocious Autobiography*, 10.

For any poet, of course, experiences with words are as important as those with worlds. Ó Searcaigh favours Auden's definition of poetry as an exploration of the possibilities of language because words, as well as things, invite the gesture that attempts to connect the two, to bridge the gap 'between thought and word'.[100] Ó Ríordáin wrote that 'níorbh é an t-ábhar amháin a chorraigh mé agus a bhíog mé chun véarsaí a scríobh. Do chorraigh an teanga féin. Is mó dán díobh, pé acu olc maith iad, a tháinig as líonrith, as *excitement*, na teanga féin (e.g. 'Scagadh').[101] Ó Searcaigh's exploration of language includes the living language of his people in the Donegal Gaeltacht whom he so often quotes with pleasure and pride; and also the work of other writers in the Irish language and in languages from around the world.

Cited at the back of *Suibhne*/Sweeney, for example, are nine Lowell-like imitations (since they are not, strictly speaking, translations) which the poet naturalizes into expressions of his own viewpoint from the angle of his home terrain.[102] Perhaps the most interesting is 'Johnny Appleseed' by the American poet, Mary Oliver. Ó Searcaigh's version is dedicated to another poet, Nuala Ní Dhomhnaill, for its allegorical insistence on the value of 'keeping going':

> Ach in ainneoin chianfhulaingt sin na péiné
> níor lig sé dá léas dóchais a dhul as.
> Sin cinneadh; an spréach atá ionat a mhúchadh

---

[100] This is the title of a sub-section in *Suibhne*; the phrase is taken from the poem 'Transubstaintiú', *S* p. 95.

[101] 'It wasn't the subject alone that moved me, that spurred me into writing verse. The language itself moved. Many a poem, good or bad, came from a sudden start, an *excitement* of the language itself (for example, "Scagadh/Refinement").' Ó Ríordáin, quoted in Ó Coileáin, *Seán Ó Ríordáin*, 209.

[102] For an explanation of the distinction Ó Searcaigh makes, see *NBB* pp. 91–2:

There's a handful of poems in the second section, *I bhFianaise na Bé*, which are versions of foreign poems. They are not translations but retellings. In as much as that, I came under the influence of Robert Lowell. 'I believe that poetic translation—I would call it an imitation—must be expert and inspired, and needs at least as much technique, luck and rightness of hand as an original poem.' Something in the originals inspired me—a playful line, perhaps, a moving thought or an extraordinary image. My aim, like that of Robert Lowell, was to compose a new poem out of whatever it was in the original that sent my mind racing; a live-and-kicking poem that had enough sense to stand up for itself on its own feet and face the world, naturally, in Irish. There are foreign-language poems here in languages I don't know at all but I understood from the poems—having read them in English—that they sprang from the same sources of inspiration from which I tend to draw. I am indebted to these poets who swapped jerseys with me, gave me inspiration and lightened the dark. [My translation.]

nó í a spreagadh chun solais is déine.
Chinn sé a chroí a chur i gcrainn úll anois
is iad a shíolú is a scaipeadh in ainm an dóchais
a d'adhain istigh ann go fuarintinneach.

Despite that long pain,
he never let despair darken
his door. Fate can either
stir the embers or smother
the flame. He put his heart
into apple-trees after that,
laying seed-bed after seed-bed
of hope that sprung in hundreds.

(*OO* pp. 186–7)

The strange spell on Johnny Appleseed which sends into bloom any apple-tree he passes, indicates the power that people (including poets) have to curse or bless, to spread the light of growth and creativity or cast the shadow of death and disillusion. But what if there is more than just 'a hint of frost' blighting the individual? Or what if the entire rich soil of language has been choked by a deadly winter?

That possibility is explored in 'Caoineadh/Lament' (*ABB* p. 208) which concludes the *Suibhne* collection on rather a sour note. The poet compares his native language, which he terms 'the language of [his] emotions', to an old pet sheep being eaten alive by crows on the ledge of a cliff: 'Ó dá ligfeadh sí liú amháin gaile—liú catha'/O, if she could let out one furious war-cry', he cries and, of course, his cry is the poem, this book of poems. 'Ní dhéanfaidh gealladh an phian a mhaolú/promises now won't ease the pain', Ó Searcaigh concludes in 'Caoineadh'; nor have they yet, but it could be argued that alive and kicking literature such as this proves that Irish, despite the flogging, is no dead horse or ewe.

Indeed, the *Suibhne* collection as a whole leaves one feeling that the horse of Ó Searcaigh's poetry still has a race to run. He travels quite far running with the 'wind of memory/leoithne na cuimhne', significant memory that lasts and grows into an epiphany of some kind. This enables the poet, for example, to compare a fresh blanket of snow at the mercy of a child-self to the susceptibility of a sheet of paper in the hands of a poet-self; or to discover the life-likeness of a snowman, second time around, in his death and disappearance back into the earth. Some of these connections span years and surprise the reader like a web stretching from one object to another so far away that one has to follow the web to reach it. However, such delicately wrought connective webs start to form a repetitive pattern in the expanding 'text' of the poet. Already, by this stage, Ó Searcaigh needed new subject matter and a new method. 'It takes little talent to see clearly what lies under one's nose, a good deal of it to know in which direction to point that organ.'[103] Treating Auden's advice on poetry like a tip from the horse's mouth, Ó Searcaigh sets off in two new directions in the course of this collection: writing about writing and writing about love.

With poetry as subject, Ó Searcaigh's Pegasus is not at this point a trail-blazer like that of Ó Direáin, 'liberator' of the word in 'An Fuascailteoir' (*ABB* p. 186). Ó Searcaigh does, however, pledge and apprentice himself to the lonesome, uncertain terrain where 'idir an smaoineamh agus an briathar/tá dúichí oighir agus ceo.'[104] This is from 'Transubstaintiú/Transubstantiation' (*ABB* p. 184), one of several poems which owe much to Ó Ríordáin and to conventional identification of artistic creativity with religion or, in some cases, sexuality. A more original and organic poem on this subject is 'Dordánta' which I can only translate as 'Po-hums':

As coirceog na cloigne	*From the hive of the head,*
caolaíonn siad amach	*out they slip,*
ina mbeach ina mbeach	*bee by bee*
ag tarraingt caol díreach	*in a thin straight line*
ar bheachlus an phinn	*to the bee-plant pen*
is puinn ní fhágaid ann	*where they'd leave not a drop*
de dhúchlón neachtair	*of the inky nectar*
ach é dhiúl go dríodar	*but drain it to the dregs*
i gcomhair mhil na héigse.	*for the sweet honey of poetry.*

(S p. 89)

This poem is truly an exploration of the possibilities of (Irish) language and has a timeless quality retaining some of the metaphorical daring and surprise of early Irish, metaphysical, *and* contemporary, poetry.

Ó Searcaigh's love poetry at this point is far less innovative and much more self-consciously traditional. He follows Auden and Ó Ríordáin by treating sex in his poetry with religious intensity: in 'Laistiar/Beyond', the lover's blue eyes are preferred to the blue of the Virgin Mary's sash

---

[103] Auden quoted by Ó Searcaigh, *S* p. 148.
[104] 'Between thought and word/there are lands of ice and mist.' *ABB* pp. 184–5.

(*ABB* p. 150); while sharing a laugh with, presumably, a lover in 'Dhéanfainn an Ní Dodhéanta/I Would Do the Impossible' is compared to a waltz with Her (*S* p. 101); also in 'Aoibh/Beauty', the lover's heart is a veritable heaven, a Tír na nÓg of eternal summer (*ABB* p. 152). There is some experimentation with rhyme in these poems but this merely adds to the impression that they are quite conventional and even sentimental.

Other new poems in the collection celebrate love with images drawn from nature and the elements. If many dramatize a rejection of religion in favour of more physical relationships, they also show how religions can lack room for the variety of human loves:

> A cheann dubh dílis dílis dílis
> d'fhoscail ár bpóga créachtaí Chríosta arís;
> ach ná foscail do bhéal, ná scéith uait an scéal;
> tá ár ngrá ar an taobh tuathal den tsoiscéal.
>
> *My dark, dear, dear dark-haired love,*
> *our kisses open Christ's wounds up;*
> *don't open your mouth, don't tell a soul;*
> *our love's on the wrong side of the gospel.*

Here, 'Ceann Dubh Dílis/Dear Dark-Haired Love' (*OO* p. 112) deliberately echoes the traditional love-song by the same name to stress that love is older and wider than any gospel. The poem is inclusive in that, most likely concerned with homosexual love, it could also refer to an 'illicit' heterosexual affair, for example. However, this is an early indication of the homo-eroticism which becomes a central theme of Ó Searcaigh's later poetry.

2.3 *AN BEALACH 'NA BHAILE/HOMECOMING* (1993)

An Bealach 'na Bhaile/Homecoming was first published in 1991 with an audio-cassette of readings by the author. A larger bilingual version appeared in 1993, an attempt by the publishers, Cló Iar-Chonnachta, to emulate the success of Nuala Ní Dhomhnaill's bilingual collections from Gallery Press, *Pharaoh's Daughter* and *The Astrakhan Cloak*.[105] The Ó Searcaigh volume followed the format of the former by employing a variety of translators.

---

[105] Ní Dhomhnaill, N., *Pharaoh's Daughter* (1990) and *The Astrakhan Cloak* (1992).

Coming six years after *Suibhne*, *An Bealach 'na Bhaile/Homecoming*
contains a disappointingly small number of new poems. Most of these
rehearse familiar themes of the poet, including celebrations of local
characters such as the impish but god-like seanchaí/storyteller who
taught the poet to say more than his prayers and to be wider than the
narrow road of 'opinion', in 'Cré/Creed' (*ABB* p. 128). The poem 'Lá de
na Laethanta/A Day to Remember' restores a day of 'miracles' from the
'luanscrios/carnage' of time, recreating some of the psychedelic feel of
an acid, rather than just a mountain, trip:

Bhí na néalta ag méileach ar na bánta. Ní raibh oiread agus caora le feiceáil sa
spéir [. . .] Thug na clocha cuireadh domh suí ina gcuideachta is nuair a chiú-
naigh siad thart orm go cainteach thuig mé cad is tost ann. D'éist mé le bláth
beag bhí ag seinm 'sonata' ar 'phianó' a piotail, ceol a chuir aoibhneas ar mo
shrón. Tharraing an loch mo phictiúr.

The clouds were bleating in the pastures. Not one sheep was in the sky [. . .] The
stones invited me into their company and when they quietened talkatively about me
I understood the meaning of silence. I listened to a small flower playing a sonata on
her petal-piano, music that pleased my nose. The lake drew my picture. (*ABB* p. 48)

The estrangement technique employed in this poem may no longer be
new but this does not detract from the surprise and delight of many
young readers at finding such cheeky and chancy redeployment of
natural imagery in Irish (language) poetry which is usually regarded as
more conservative.

Two of the new poems in *An Bealach 'na Bhaile/Homecoming* revisit the
city. 'Is Glas na Cnoic/Faraway Hills' takes, for once, a much more positive look at the urban landscape, concluding: 'don chéad uair braithim sa
bhaile i gcéin/for the first time I feel at home abroad' (*ABB* p. 206).
However, the poet feels more 'at home' because he makes himself more at
home, turning the traffic—through the use of metaphor—into a flock of
sheep, the office-blocks into mountains. The development marked in this
poem is not the attainment of a less leafy view of the city but the poet's
growing self-confidence, his step out of Ó Ríordáin's narrow band of
listeners or listen-*ing*, in 'Éisteacht Chúng'/Minority Audience,[106]
towards his own éisteacht leathan/wide audience [listening or reception].
Ó Searcaigh's walkman or personal stereo, for example, 'picks up' and
blends Radio One *and* Ráidió na Gaeltachta:

[106] Ó Ríordáin, *Brosna*, 38.

Anois piocaim suas Mín 'a Leá agus Mayfair
ar an mhìnicíocht
mhire mhíorúilteach amháin i m'aigne
sa *bhuzz* seo a mhothaím i mBerkley Square;
agus mé ag teacht orm féin le dearfacht
nár mhothaigh mé go dtí seo
mo *vibe* féin, mo rithim féin,
rithim bheo na beatha ag borradh agus ag *buzzáil*
i bhféitheacha mo bhriathra.

Now I pick up Mín 'a Leá and Mayfair
On the same mad miraculous
Frequency in my mind
In this buzz I feel in Berkeley Square;
While I discover myself with a positiveness
I haven't already felt
My own vibe, my own rhythm
The exciting rhythm of life increasing and buzzing
In the arteries that are my words. (ABB p. 206–20)

'Mise Charlie an Scibhí/I am Charlie the Scivvy' marks a further departure. Here, the city is seen in both a good and a bad light. In either case, the subjectivity of the poet is foregrounded as the place itself becomes a backdrop for an open-ended discussion of the poet's, and his language's, future:

tá sí [an Ghaeilge] chomh saonta
liom féin, i *slickness* na cathrach;
chomh hamscaí faoi na soilse seo
le damhsóir bróga tairní
i mballet Rúiseach. Ach lá inteacht
tiocfaidh muid beirt, b'fhéidir,

Ar phéirspicíocht dár gcuid féin
a bhéarfas muinín dúinn
ár n-aghaidh a thabhairt go meanmnach
ar ár ndán [. . .]

She [Irish] is as gullible as myself
In the city slickness;
As ungainly under these lights
As a hobnailed stepdancer
In a Russian ballet. But some day
Perhaps we will both discover

> *A perspective of our own*
> *Which will give us confidence*
> *To face our destiny with courage.*
> (*ABB* pp. 202–5)

The poem ends on a cheerful note in which the uncertain present is at least brightened and warmed by some sun-rays from the past: 'cuimhní/memories' on which this poet and his poetry so often depend.[107]

The newer love poems in *An Bealach 'na Bhaile* turn to the loss and pain that time can inflict on friendship and romance. 'Cumha na gCarad/Lament for Friendship' (*ABB* p. 170) is an updated version of 'An Osna/The Sigh' (*MC* p. 73), a translation of a poem by Yevgeny Yevtushenko. This time Ó Searcaigh assimilates the poem further into his own experience and home territory, making it more alive and convincing in one. 'Tá mo Chéadsearc i Londain/To my Heart's Desire in London' (*ABB* p. 144) is a moving lyric about separation written in the form of a traditional amhrán ghrá/love-song.

One poem first published in *An Bealach 'na Bhaile*, 'Laoi Chumainn/Hound of Ulster' or in my own English version 'Serenade', heralds the path that Ó Searcaigh's most recent work has taken:

> Agus is toil liom, a mhacaoimh óig,
> gurb é anseo ar léana mo leapa
> a dhéanfá le barr feabhais
> do mhacghníomhartha macnais,
> gurb anseo i ngleannta is i gcluanta
> mo cholla, a thiocfá i dteann is i dtreise
> is go mbeadh gach ball
> do mo bhallaibh, ag síorthabhairt grá duit
> ar feadh síoraíocht na hoíche seo.
>
> Anocht chead ag an domhan ciorclú
> leis na beo is leis na mairbh:
> Anseo i dtearmann dlúth na bpóg
> tá an saol ina stad [. . .]
>
> *And, yes, it is my will, brave youth,*
> *that on the field of my bed*
> *you do your utmost*

---

[107] 'Níl de chara ag Cumhaidh ach Cuimhne'/Loneliness [a sense of loss or of missing someone or something] has no friend but Memory'. See 'Piccadilly: teacht na hoíche/Piccadilly: Nightfall', *ABB* pp. 68–77 (p. 72).

> *to perform your manly deeds,*
> *that here in the hills and hollows*
> *of my flesh, you grow hard and strong*
> *as I give all*
> *my all in limitless love to you*
> *for the eternity of this night.*
>
> *For, tonight, the world can beat about*
>   *with life and death.*
> *Here, safe in the sanctuary of our kiss,*
>   *time cannot catch up with us.*
>
> (*OO* p. 88)

Despite the lingering objective co-relative of the 'champion' on the battlefield, this poem marks the shift in Ó Searcaigh's poetry to even more heightened sensation and to frank representation of sexuality. The poem could stand as both a dramatic monologue from some historic fe/male character to her/his knight and as an overtly gay poem of seduction. While both interpretations are possible, and intended, since the gender of the speaker is not specified, the second takes precedence because the reader familiar with Ó Searcaigh's work is aware that the 'I' of his poems refers almost always to himself in the first instance, and that he is both gay and male. Yet, most importantly, in this poem, Ó Searcaigh hits upon a new poetic theme and agenda; a way of extending the conventional love-poem by opening up the windows of the stanza (literally, room) and applying some aesthetic *glaznost* to the variety and sheer physicality of love.

2.4 *NA BUACHAILLÍ BÁNA* (1996)

While many of Ó Searcaigh's latest poems deal with the period that could be described as 'afterlove', they are usually illumined with the 'afterglow' of vivid and lingering memory. Is the poet's stoical and all-inclusive philosophy determining the poetry, or the poetry directing the philosophy? Both; for they cannot be separated since Ó Searcaigh belongs to the school of Yevtushenko who comments: that 'if the poet tries to split himself in two between the man and the poet, he will inevitably commit suicide as an artist.'[108]

Consequently, what draws some readers to Ó Searcaigh's work is the

---

[108] Yevtushenko, *A Precocious Autobiography*, 7.

freshness of a real human voice talking about real things, real encounters and experiences which the surreal language and imagery of his poems come tantalizingly close to re-creating, re-experiencing through language.[109]

Also at work in Ó Searcaigh's poetry is what the sculptor Louise Bourgeois[110] calls a 'mechanism of seduction':

> Bhí gach cead agam, an oíche úd, ar do chaoinchorp caomh;
> ar ghile cúr séidte do bhoilg; ar do bhaill bheatha
> a ba chumhra ná úllaí fómhair 'bheadh i dtaisce le ráithe;
> ar mhaolchnocáin mhíne do mhásaí, ar bhoige liom go mór iad
> faoi mo láimh, ná leithead d'éadaigh sróil, a mbeadh tomhas
> den tsíoda ina thiús . . . Anois agus mé 'mo luí
> anseo liom féin i leabaidh léin an díomhaointis
> tá mé ar tí pléascadh aríst le pléisiúr . . . le tocht
>
> ag cuimhne ortsa, a ógánaigh álainn, deargnocht
> a d'aoibhnigh an oíche domh . . . ocht mbliana déag ó shin anocht.
>
> *that night I could do anything with your slender*
> *smooth body your belly bright as a foaming wave*
> *and below more tempting than autumn apples*
> *in store mine were the rolling drumlins of your cheeks*
> *soft under my hand and light as the scantiest silk*
> *now alone on a no-such-lucky bed in pain*
> *in joy I remember you beautiful naked*
>
> *transforming my night eighteen years ago tonight*
>   (from 'Oíche/Night' *OO* p. 90)

Ó Searcaigh affirms the value and delight of passing moments by unsparingly commemorating them, using words not in Ó Ríordáin's defiant way as 'stones to throw at fate'[111] but in a manner closer to what William Wordsworth really meant by emotion recollected in tranquillity: 'the emotion is contemplated till, by a series of reactions, the tranquillity gradually disappears, and an emotion, kindred to that which

---

[109] 'Re-creating' in Ó Ríordáin's sense that a poem is a being, not a telling (*ES* p. 11); and 're-experiencing' satisfying Adrienne Rich's wish that poems should *be* experiences, not *about* them. See Boland, E., 'Outside History', *Object Lessons: The Life of the Woman and the Poet in Our Time* (London: Vintage, 1996), 123–53 (p. 131).

[110] 'When the thing [a sculpture or poem] is successful, when harmony has been accomplished [. . .] the artist achieves something that seduces, something that convinces. And if seduction is convincingly achieved, then sex occurs' (Louise Bourgeois). See Meyer-Thoss, C., *Louise Bourgeois: Designing for Free Fall* (Zurich: Ammann, 1992), 129.

[111] Ó Coileáin, *Seán Ó Ríordáin*, 2.

was before the subject of contemplation, is gradually produced, and does itself actually exist in the mind.'[112] In poems such as 'Gorm/Blue' (*OO* p. 102), 'Samhain'/November (*OO* p. 106), and 'A Mhianta m'Óige/Passions of my Youth' (*OO* p. 132), the poet recollects passion with a passion that can still thrill at the recollection. Consequently, he is writing the most sensually charged poetry in either language in Ireland today, encouraged by the example of Ní Dhomhnaill at home, and of outspoken gay writers from abroad, such as Cavafy.

A number of Ó Searcaigh's most recent poems also reveal a welcome diversity of subject matter and technique. Perspective not only changes but deepens as if he has combined Heaney's concept of 'seeing things' through the window or gateway of a 'Field of vision'[113] with Aldous Huxley's mind-opening *Doors of Perception*:

I took my pill at eleven. An hour and a half later I was [. . .] looking intently at a small glass vase. The vase contained only three flowers—a full-blown Belle of Portugal rose, shell pink with a hint at every petal's base of a hotter, flamier hue [. . .] I was seeing what Adam had seen on the morning of his creation—the miracle, moment by moment, of naked existence [. . .]

Istigkeit—wasn't that the word Meister Eckhart liked to use? 'Is-ness.' The Being of Platonic philosophy—except that Plato [. . .] could never, poor fellow, have seen a bunch of flowers shining with their own inner light and all but quivering under the pressure of the significance with which they were charged; could never have perceived that what rose and iris and carnation so intensely signified was nothing more, and nothing less, than what they were—a transience that was yet eternal life, a perpetual perishing that was at the same time pure Being, a bundle of minute, unique particulars in which, by some unspeakable and yet self-evident paradox, was to be seen the divine source of all existence.

I continued to look at the flowers, and in their living light I seemed to detect the qualitative equivalent of breathing.[114]

Ó Searcaigh substitutes 'Muse' for mescalin and finds:

An brú atá ormsa le mé féin a chur in iúl faoi scáth na bhfocal;
níl aon ghá ag an lilí

---

[112] Wordsworth, 'Preface', *The Lyrical Ballads 1798–1805*. See Sampson, G. (ed.), *William Wordsworth and Samuel Taylor Coleridge: The Lyrical Ballads 1798–1805* (London: Methuen and Co. Ltd., 1903, repr. 1965), 33.
[113] Heaney, *Seeing Things*, 22.
[114] Huxley, A., *The Doors of Perception/Heaven and Hell* (London: Granada Publishing Ltd. /Panther Books, 1977, 1978), 15–16.

lena leithéidí. Ní theastaíonn ealaín na bhfocal uaithi le í féin
    a nochtadh, a chur in aithne.
Is leor léithe a bheith mar atá sí, socair, suaimhneach, seasta,
    ansiúd sa tsoitheach chré.
Í féin a deir sí agus deir sí sin go foirfe, lena crot, lena cineáltas,
    lena cumhracht, lena ciúnas.
Má shiúlaim róchóngarach dithe cuirim ar crith í, ar tinneall.
    Mothú ar fad atá inti
agus í ag breathnú agus ag braistint, ag ceiliúradh na beatha
    le niamh dhearg a hanama.[115]

Heaney's formal gateway of poetry and Huxley's swinging doors of
perception can lead to remarkably similar visions and insights. When the
object of contemplation is a chair, for example, Ó Searcaigh imagines

amanta	*sometimes,*
ba mhaith léithe	*she would like*
suí síos,	*to sit down,*
a scíste	*take a break*
a dhéanamh,	*and put her feet up,*
na cosa a chrúpadh	*yawn and stretch*
fúithi,	*her stiff wooden bones,*
osna faoisimh a ligean	*cross her arms*
as adhmad cruaidh	*and listen to the woodwind*
a cnámh,	*of her memory,*
a huilleanacha	*reflecting on the tree-god,*
a thrasnú ar a chéile;	*she sprang from.*
éisteacht le ceol na Coille	
ina cuimhne;	
meabhrú ar an Dia-Chrann	*Now, with the cat*
as ar foinsíodh í.	*licking at her legs,*
	she feels
	the whiskey
Anois agus an cat	*of the woods*
ag lí na cos aici	*pouring through her veins,*
mothaíonn sí sú na Coille	*the wind*
ag sní aríst ina cuislí;	*tickling her limbs.*
an ghaoth	*Trembling,*
ag slíocadh a géag—	*she all but leaps*
Ar crith,	*for joy . . .*
is beag nach bpreabann sí as a seasamh	
le pléisiúr.	(*OO* p. 202)

---

[115] Translation I in Appendix. See also *OO* pp. 236–9.

With the power of concentration and imagination, the poet (in Ó Ríordáin's terms) flies to the 'self' of the chair, becomes 'bottled' or, in this case, 'chaired' in it and is then able to look out from its vantage point. With mescalin, Huxley makes a similar trip into

a world where everything shone with the Inner Light, and was infinite in its significance. The legs, for example of that chair—how miraculous their tubularity, how supernatural their polished smoothness! I spent several minutes—or was it several centuries?—not merely gazing at those bamboo legs, but actually *being* them—or rather being myself in them; or, to be still more accurate (for 'I' was not involved in the case, nor in a certain sense were 'they') being my Not-self in the Not-self which was the chair.[116]

I am trying to suggest that Ó Searcaigh's mysticism[117] and Huxley's mescalin open doors between 'the universe of reduced awareness [. . .] petrified by language' and that of 'the totality of awareness belonging to Mind at Large'. For Huxley, Mind at Large is exhibited by certain people (such as artists, poets, and mystics) who are 'born with a kind of by-pass that circumvents the reducing valve'[118] which normally protects the individual from an over-bombardment of perceptions. Mescalin seems to link up with this 'by-pass' by causing the brain to run out of sugar, and the undernourished ego to weaken. Consequently, the ego can travel out to and identify more easily and fully with the other or otherness of external entities: ' "I" was not involved in the case [. . .] being my Not-self in the Not-self which was the chair.'[119] Finally, the experimenter is transformed into a state of heightened awareness which uncannily resembles that of a pantheist poet, a Wordsworth or Ó Searcaigh:

as Mind at Large seeps past the no longer watertight valve, all kinds of biologically useless things start to happen. In some cases there may be extra-sensory perceptions. Other persons discover a world of visionary beauty. To others again is revealed the glory, the infinite value and meaningfulness of naked existence, of the given, unconceptualised event. In the final stage of egolessness there is an 'obscure knowledge' that All is in all—that All is actually each. This is as near, I take it, as a finite mind can ever come to 'perceiving everything that is happening everywhere in the universe.'[120]

---

[116] Huxley, *The Doors of Perception*, 19.
[117] Ó Searcaigh, from the start, shared with other *INNTI* poets, including Gabriel Rosenstock, a fascination with Eastern philosophy and religion. Lama Anagorika Govinda and Krisnamurtí are among his many gurus—western *and* eastern (*S* pp. 145–51).
[118] Huxley, *The Doors of Perception*, 20.   [119] Ibid. 19.   [120] Ibid. 22.

The discoveries which Huxley mentions occur when the true artistic impulse stirs and moves, when the everyday mind expands from the universe of reduced awareness into Mind at Large and 're-cognizes',[121] vis à vis the self, the *istigkeit*, the Edenic quidditas of, for example, a pink Belle of Portugal rose—singled out by Huxley—or a naked lily in Donegal:

> An é go bhfuil mé gafa i gciorcal draíochta an bhlátha seo, go bhfuil
>   ciapóga ag teacht orm?
> Ní hé go dteastaíonn uaim a bheith i mo lilí, cé go mbeinn sásta
>   leis an chinniúint sin
> in cé bith ioncholnú eile atá i ndán domh sna saoltaí romham amach.
>   Níl uaim i láthair na huaire
> ach a bheith chomh mór i dtiúin le mo nádúr daonna is atá
>   an lilí seo lena dúchas lilíoch.
> Níl uaim ach a bheith chomh mór i mo dhuine agus atá an lilí
>   ina lilí—an lilí bhándearg.

> *Has this flower overpowered me? No.*
> *Even though I'd be happy with that incarnation*
> *in some future life, all I want now*
> *is to be as human as the lily is lilium,*
> *as much myself as that lily, in the pink.* (*OO* p. 238)

CONCLUSION

Hopkins wrote that each thing

> Selves—goes itself: myself it speaks and spells:
> Crying, what I do is me: for that I came.[122]

I draw attention to that 'goes itself', not *is* itself. When a poet 'goes' him/herself, the journey is physical, psychological, and formal. S/he explores the possibilities of the phenomenological world, of the mind that interacts with it, and of the language with which s/he tries to keep a log-book of the journey. This voyage is, of course, a life, beginning with the poet's first home which is always his/her starting point. Note

---

[121] 'The thing and the language are separate, of course, and the separateness is recognised, or as Heidegger would say "re-cognised", known again: only through such separateness, only in such a separation, can there be the gesture which invites.' Welch, 'The Loutishness of Learning', 69.

[122] Quoted by Ó Ríordáin. See *Eireaball Spideoige*, 14.

how Yevtushenko concluded his early but far-reaching poem about his own home town, 'Zimá Station':

> Then Zimá Station spoke to me.
> And this is what Zimá Station said:
> 'I live modestly, crack nuts,
> smoke quietly with steam-trains,
> but I also think a lot about life,
> I love it—for real, not for show.
> You're not the only one,
> like you now in the world,
> who is searching, scheming, struggling.
> It's OK, son, that you didn't answer
> the particular question asked of you.
> Be patient, look about you, listen.
> Keep searching the whole world over.
> Yes, truth is fine, but happiness is better,
> though without truth, you'll never be happy.
> Go through life with your head held high.
> Be up-front. Let rain-wet pine-needles lash
> your heart, your eyes, your face, let
> tears and troubles wash your eyelashes.
> Love people—for love looks after its own.
> Remember.—
>   I'm keeping you in mind.
> It won't be easy—you can come back to me . . .
> Go on!'
>   I went.
>   And I am still going.[123]

Ó Searcaigh is still going, too; spinning the web of his poetry ever wider, making new connections and patterns. Gradually, he is putting Caiseal na gCorr Station on the same literary map as Zimá Station. The Irishman has established a direct line with the Russian by sharing the latter's belief that 'no people are uninteresting./Their fate is like the chronicle of planets' and by adding his own 'laments against destruction';[124] by his adoption of numerous forms and production of original,

---

[123] My translation. For an alternative version, see *Yevgeny Yevtushenko: Selected Poems*, ed. by Milner-Gulland and Levi, 51.

[124] Ibid. 85–6. For an example from Ó Searcaigh's work, see 'Do Narayan Shrestha', *OO* pp. 188–93.

startling work such as the phantasmagoric nightmare-like narrative of 'Dreimire/Ladder' (*OO* p. 232); and lastly, by writing a poem that *had* to be written, one that—in Kirsánov's terms—was needed like 'an ambulance rushing to someone's aid'.[125]

Ó Searcaigh's 'Gort na gCnámh/Field of Bones' (*OO* pp. 65–76) is a powerful poem in seven sections each with thirteen long lines spoken by a middle-aged female character. Set in Donegal, the poem relates how the main character and narrator has been imprisoned and rendered voiceless—barr the conceit of the poem itself—in the fields where she suffered hardship and sexual abuse. The poem contains graphic accounts of domestic violence, incestuous rape of a minor, and the murder of the resulting off-spring. The realism and down-to-earth language of the female victim/narrator render this account justly shocking and disturbing.

Too long and unified to quote from, it is not surprising that 'Gort na gCnámh' has had a mixed reception: while one Donegal priest has condemned the poem as 'immoral', a local library has offered to put it on display. 'Russian poets have always been the spiritual government of their country', Yevtushenko declares in his autobiography;[126] perhaps, with power and trust slipping from the hands of priests and politicians in Ireland, it is for poets, like Heaney and Ó Searcaigh, to maintain— as they have done—responsible citizenship, and to turn, occasionally, from the 'private Japanese garden of poetry'[127] to attack the weeds and dangerous growth, for example, of injustice and of reluctance to face disturbing home truths, realities and contradictions.

Yevtushenko once wrote: 'we had flutes in plenty, what we needed now was the bugle',[128] the bugle to drive people not from failed faith to no faith but to new faith in the necessary 'struggle for the future'.[129] One thing I have noticed about Ó Searcaigh's work is that, ultimately, it sounds a note of hope.[130] It does so not by being childishly naive or fanatically positive but by facing the dark, the 'duibheagán' or abyss, head on in the same way that it faces the sun. For example, consciously or not, Ó Searcaigh has risen to the challenge laid down by Eiléan Ní Chuilleanáin in her essay 'The borderlands of Irish poetry':

[125] Yevtushenko, *A Precocious Autobiography*, 74.
[126] Ibid. 99.   [127] Ibid. 100.   [128] Ibid. 104.
[129] Ibid. 137.
[130] This note has been picked up on and welcomed by a variety of readers, including the English poet Carol Rumens.

the events which shocked the consciences of Southern people in the middle 1980's had nothing to do with a war between Catholics and Protestants. They were the discovery of an infant's body in Kerry and the subsequently published story of a local girl who falsely confessed that it was hers and that she had murdered it. Later a public inquiry found that, while the original baby could not have been hers, she had indeed had a child which died at birth. A few months later a schoolgirl was found dead outside a church in Co. Longford, having given birth there to a dead child [. . .] While nobody has yet written a great poem about Joanne Hayes or Ann Lovet, who with their children were the victims of these episodes just mentioned, the public wants somebody to do it. The public would probably like the job done with simplicity and direct-ness.[131]

Ó Searcaigh's 'Gort na gCnámh/Field of Bones' does the job, I believe, 'with simplicity and directness' although it does not deal specifically with the cases mentioned, choosing instead to relate to them not by name but as part of a wider and continuing legacy.[132]

---

[131] Ní Chuilleanáin, E., 'The Borderlands of Irish Poetry', in E. Andrews (ed.), *Contemporary Irish Poetry: A Collection of Critical Essays* (Houndmills: MacMillan Press Ltd., 1992), 25–40 (pp. 34–5).

[132] The poem, incidentally, was chosen by Nuala Ní Dhomhnaill as one of the *ten* most significant Irish poems of the 1990s. See *Watching the River Flow: A Century in Irish Poetry*, ed. by Noel Duffy and Theo Dorgan (Dublin: Poetry Ireland, 1999), 223 and 232–9.

CHAPTER 3

Máirtín Ó Direáin: Departures You Cannot Go Back On[1]

In med do connac ni fhacim	*That which I saw I do not see*
agus in med do cim ni fhaiceb	*and that which I see I shall not see*
agus in med do bi ni fhuil	*and that which was is not*
agus in med atá ni bia	*and that which is shall not be*
agus in med bias ni beid.	*and that which shall be shall not be.*[2]
Ní críoch ach athfhás.	*Not the end but new growth.*[3]

INTRODUCTION

Máirtín Ó Direáin's poetry, like that of Seán Ó Ríordáin and Cathal Ó Searcaigh, is also, for the most part, a poetry of self. Notably, the 'I' of his poems first speaks as a (past) member of an Aran community; then as one of Ireland's community of exiles, uprooted in the 'cathair fhallsa/deceitful city' (*D* p. 90); and ultimately as the voice of a lone individual or artist culturally and linguistically displaced by the experience of modernity. Throughout his career, however, his private concerns mainly of love and loss (in a word: change) mirror, in varying degrees, those of the contemporary Irish public and of humanity in general. For example, Seán Ó Tuama writes that 'Ó Direáin's poetry speaks to us not only of his own personal longing for the old ways of life on Aran, but also of the longing of all of those of his contemporaries who were concerned about the devastation of an old-world culture.'[4]

---

[1] Heaney, 'Making Strange', *New Selected Poems*, 154–5.

[2] Riddle set by Ciothruadh Mag Fhiongaill, Tory Island, *circa* 1513. See de Blacam, *Gaelic Literature Surveyed*, 196.

[3] From 'Ag Críost an Síol', trad. Irish, Hymn No. 254 in *Hail Christ Our King: Hymnal* (Dublin: Cedar Media and Communications Ltd., 1993).

[4] Ó Tuama, 'Modern Poetry in Irish' (1991), *Repossessions* (Cork: Cork University Press, 1995), 3–9 (pp. 6–7).

In a poetry of self, moreover, private and public worlds merge so that Ó Direáin felt this 'devastation' personally in his own life, symbolized or made manifest by the death or loss over time of friends, loved ones, family, customs and, he feared, even his native language. Therefore, it is as true of Ó Direáin as it is of any of Ireland's poets 'from Muiríoch Albanach Ó Dalaigh (*c.* 1200) to Seán Ó Ríordáin' that 'the game of poetry became their survival weapon. To "survive" each had to develop a personal insight into his own special disturbance.'[5] Ó Direáin's special disturbance was his sense that his identity (and that of Ireland) was under threat. For him, constant change meant annihilation because the natural resources of selfhood (language, custom, culture, etc.) were fast running out. How could a depleted citizen or state partitioned from him, her, or itself, stand up to life in which one is never quite 'together' or even entire but always, as Julia Kristeva has described, a 'subject in process'?[6]

Ó Direáin's answer or defence was to summon up the remaining reserves of selfhood, plumbing deep into the (re)sources of language, memory, and tradition with the roots of poetry. What Ó Direáin sought was preservation of the self's autonomy, symbolized by his defiant image of the upright or 'standing tree/crann seasta'.[7] He would certainly have agreed with John Hewitt's dictum that the writer 'must be a rooted man, must carry the native tang of his idiom like the native dust on his sleeve: otherwise he is only an airy internationalist, thistledown, a twig in a stream.'[8] However, since the experience of modernity[9] continues to uproot large numbers of the world's population, is identity better symbolized by Ó Direáin's still-standing tree or by the well-travelled twig riding the back of the stream?

Emerson opted for endless, energizing, zigzagging flux: 'power ceases in the instant of repose; it resides in the moment of transition from a

   [5] Ó Tuama, 'Three Lyrics I Like' (1990), *Repossessions*, 267–73 (p. 268).

   [6] Kristeva, for example, concluded from Antonin Artaud's French texts that 'all identities are unstable [. . .] constantly called into question, brought to trial, over-ruled'. See Kristeva, 'A Question of Subjectivity—an Interview' (1986), from *Women's Review*, No. 12, pp. 19–21, re-printed in P. Rice and P. Waugh (eds.), *Modern Literary Theory: A Reader* (London: Edward Arnold, 1989), 128–34 (pp. 128–9).

   [7] See, *FB* p. 23, and the poem 'Bí i do Chrann'/Be Tree-like, *D* p. 128.

   [8] See 'Introduction', *The Collected Poems of John Hewitt*, ed. F. Ormsby (Belfast: Blackstaff Press, 1991), xli–lxiv (p. li).

   [9] Berman, M., *All That Is Solid Melts Into Air: The Experience of Modernity*, 2nd edn. (London: Verso, 1983, repr. 1995), 13–15.

past to a new state, in the shooting of the gulf, in the darting to an aim [. . .] Nothing is secure but life, transition, the energising spirit.'[10] For Kristeva, not only power resides in the moment of transition but being itself: 'a "fixed identity": it's perhaps a fiction, an illusion—who amongst us has a "fixed" identity? It's a phantasm; we do nevertheless arrive at a certain type of stability.'[11] Using the psychoanalytic theory of Jacques Lacan, Kristeva concludes that stabilization of the self in relation to the 'other' first occurs in an individual on their passing through the mirror and Oedipal phases whereupon utterance is made possible; the subject can then tell his/her own story.

Yet, that, in my opinion, would only be the story so far. New changes and confusions will appear against which poetry, for one, may act as a temporary stay (as Frost put it) or as a method of interpretation in the continual search for meaning, for self-knowledge. A subject engaged in such stabilizations of self really is 'in process' and their creativity, of course, a triumph of self-affirmation over self-doubt. This is often made necessary for writers because, as Kristeva has pointed out, 'the creative act is released by an experience of depression without which we would not call into question the stability of meaning or the banality of expression. A writer must at one time or another have been in a situation of loss—of ties, of meaning—in order to write.'[12]

Post-structuralists would attribute this loss and/or depression to the realization or sense that humanism's autonomous and unified man is dislocated from the centre of meaning and action. In this view, 'the subject, and that sense of unique subjectivity itself, is constructed in language and discourse; and rather than being fixed and unified, the subject is split, unstable or fragmented.'[13] How much more acute this 'ontological insecurity'[14] must be for the minority-language writer, especially when s/he writes in the pre-colonial language of her/his country. Ó Tuama saw Seán Ó Ríordáin as one such subject. Quoting the psychologist R. D. Laing, he noted that such a person 'is forced into a continuous struggle to maintain a sense of his own being . . . The total self, the "embodied self", faced with disadvantageous conditions, may

---

[10] *Ralph Waldo Emerson: Essays and Poems*, ed. Tony Tanner (London: J. M. Dent LTD./Everyman, 1992), x.

[11] Kristeva, 'A Question of Subjectivity', 129–30.   [12] Ibid. p. 133.

[13] (Eds.) Rice, P. and Waugh, P., 'The Subject', *Modern Literary Theory: A Reader* (London: Edward Arnold, 1989), 119–21 (p. 119).

[14] Ó Tuama, 'Seán Ó Ríordáin, Modern Poet' (1978), *Repossessions*, 10–34 (p. 29).

split into two parts, a disembodied "inner self" felt by the person to be the real part of himself, and "a false self" embodied but dead and futile, which puts up a front of conformity to the world.'[15] This description also fits, in my view, the Aran poet and exile Máirtín Ó Direáin who felt himself to be a 'prisoner' in the metropolitan centre of Dublin during a 'wretched era' in which Ireland was busy modernizing itself out of recognition, doing violence to the family tradition.[16]

Joyce once described Ireland as a 'split little pea'[17] but it seems to me that Ó Ríordáin and Ó Direáin are like split peas in the pod of a split country. Their individual struggles (personal and literary) are tragic but the resulting poetry sheds much needed light on some of the fissures, cracks, and fault-lines on the cultural map of Ireland.

3.1 *Ó MÓRNA* (1957)

Ó Direáin's two most important mature collections of poems are *Ó Mórna* (1957) and *Ár Ré Dhearóil* (1962). The former contains a large body of poems and a much quoted foreword, 'Mise agus an Fhilíocht'/Myself and Poetry (*D* pp. 215–17). The volume itself is dominated by the long title poem 'Ó Mórna' (*SP/TD* pp. 20–31).

This poem is based on the life of James O'Flaherty (d. 1881), a landlord whose cattle were driven over a cliff during Land League agitations. Ó Direáin has stated that 'since the creative bug ["cruimh"/worm] started goading me more and more, I took an interest in the O'Flaherty as a man [. . .] There's definitely a novel, play or long poem, perhaps all three, over there in Reilig Chnocán na mBan, waiting to be written by someone.'[18] Ó Direáin's characterization of O'Flaherty in the form of Ó Mórna provides, all in one, an unforgettable depiction of a sexually charged Gothic monster, a realistic portrayal of one of Yeats's hard-riding country gentlemen, and a sympathetic account of a lonely outsider whose birth and nature (not his nurture) drive him beyond the pale of the community. Somewhat surprisingly, this dissolute landlord who drinks, whores, and curses himself into the ground maintains Ó

---

[15] Ibid. This 'false self' is, indeed, what Ó Ríordáin would call a 'halla' [punning on 'hollow'] man. See Ó Coileáin, *Seán Ó Ríordáin*, 79.

[16] O'Flaherty, Tom, *Aranmen All* (Dublin: The Sign of the Three Candles, 1934), 86.

[17] See Ó Tuama, 'Synge and the Idea of a National Literature' (1972), *Repossessions*, 219–33 (p. 230).

[18] O'Flaherty's remains lie buried in the churchyard mentioned. See *FB* p. 57.

Direáin's sympathy throughout. Consequently, the poem has been read by various critics as amoral, a product of Ó Direáin's reading of Nietzsche:

the primacy assigned to 'will' and 'passion' in the philosophy of Friedrich Nietzsche no doubt encouraged the poet in his portrait of a 'hard-riding country gentleman' but the creation of *Ó Mórna* as an alter ego enabled the poet to give expression to what can only be described as a glorification of the male sexual drive. (Mac Síomóin and Sealy, *SP/TP* pp. xv–xvi)

Ó Mórna certainly lived outside the conventional morality of his day, his horses or passions driving him beyond the good and evil of the church, but he was no Nietzschean Superman. He is consumed with passion and out of control, as his drunken appearance on horseback suggests. The real Superman, on the other hand, is 'master of *himself*. But to master *oneself* is the hardest of all tasks, that which requires the greatest amount of power.'[19] Before power must come the will to power, and in society, this will is sublimated: 'a table of values—i.e. a *morality*—"hangs over every people": it is the table of the self-imposed commands which have turned a herd and rabble into a nation: primitive aggression has been directed back upon itself, sublimated into *self*-control.'[20] As a hereditary landlord, Ó Mórna's power is not willed but long since pre-determined and, naturally, corrupts. Throughout the poem, Ó Direáin stresses Ó Mórna's 'ceart/right' to power and property, 'glac'. His heredity, his name, set him apart on the island and seem to have determined his nature and downfall. Could he have had an alternative fate?

Instead of using his early insights gained from working alongside his people to apply a fair and mutually beneficial system of management, he used his inside knowledge to exploit them (*SP/TD* p. 22) in a way that neither increased his power nor his joy but magnified his appetite and the greed of his stewards:

> An t-úll go léir acu dóibh féin   *The whole of the apple to themselves*
> Is an cadhal ag gach truán.   *and the peel to the poor.*
>
> (*SP/TD* p. 26)

Ironically, the poor may have obtained more from the peel than Ó Mórna from his cut of the apple which in a biblical twist surely goes to 'the worm in his flesh he could not defeat' (*SP/TD* p. 29).

---

[19] Nietzsche, F., *Thus Spoke Zarathustra: A Book for Everyone and No One*, trans. R. J. Hollingdale (Harmondsworth: Penguin, 1961, 1978), 27.
[20] Ibid. 26

This worm, finally gnawing him *in* the grave, suggests that there is a horrific, vampire-like determinism operating in the life of Ó Mórna. He appears doomed from the start to feed with flesh the fleshworm feeding on his flesh. The reader knows that Ó Mórna can not last and, in fact, hasn't since the poem (in the past tense) begins and ends at his grave. Yet, for me, the fact that Ó Mórna feeds the worm of his insatiable desires is not what is most significant and disturbing about the poem. Crucially, the worm that gnawed him '*istigh* san uaigh/*in* the grave' stands also for a curious mixture of time and destiny (including decay) which affects everyone, the 'high' and the 'low'.

Ó Mórna, high on his horse, has a terrible fall: 'tháinig na pianta ar áit na mianta'/ pains overcame where desire had reigned until he died in his family house which knew neither grace nor laughter. It is significant that with him was buried the last male heir, the last who could keep up the family name and birthright. The hard-riding gentleman's race had literally degenerated.

Notably, during the writing of this (and his next) collection, Ó Direáin was under the influence of the German philosopher Oswald Spengler (*SP/TD* p. xii). It is no coincidence that the latter's major work is called *The Decline of the West*,[21] a book that would have simultaneously attracted and unnerved Ó Direáin, set his thoughts dancing as he said poetry should do for words. Spengler stressed the transience of every society, the 'morphology of culture', applying to the study of history the biologist's concept of living forms: 'each culture, in this view, was an organism, which like any other living thing went through a regular and predictable course of birth, growth, maturity, and decay. Or, in more imaginative language, it experienced its spring, summer, autumn, and winter.'[22] Moving from the cultural scale to that of the individual human life (and back), Ó Mórna's (the protagonist's) rise and fall in the poem could be seen as charting morphological stages common to all individuals, to his class and to all classes and societies who sooner or later have to encounter the 'cruimh gur cuma léi íseal ná uasal'/worm that heeds not birth nor blood (*SP/TD* p. 30). What interests Ó Direáin, then, is Ó Mórna's fate or destiny/'dán'. The latter was central

---

[21] Spengler, O., trans. Charles Francis Atkinson, *The Decline of the West 1: Form and Actuality* (New York, 1926); *2: Perspectives of World History* (New York, 1928).
[22] Hughes, H. S., *Oswald Spengler: A Critical Estimate* (New York: Charles Scribner's Sons, 1952), 10.

to Spengler's approach to history but the notion was problematic to him: 'destiny is a word whose content one *feels*'.[23]

The most that one commentator could say of Spengler's notion of destiny was that it 'obviously bears a close relation to the question of determinism in history'.[24] The question interested Ó Díréain because what if, for example, Ó Mórna's death without an heir, his—and/or his people's—degeneration was *determined*? How long, Ó Díréain surely wondered, before another 'deireadh'/'winter' (signifying death, decay, the end) comes to remaining individuals, classes or peoples, including his own former Aran community?

Ó Mórna's story, in this light, is one of transition: 'so long as the culture phase lasts, the leading figures in a society manifest a sure sense of artistic "style" and of personal "form". Indeed, the breakdown of style and form most clearly marks the transition from culture to civilisation.'[25] For thinkers such as Spengler, Nietzsche, and Mann, 'culture' is the spring, summer, and autumn of a society, and 'civilization' the winter: 'in the former the "soul" predominates, in the latter the "intellect" of the city.'[26] Ó Direáin appears to me to have interpreted such views in his own Aran language and style, substituting 'Eascar', 'Fás', 'Feochadh', and 'Deireadh',[27] respectively, for the aforementioned seasons. Therefore, for Ó Direáin, 'civilization', often symbolized by the city, equals winter or rather 'deireadh'/the end or final 'morphological' stage for an individual or culture. Any profit from the supposed 'intellect' of the city merely amounts, in this view, to 'ciall ceannaigh'/the hard-bought or hard-earned knowledge that passage from 'culture' to 'civilization', from spring to winter, youth to age, small island or rural community to international city, is costly, even fatal: *partir c'est mourir un peu/on laisse un peu de soi-même.*[28]

One curious aspect of 'Ó Mórna' is the surprising degree to which the poet actually identifies with the landlord, the anti-hero. How conscious Ó Direáin was of the degree of his merging or 'malairt', in Ó Ríordáin's sense,[29] with Ó Mórna is difficult to gauge. However, there

---

[23] Ibid. 70.

[24] Ibid.

[25] Ibid. 72; see also 10.

[26] Ibid.

[27] 'Budding-time', 'Growing-time', 'Withering-time', and 'The End'. These, Ó Direáin likes to recall, are one old Aran Islander's translation or understanding of Spring, Summer, Autumn, and Winter. See *FB* p. 115.

[28] 'To leave is to die a little/One leaves behind a little of oneself.' Edmond Haraucourt, 'Rondel de l'Adieu', discussed by Ó Direáin in *FB* pp. 143–5.

[29] Ó Ríordáin, 'Malairt', *Eireaball Spideoige*, 63.

are passages of the poem which describe exactly the poet's own life and even his work: the opening lines stress the need to take into account Ó Mórna's background just as one must in the case of Ó Direáin when reading his work; certain stanzas show Ó Mórna storing the knowledge which he gained in the people's cabins and putting it to his own use just as Ó Direáin does; also, we find that Ó Mórna, like Ó Direáin, is 'prey to melancholy's assaults . . . odd man out . . . yearning for ease and alleviation' (*SP/TD* p. 25); also, while Ó Mórna's desire was partly to procreate, to continue the (family) line, Ó Direáin's was to keep his own poetic line going, his creativity; finally, the critic Liam Prút writes of Ó Mórna as an odd bird/'éan cuideán',[30] as someone who is emotionally linked to the people of his society but destined to be isolated from them when he assumes his power and title. This is a perfect description of Ó Direáin's gradual adoption of the poet's mantle, of his own fateful inheritance of artistic sensibility:

Ghreamaigh díom an galar úd	*That disease stuck to me*
Is ní saor mé uaidh go fóill,	*and I'm not free of it yet,*
Is é a sheol ar bhóthar na n-aisling mé	*it sent me off on the road of visions*
Is a dhealaigh mé ón sló.	*and set me apart from the crowd.*

(*D* p. 26)

Ó Direáin himself was quite an 'éasc aduain'/strange fish, his artistic sensibility driving a wedge between himself and Aran (*FB* pp. 58–9). Indeed, for him, the consequences of assuming the role of poet were similar in some ways to those for Ó Mórna when the latter assumed *his* title and authority:

Ó Mórna was completely isolated from them [the people] and it could not be expected that he would act according to any conventions but those that reflected his station, his authority, his proper historical place in the system. It happened that 'of his own kind, he heard nothing'; he had no historical connection with an exemplar who would have trained him in the behaviour befitting his position as new master.[31]

Much of the above could be applied to Ó Direáin. Not quite as isolated from his community as Ó Mórna, the poet certainly did not fit in either. Ó Direáin did hear a lot about 'his own kind', but in common

---

30 Prút, Liam, *Máirtín Ó Direáin: File Tréadúil* (Maigh Nuad: An Sagart, 1982), 50. All translations into English from this text are mine.   31 Ibid. 49–50.

with the *fictional* Ó Mórna,[32] he suffered from the lack of an exemplar through the early loss of his father. Their similarities prompt Prút to unite the two in one symbol: that of the isolated 'éan cuideáin',

> the odd bird, the symbol of Ó Mórna vis à vis his people, the symbol of the poet who sustains his art off the backs of other people but who enriches the whole people with his gift of poetry.[33]

The last comment, however, highlights the essential difference between the two: Ó Mórna has the 'aithinne is lasair'/fire and spark (*D* p. 145) that Ó Direáin admires and he also stands out from the crowd but he uses his knowledge of the underclass to exploit them—his path is, therefore, destructive to himself and others. Ó Direáin, on the other hand, uses his knowledge of the people (including Ó Mórna or, in real life, the O'Flaherty) creatively, remembering and sometimes celebrating them in his poems. But how are 'the poeple' represented in 'Ó Mórna'?

The people's direct political intervention in the real Ó Mórna's/O'Flaherty's life (the driving of his cattle over a cliff by the Land League) is not reported in the poem. This may seem surprising but this event was not what interested the poet and, after all, the action was ineffectual since the landlord simply exacted compensation from then on. The people's prayers and curses in the poem seem equally ineffective: Ó Mórna's fall has more to do with a Spenglerian notion of destiny than with divine intervention. For once, however, the crowd in Ó Direáin's poem exhibits, significantly, a variety of characteristics: they have both their charms *and* weaknesses from the bare-calved washing women to the bare-clawed Cáit an Ghleanna/Kate of the Glen, from the knock-kneed serf to the stiff-necked rebel.

Liam Prút, however, writes that 'full or proper humanity is not revealed in "Ó Mórna", just fallen humanity.'[34] I disagree because the poem highlights not a 'fallen' but an unidealized humanity, honestly portrayed. In the poem, for example, Ó Mórna receives a wide variety of reactions from the locals: his sexual advances are welcomed by some of the local girls though forced on others; the local men's attitude towards him ranges from the stiff-necked to the obsequious; his wife turns out to be a cold but not necessarily 'fallen' partner; also his sinful

---

[32] The real-life Ó Mórna, i.e. the landlord O'Flaherty, didn't lose his 'fond father' until he was forty-seven. See *SP/TD* p. 127.
[33] Prút, *Máirtín Ó Direáin*, 54–5.
[34] Ibid. 53.

stewards and bailiffs are counter-balanced with the apparently innocent priest and flock at whom Ó Mórna flings curses and coins. In return, priest and flock curse and denounce him until death again has the last word, or almost:

> An chruimh a chreim istigh san uaigh tú,
> A Uí Mhórna mhóir, a thriath Chill Cholmáin,
> Níorbh í cruimh do chumais ná cruimh d'uabhair
> Ach cruimh gur cuma léi íseal ná uasal.
> Go mba sámh do shuan sa tuama anocht
> A Chathail Mhic Rónáin Mhic Choinn.

> *The worm that gnawed you in the grave,*
> *Great Ó Mórna, lord of Kilcolman,*
> *Was not the worm of your vigour nor of your hauteur*
> *But a worm that heeds not birth nor blood.*
> *Calm be your slumber in the tomb tonight,*
> *Cathal, son of Rónán son of Conn. (SP/TD* pp. 30–1)

The final lines actually wish the degenerate landlord well; thus the dead Ó Mórna dominates the poem from beginning to end. He 'ploughs' through the poem and 'an chré labúrtha'/the labouring flesh with power and force. That 'cré labúrtha' likens the people to clay, an ancient Irish pun carried into the twentieth century by writers such as Joyce and Kavanagh. As in the latter's 'The Great Hunger', the 'peasants' of Ó Direáin's poem seem to be weighed down with boulders like morality,[35] with what Berdyaev called 'a morality of obedience' which, *by itself,* makes it 'impossible to live in the world and create new life'.[36] Ironically, though, it is Ó Mórna who fails (in the finished version of the poem[37]) to create new life, any 'proper heir', while the people in their time-honoured custom sow and reap as well as 'plough'. Metaphorically, then, Ó Direáin's creativity keeps him closer to his own people than to the firebrand Ó Mórna. The poet shares with the people what Berdyaev called an 'ethics of creativity' which 'lays upon man [. . .] the responsibility for his destiny and the destiny of the world.'[38] While

---

[35] Kavanagh, 'The Great Hunger', in P. Muldoon (ed.), *The Faber Book of Contemporary Irish Poetry,* 26–55 (p. 29).

[36] Nikolai Aleksandrovich Berdyaev, quoted in Zenkovsky, V. V., *A History of Russian Philosophy,* 2 vols. (London: Routledge & Kegan Paul Ltd., 1953), ii, 767. Note: Berdyaev, like Spengler, was interested in 'destiny' and 'creativity'.

[37] For the earlier version, see *D* pp. 221–4.

[38] Berdyaev, quoted in Zenkovsky, *A History of Russian Philosophy,* ii, 767.

Ó Direáin shares with Ó Mórna the *desire* for creativity, Ó Mórna lacks the ethics of creativity, the responsibility or, in Nietzschean language, the sublimated will to power without which he loses control and falls.

What troubles Ó Direáin, however, is the fact that some kind of 'fall' seems predetermined for everyone. Prút usefully draws attention to the fact that 'Ó Mórna' is closely connected to another poem, 'Sic Transit',[39] which focuses on

> Mana a bheireann dúshlán Flaitheartach:
> *Fortuna favit fortibus—*
> Ach tá meirg ag creimeadh an ráille.
>
> *A slogan that bears the O'Flahertys' challenge:*
> Fortuna favit fortibus—
> *But rust is gnawing at the rail.*   (SP/TD p. 59)

Here, rust gnaws like the worm that keeps turning up in Ó Direáin's poems; the nagging worry that brave or cowardly, good or bad, we all face Spenglerian decline and the worm that heeds not birth nor blood. Ó Direáin, while he favours the brave, fears, like Larkin, that 'death is no different whined at than withstood'.[40] In this context, Ó Mórna at least has the quality of standing out as a spectacle; we watch his descent with awe as he flares up and out like one of Kerouac's fabulous roman candles, all bang and very little whimper,[41] although the reader is never in any doubt that the trajectory of his trail-blazing path will be down and out. There is a price for every performance.

Ó Direáin was mesmerized by the Faustian figure cut by Ó Mórna and stirred up from the burnt-out ashes of Ó Mórna (his 'Eros and dust'[42]) perhaps his best, certainly his most memorable and sustained, poetic achievement. The poem 'Ó Mórna' is actually a microcosm of Ó Direáin's work and it is for this reason that I have discussed it at such length. It charts the fate, the budding-time, growing-time, withering-time, and end of an individual but also, by implication, perhaps of a

---

[39] Prút, *Máirtín Ó Direáin*, 41.

[40] Heaney, 'Joy or Night: Last Things in the Poetry of W. B. Yeats and Philip Larkin', *The Redress of Poetry: Oxford Lectures* (London: Faber and Faber, 1995), 146–63.

[41] References to Ó Searcaigh, 'Do Jack Kerouac', *Out in the Open*, 180; and also Eliot, 'The Hollow Men' Part V, *Collected Poems 1909–1962* (London: Faber and Faber, 1963, 1974), 87–92 (p. 92).

[42] Auden, 'September 1, 1939', in R. Skelton (ed.), *Poetry of the Thirties* (London: Penguin, 1964), 280–3 (p. 283).

class, people, culture, or civilization. The poem highlights the passage of a life and, potentially, the morphology of a culture as brightly as the path of a comet coming to nothing. Nevertheless, we see it in the light of an art-form which doesn't just 'cry out' but provides food for 'thought'.[43]

A common phrase in Aran is 'many a thing is more lasting than man', and frequently one finds Ó Direáin addressing *things* such as 'Teampaill an Cheathrar Álainn/The Church of the Four Beautiful Ones (*SP/TD* p. 42), his 'Buaile Bheag'/Small Grassy Hideaway (*D* p. 57), the ruins of St Enda's monastery in 'Teaghlach Éinne/Éanna's Community' (*SP/TD* p. 46), 'An Bhró'/The Stone Hut of an ancient hermit (*D* p. 74). He questions these silent, lonely, eerie/'uaigneach' places for their secret, the knowledge he feels that they have absorbed from witnessing and outlasting generations of human life; but, of course, they keep their mysterious secret/'rún', their grave silence which allows the poet's imagination to speculate and wonder.[44] These poems operate in much the same way as 'Rún na mBan/The Women's Secret' (*SP/TD* p. 10). A fog of separation, of unknowing, creates the desire for knowledge,[45] prompts the inquiry of the poem: 'Do scéal, a chloch, dob áil liom/Your story, stone, is what I want' (*D* p. 67). Having the story would not make Ó Direáin a great poet (despite Liam O'Flaherty's comment[46]) although it did help him in the case of 'Ó Mórna'. More often, Ó Direáin makes a poem out of longing or reaching for the story, causing this reader to feel that he would have been a better poet if he made up a story of his own as he almost does in 'Clochán na Carraige'/Stone Shore-Dwelling (*D* p. 74). But what attracted Ó Direáin to such secluded, often holy, places?

Writing of American primitive or naive painters, Tom Paulin finds that

they have a salving delight in what Hardy termed 'the beauty of association'— the wear on a threshold, a beloved ancestor's old battered tankard are his examples—and they often infuse their work with what a native American might term the Great Spirit. These painters possess an animist vision—as small chil-

---

[43] For the distinction, see Heaney, 'Joy or Night', *The Redress of Poetry*, 146–63 (p. 162).

[44] 'Bhí mé chomh práinneach i nithe neamhbheo nuair a bhí mé i mo ghasúr is go ndéarfá go raibh dáimh agam leo./I was so obsessed with unliving things when I was a boy that you could say that I empathised/identified with them' (*FB* p. 13).

[45] Welch, 'The Loutishness of Learning', *Writing Ulster*, 69.

[46] 'If Ó Direáin had the women's secret, he'd be a great poet'—my translation. Liam O'Flaherty quoted by Ó Tuathail, E., 'Cloichín ar Charn', in *CMC* pp. 105–26 (p. 109).

dren's drawings do—of natural and man-made objects that gives their work a type of mute sanctity which at times is almost unbearably haunting.[47]

Paulin is haunted by the same mute sanctity with which Aran-of-the-Saints haunted Ó Direáin. The latter felt a strong 'dáimh'/empathy or identification with various hermitages and monasteries, natural objects (especially stone) and their associations whose ghostly effect on him is relayed in many of his poems.[48] Typically, Ó Direáin takes (what Paulin calls) his 'salving delight' in holy places associated with asceticism and scholasticism which, having fallen into neglect, are unsullied by mass contemporary use. The poems he composes for or about these areas and buildings could be compared to Larkin's 'Church Going' except that 'the brass and stuff up at the holy end' in, say, Mac Conaill's church have long since been eaten by rust and sand.[49] Significantly, Ó Direáin could never indulge in Larkin's ironies or mock-indifference: Éanna's Church, for example, links the Aran poet to his forefathers and not just, as in Larkin's poem, to the general mass of the dead. For Ó Direáin, therefore, such places are even more 'serious', haunting, or 'uaigneach' than they appear to Larkin.

Obsessed with unliving things and with death itself, Ó Direáin distrusted living things for being potentially dishonest (*SP/TD* p. 120) or ridiculous (*FB* p. 19). Mac Síomóin and Sealy, for example, referring to the influence of Spengler on Ó Direáin, write that the poet increasingly saw himself as 'the last voice of a doomed culture'.[50] The result is that, too often, what one hears in his poems is the unremitting voice of doom. Whereas the key-word of his early poetry was 'buan'/permanent, the word 'deireadh'/the end gradually usurps it. For example, the feeling that his communion with Aran is slipping away from him is interpreted by Ó Direáin as the 'end of an era' (*SP/TD* p. 36) not just for himself but for the island, too:

> Tá an saol céadra i ngach áit   *Everywhere the old way of life*
> Ag meath go mear gach lá.   *is dying out fast every day.*
>
> (*D* p. 62)

---

[47] Paulin, T., 'American Primitives', *Writing to the Moment: Selected Critical Essays 1980–1996* (London: Faber and Faber, 1996), 268–72 (p. 269).

[48] See 'Teampall an Cheathrar Álainn/The Church of the Four Beautiful Ones', *SP/TD* pp. 42–3.

[49] Comparing Philip Larkin's 'Church Going', *Collected Poems*, 97–8, with Ó Direáin's 'Teaghlach Éinne/Éanna's Community', *SP/TD* pp. 46–7.

[50] See Introduction, *SP/TD* p. xii.

In Ó Direáin's poetry, not only the elements but wind, sand, sea, and even stone appear to be driving his people into the ground or away, leaving only a few old bachelors paired with 'cian'—a word which ingeniously weds 'grief' to 'time'. Everywhere Ó Direáin looks, almost, he sees death. Why? How accurate a picture was this?

The poet was forty-seven and settled in Dublin by the time the *Ó Mórna* volume was published in 1957. His contact with Aran was greatly reduced and in the visits that he does record he characterizes himself as an

[. . .] Oisín ar na craga,	*[. . .] Oisín on the crags,*
Is fós ar fud an chladaigh,	*and all along the beach, too,*
Mé ag caoineadh slua na marbh.	*lamenting the many who are dead.*

('Deireadh Ré/End of an Era', *SP/TD* p. 36)

Ó Direáin was certainly prone to seeing the 'skull beneath the skin'[51] but this was due, I feel, to the extent to which the early demise of his father sensitized him to loss. This first separation seems to have magnified the poet's future grief at the parting of individual friends or lovers (*FB* pp. 143–5), and at the deaths of old neighbours, acquaintances, and his own brother (drowned at sea in May 1946).

A North American tribesperson once explained to me the thinking behind the Ghost Dance, aimed at summoning back the dead: 'too many dead tipped the scales of the imagination.' For Ó Direáin, the poet's duty was 'to set words dancing before us'. Consequently, *his* words appear to me to 'ghost dance', to try imaginatively to re-unite him with the dead or dying, and to hold back the sands of time and sea-changes that threaten his and his people's foundations, their world and world-view.[52] Yet, it appears that Ó Direáin himself had already 'given up the ghost'. The defiance, for example, of 'Gleic Mo Dhaoine'/My People's Struggle[53] is surrounded, outnumbered, and shouted down by dark defeatist poems such as 'Bua na Mara'/The Sea's Victory (*D* p. 51) which prematurely foretells the total depopulation of the island and its Hy-Brazilian disappearance.

To be fair, Ó Direáin had some reason to be worried about the breakdown of Aran society as he knew and valued it. There were clear signs of decay. For example, the population in 1841 of 3,521 fell to 1,386 by

---

51 Eliot, 'Whispers of Immortality', *Collected Poems*, 55–6.
52 See 'Teaghlach Éinne/Éanna's Community', *SP/TD* pp. 46–7.
53 See *SP/TD* p. xiv and *D* p. 49.

1981.[54] 'What the famine left, America took', a character remarks in a story by Tom O'Flaherty.[55] Along with decline in population came economic change which badly affected traditional trades such as kelp-burning and fishing.[56] Yet, while land and native language use have fallen,[57] they have not done so quite to the degree that Ó Direáin predicted in his homage to Synge (*SP/TD* p. 40).

What particularly disturbed Ó Direáin was that as he changed and aged, so did Aran: 'the past is a foreign country: they do things differently there'.[58] Increasingly, Ó Direáin found that time and distance were estranging him from the land of his youth. Even in this relatively early volume, *Ó Mórna*, the island begins to turn secretive on him and slip away. Seeing only the end in sight, memory becomes a painful burden,[59] and despair makes the poet ask death to collect all of 'us children' as gently if not as soon as possible.[60] Is Ó Direáin simply lamenting a lost Eden, the end of innocence and the coming of age as symbolized by his move from traditional rural community to the city?

Not quite. He increasingly stresses the hardship as well as the beauty of the island: in 'Mo Mháthair'/My Mother (*D* p. 66), he curses the fate that left his family so poor; and in 'Cuimhne an Domhnaigh/A Sunday Memory' (*SP/TD* p. 38), it is only the sunbeams on the island that are described in glowing terms since

Mórchuid cloch is gannchuid cré	*Wealth of stones and dearth of clay*
Sin é teist an sceirdoileáin,	*Are the signature of the rugged island,*
Dúthaigh dhearóil mo dhaoine.	*The bleak ancestral land of my people.*

The grief-struck mother of this poem who holds on to her brood with the thread of her memory provides a mirror-image for Ó Direáin himself trying to hold on to his motherland, to a rock of integrity which, he admitted, was also a hard place of poverty and cold. Therefore, his attitude to Aran was not always as uncritical and uncomplicated as is sometimes thought.

Nevertheless, too many poems in *Ó Mórna* help the reader neither

[54] Robinson, Tim, *Stones of Aran: Pilgrimage* 3rd edn. (London: Penguin, 1990), 7.

[55] O'Flaherty, T., *Aranmen All*, 185.

[56] Robinson, *Stones of Aran*, 148–53 and 182–5. See also O'Flaherty, T., *Aranmen All*, 176–7.   [57] Robinson, *Stones of Aran*, 7–8.

[58] Hartley, L. P., *The Go-Between* (London: Hamish Hamilton, 1953, 1966), 9.

[59] 'Mí an Mheitheamh'/Month of June, *D* p. 79.

[60] 'An Bás'/Death, *D* p. 71.

to enjoy nor endure and certainly not to overcome life's challenge/'dúshlán na ndúl' unless they do so by goading us into action by presenting an alternative of total negation and despair. This, however, seems doubtful. The 'twilight ambience' of the poems suggests that Ó Direáin was resigned to the Spenglerian decline of 'Gaelic' or Irish culture in Ireland and to the annihilation of Aran itself.[61] The population rate *was* falling, land and language use *were* decreasing, but wasn't Ó Direáin premature and out of order in addressing this 'creill an oileáin rúin'/death-knell of the secret island *to* the fishermen of Aran?

> Éistíg le fead na hadhairce
> Ag fuagairt cath ar bhur gcleacht,
> Thoir sa gcathair a séidtear í,
> Is í creill bhur gcleacht an fhead.
>
> Ná bíodh bhur dtnúth le muir feasta
> Ach tugaíg cúl léi go luath,
> Tugaíg aghaidh ar chill is ar thír,
> Ní fada uaibh anois an uaigh.[62]

Although the poem angrily puts the blame for Aran's decline and mismanagement on the East (the government, by implication), it accepts defeat. Perhaps this is inevitable: the sea was enemy enough for the brave fishermen honoured by time and by Ó Direáin. However, this poem is one of too many in which the poet unfortunately appears like the unavoidable character in a disaster-movie called *Life* who treats his hearers to the unencouraging refrains 'we're all going to die!' and 'the end is nigh!'

At this time, almost all of Ó Direáin's eulogies turn out to be elegies: for example, the story-teller Darach Ó Direáin is shut up in and by the earth (*D* p. 66); and the island's whole way of life is summed up as 'ag meath'/declining, degenerating, withering, or decaying.[63] Unfortunately, Ó Direáin loses faith in Aran's ability to *sur-vive* the modern tide and its 'torrents of English'.[64] Yet, by way of complete contrast, even as late as the mid-1980s, the geologist Tim Robinson felt able to write that 'the material destructiveness of modern life is *only now*

---

[61] See *D* p. 51, p. 53, p. 62, p. 66, p. 67, p. 70.
[62] From 'Iascairí an Chladaigh'/The Shore Fishermen, *D* p. 67. Translation J in Appendix.
[63] 'Ómós do John Millington Synge/Homage to J. M. Synge', *SP/TD* p. 40.
[64] Robinson, *Stones of Aran*, 7–8.

beginning to impinge on Aran, and until very recently the sole custo-
dian of this land of total recall has been a folk-mind of matching tenac-
ity, focused by the limitations of island life and with the powers of
memory of an ancient oral culture.'[65] Into the twentieth century, this
folk-mind could still answer the challenge of time and the elements
with a prophesy that Aran would get its turn of life's great wheel yet:
'Bl'átha an Rí bhí, Gaillimh atá agus Árainn a bhéas'/Athenry that was,
Galway that is and Aran that will be.[66]

Presently, Aran islanders run a very successful and attractive tourist
industry and, despite the continued drop in population (1,651 in 1961
and 1,368 in 1981), the percentage of Irish-speakers in the district elec-
toral division of the islands in 1981 stood at 98 per cent.[67] What a pity
Ó Direáin, who only foresaw the decline of the west, was a disciple of
Blok[68] and not of Pushkin:

> If life deceives you,
> Do not sorrow, do not rage!
> On the day of grief submit:
> The day of joy, believe, will come.
>
> In the future lives the heart [. . .][69]

Ó Direáin had no heart for the future because he didn't feel that there
was room in the future for his kind. He only saw winter and death
ahead, not the death of winter.[70] Too many of the people he looked up
to as a boy, his 'crainn seasta'/steadfast trees, had fallen and this tipped
the scales of his imagination towards cultural despair.

Brushes with death, however, are common in the lives of Aran fishermen and cliff-climbers.[71] Ó Direáin had been warned off the sea by
his worrying mother. This he felt was responsible for the 'softness'

---

[65] Robinson, *Stones of Aran*, 4. My italics.   [66] O'Flaherty, T., *Aranmen All*, 172.

[67] Moran, G. (ed.), *Galway History and Society: Interdisciplinary Essays on the History
of an Irish County* (Dublin: Geography Publications, 1996), 672.

[68] Blok, Alexander, 'There is no refuge, no peace, none.' From 'Earth's Heart is
Growing Cold Again', in *Alexander Blok: Selected Poems*, ed. by Jon Stallworthy and Peter
France (Harmondsworth: Penguin, 1974), 93.

[69] Pushkin, Alexander, *Pushkin Threefold*, trans. W. Arndt (London: George Allen and
Unwin Ltd., 1972), 197.

[70] See excerpts from Liam O'Flaherty's *The Black Soul* and *Thy Neighbour's Wife*, in
An Aran Reader, ed. by B. and R. Ó hEithir (Dublin: Lilliput Press Ltd., 1991). Compare:
'In winter all things die' and 'Winter died with a melancholy roar of all the elements',
140 and 147, respectively.

[71] Ó hEithir (eds.), *An Aran Reader*, 112.

which had shaped him to his own dissatisfaction.[72] 'Soft' or just sensitive, the loss of his father at the age of seven had, I believe, put a 'cor i leamhnacht a shaoil'/a sour turn in the fresh milk of his life, set Ó Direáin on a road off the island of Aran to Galway and Dublin—Kavanagh's 'City of the Kings/Where art, music, letters are the real things'.[73] The Aran poet's companion on this road was not tradition, as it was for the divided Ó Ríordáin, but death with and about which he struck up a conversation that turned into art: 'scéal, is nath, is gáire'/story, quip and laughter.[74]

Ó Direáin's artistic vision, a source of pride and solace to him, also set him apart from the crowd in the negative sense that it isolated him. In the *Ó Mórna* volume, artistic insight is first presented as a privilege to the possessor. In 'Fís an Daill/The Blind Man's Vision', it miraculously permits the blindman to see, with his imagination or sixth sense, wider and further than those with 'normal' sight dulled by habituation and confined to experience. As with Emerson's thought, the blindman's view expands at limit.[75] The reward is a limitless view and near-Beatific vision:

Is chonaic mé gné	*And I saw the face*
An tseanchaí léith	*of the grey-haired storyteller*
Is í ar lasadh ag fís na háille.	*shining with visionary delight.*
	(*SP/TD* p. 32)

In 'An tÓinmhid/The Buffoon' (*SP/TD* p. 44), heaven, eternity and full Beatific vision are attained. These two poems reveal extreme animosity to the worldly crowd whose materialism and lack of imagination condemn them to (eternal?) darkness and send them (by implication) to hell. Is the priest *manqué* in Ó Direáin emerging?

The poet doesn't just set himself up as a priest, god, or judge in order to condemn or admonish his people. Rather, out of deep concern, he genuinely assumes the traditional role of *file* or seer to point them and us back towards the light as he perceives it. However, while the (Irish) people were exposed to lashings of this poet's tongue, Ó Direáin left himself open to the devastating disinterest of a people immune to any

---

[72] See 'Boige'/Softness, *D* p. 143; and Muiris Mac Conghail, 'Agallamh le Máirtín Ó Direáin', in *CMC* pp. 135–6.

[73] Kavanagh, 'Temptation in Harvest', in Muldoon (ed.), *The Faber Book of Contemporary Irish Poetry*, 57–60 (p. 59).

[74] 'Leigheas na hEagla/Salve for Fear', *SP/TD* pp. 52–3.

[75] Tanner (ed.), *Ralph Waldo Emerson: Essays and Poems*, xi.

bard-like reproach, a generation who—he despaired—lacked the discernment, love, and generosity that real Irish chiefs of the past, and even the Ascendancy, had shown to the Arts.[76] So why did he bother haranguing 'unremembering hearts and heads'[77] with his songs?

For Ó Direáin art and literature had a purpose best revealed perhaps by his 'Ómós do/Homage to John Millington Synge' (*SP/TD* p. 40). Although he never made the same claim for his own work, Ó Direáin believed that the words and some of the ways of his people had been preserved 'till Coill Chuain comes to Inis Meáin' by Synge's translation of them into art. Literature, for Ó Direáin, was not only a means of reclaiming, repossessing the secrets of his island but also of preserving them:

> Fóill, a ghaineamh, fóill!   *Wait, sand, wait!*
> Fearann tearmainn, seachain!   *Avoid this place of sanctuary!*
> (from 'Teaghlach Éinne/Éanna's Community', *SP/TD* p. 46)

Rather than let the islands' unsung heroes, secret places, and histories be buried in oblivion, Ó Direáin casts them in what Ó Searcaigh calls 'cré na cuimhne/the clay of memory', refashioning and exhibiting them in poetry.[78] They constituted the 'leac ionraic'/rock of integrity on, for and by which he stood, touchstones that gave him Whitman-like tokens of himself.[79] Upon this base and with these tokens, Ó Direáin shaped and carved out his body of work just as in youth he had sculpted figures using Aran stones as material.

However, no matter how much Ó Direáin wanted to stay true to the shore, he reluctantly accepted that it eventually became necessary to 'go on the deep'.[80] In the fine poem 'Cranna Foirtil/Stout Oars' (*SP/TD* p. 54), the poet is still not sure, however, where the shore ends and sea begins (*FB* p. 58) in the icy, foggy regions between thought and word.[81]

---

[76] See 'Éamh an Éigis', *D* p. 53; and 'An Sméis', *D* p. 61.

[77] Yeats, 'Under Ben Bulben', *W. B. Yeats: Collected Poems*, ed. by Augustine Martin (London: Vintage, 1992), 341–4 (p. 343).

[78] Cathal Ó Searcaigh, 'Cré na Cuimhne', *Na Buachaillí Bána*, 79–83.

[79] Whitman wrote of living animals: 'So they show their relations to me and I accept them,/They bring me tokens of myself, they evince them plainly in their possession./I wonder where they get these tokens,/did I pass that way huge times ago and negligently drop them?' From 'Song of Myself' Part XXXII, *A Choice of Whitman's Verse: Selected with an Introduction by Donald Hall* (London: Faber and Faber, 1968), 23–83 (pp. 53–4).

[80] 'Berkeley', *SP/TD* p. 106.

[81] Ibid. See also, Cathal Ó Searcaigh, 'Transubstaintiú', *An Bealach 'na Bhaile/Homecoming*, 184.

He wants his soul to hold or keep its ground but his arms, it seems, to press back on the 'stout oars' of the title. This does not leave the poem 'at sea' in the negative sense; clearly, such a poem is called to life by the tension between elements such as land and sea, the tendency for their boundaries to shift and change, and by the human necessity and experience of crossing back and forth. Sometimes, however, Ó Direáin catches poetic sustenance/'éadail ón toinn' neither from the sea nor the land[82] and, even when he does, he still envies the Aran men of action rowing against their fate on the high breast of the sea. For example, in the poem, 'Olc Liom/Remorse' (*SP/TD* p. 56), deviation from island life has meant a kind of death to the poet who, like Ó Mórna, has produced no (male) heir to further 'our stock, our ways, our heritage'. His real legacy, of poems, is not counted in this poem; modesty, and even uncertainty as to their worth, would not allow it. Despite that, frightened by the possibility of complete extinction, of oblivion, Ó Direáin returns again and again to his only 'leigheas na heagla/salve for fear': words (*SP/TD* p. 52).

In several poems from *Ó Mórna*, Ó Direáin wistfully envies animal life—birds mainly—and expresses a longing for their freedom and apparent harmony with the elements, wind and sea. In 'A Fhaoileáin Uchtbhán/White-breasted Gull' (*SP/TD* p. 34), the poet seeks escape from the human condition. Yet, just why Ó Direáin may have envied animal life is not explored in his poems so that they are simply left grounded in sentimentality and hopeless escapism. In 'Áinlí'/Swallows (*D* p. 47), for example, the poet directs the birds back west after finding them astray like himself on mainland Ireland. The Eoghainín/little Eoghan to whom he sends them back recalls Pearse's story (based on folklore) of a dying child to whom the birds are soul-mates.[83] Ó Direáin appears to be reflecting again on his own dead youth and dreams prior to his 'fall' into adulthood and disillusionment.

One group of poems in *Ó Mórna* refers to women and tells us something of Ó Direáin's attitude towards them. In 'Ionracas'/Integrity (*D* p. 69), he agrees (with the unnamed 'great poet' Ó Ríordáin) that the island *and* a woman's love are source and subject of his poems. For its integrity, he vows to keep the island in his poem but says nothing of

---

82 For the sea: 'Cranna Foirtil/Stout Oars', *SP/TD* p. 54. For land: 'Stríog', *D* p. 68.
83 Pearse, P., *Short Stories of Padraic Pearse: A Dual Language Book*, selected and adapted by Desmond Maguire (Cork: Mercier Press, 1968, repr. 1979), 27–47.

women or their integrity. Have they been left out for lacking the island's constancy?

Many of Ó Direáin's poems about women do suggest that 'cluain'/deceit has always come naturally to their kind, as in 'A Dúchas Beiche'/Her Waspish Ways (*D* p. 46). His attitude is obviously derived from personal experience as recorded in disappointed love poems such as 'Ár gCuid dá Chéile'/Our Share of Each Other (*D* p. 64). This poem was inspired by Ó Direáin's reading of French poetry, in particular, 'Rondel de l'Adieu' by Edmond Haraucourt with the lines: '*partir c'est mourir un peu*' and '*on laisse un peu de soi-même*'/'to part is to die a little' and 'one loses something of oneself' (*FB* p. 143). Ó Direáin felt that not only departure from the island brought a mini-death to the spirit but likewise departure from a loved one or a principle. Such deviation was a death-rehearsal or build up for the final curtain (*FB* p. 145).

However, one begins to suspect that Ó Direáin made more of old endings than new beginnings, more of the deaths than the life in life, more perhaps of the skull than the skin before it. For example, whereas in Ted Hughes's 'Bride and Groom Lie Hidden for Three Days' the lovers make each other into a sexually charged 'superhuman puzzle' brought or wrought to 'perfection',[84] Ó Direáin's lovers, in 'Ár gCuid dá Chéile', typically unmake each other:

Tá cuid agat díom thall,	*You've some of me over there,*
Tá agam díot abhus,	*And I've some of you here,*
Ag Áth na Scairbhe fós	*at Áth na Scairbhe still*
Tá cuid den bheirt againn.	*there's some of us both.*

(*D* p. 64)

Notably, there is a good range and diversity in the love poems of the *Ó Mórna* volume, from the mournful 'Maith Dhom/Forgive Me' (*SP/TD* p. 18) to the post-traumatic indifference of 'Caoin Tú Féin, a Bhean'/Cry For Yourself Now Woman:

> Ar an drochuair duit
> A tharla i do dháil an fear,
> Níor dhea-earra é riamh,
> Níor dhea-thuar a theacht.
>
> Rinne cloch de do chroí íogair
> Nuair a chuir i do chluais an fríd

---

[84] Hughes, Ted, *Selected Poems 1957–1981* (London: Faber and Faber, 1982, repr. 1986), 140–1.

A chuir cor i leamhnacht na beatha ort
A rinne meadhg de do shaol.

D'eascar sé ón dream dorcha
Ar geal leo an oíche,
An oíche is an claonchogar
Bia is beatha dá bhuíon.

Caoin tú féin anois, a bhean!
Cé mall an gol sin agat,
Fadó a chaoin mise thú,
Níl deoir eile agam.[85]

Ó Direáin's ideal women, on the contrary, are those that are loyal and true; modest, discerning women like Pegg Monahan who stood by and for the 'good' with humour and resilience ('Do Phegg Monahan', *D* p. 48). He also awards special praise to the 'Women of the [1916] Rising' whose 'loving hearts were true to Ireland/thug dílse a gcroí go dil do Bhanba' in the archaic but stirring panegyric 'Mná na hAiséirí'. Any awareness that a loyalist minority might be just as loyal to the English Empire did not obstruct Ó Direáin's bardic and emotive eulogy:

Is fuagraímis gach cnáid go críoch an dearmaid,
Gach giolla, gach briolla cunórach dá maireann,
Ó táid na leoin faoin bhfód, mo mhairg!

Let us renounce every jeer to the end of oblivion,
every slave, every meddling lout that remains
since the heroes, alas, have gone under. (*D* p. 76)

Ó Direáin would never be one to speak ill of the dead but his praise for them in general—whether one feels it is justified or exaggerated—is, unfortunately, accompanied very often with contempt for the living. Like all else in his poetry, women are viewed in the light of an idyllic past while the living reality seems to him vulgar:

Mná leathnocht ag filleadh	*Half-naked women returning*
Ón trá i ngluaisteáin;	*from the beach in cars;*
Áilleacht, gráinneacht is luargacht	*beauty, ugliness and coarseness*
In iomaíocht ar an uaigneas.	*vying with loneliness.*

('Tráthnóna Samhraidh'/Summer Afternoon, *D* p. 69)

---

[85] 'Caoin Tú Féin, a Bhean'/Cry For Yourself Now Woman, *D* p. 54. Translation K in Appendix.

Generally, Ó Direáin's poems express rueful regret that there are no more terrible beauties,[86] just the—for him—noisome vision of modern sluttish consumerism on both a personal and a national scale.[87]

To read *Ó Mórna* is to follow the tracks of Ó Direáin's mind from his island community, its 'ionracas'/integrity, to the 'deceitful city' of exploitation,[88] of hopeless alienation, corruption, and usury,[89] and of 'deamhan deabhaidh na sráide'/the rat-race of the street.[90] His poems continue to work or build on simple but striking and painful contrasts of place, people, and times. However, it would be superficial and unfair simply to dismiss the poet as a Brother Michael proposing that 'culture is always something that was'.[91] Instead, one must (as with Ó Mórna himself) not condemn the poet

> Gan a phór is a chró do mheas,
> A chéim, a réim, an t-am do mhair,
> Is guais a shóirt ar an uaigneas.
>
> *Without considering his blood and lineage,*
> *His station, his power, the age he lived in,*
> *and the snares that loneliness sets for his sort.*
>
> (*SP/TD* p. 21)

Ó Direáin was of an island people who took up the challenge of the elements, who bore but continually rebelled against the tyranny of land-lordism, who were noted for their 'indomitable spirit' in the shadow of death and Anglicization.[92] No surprise then that Ó Direáin should exercise bardic authority to express bitter disappointment with his partly liberated country governed by what he termed 'dúistí dúra an tuat-achais'/dour dithering idiots[93] who, he felt, let the candle of victory and nationhood waste away in Ireland's 'dark age from the 1930s'.[94]

---

[86] See 'Do Mháire Nic Giolla Mhártain', *D* p. 52.

[87] See 'De Dheasca an Úis . . ./Because of Usury' and 'Cuid Caidéise/Curiosity', *SP/TD* pp. 60–3.

[88] 'An Stailc/The Strike', *SP/TD* p. 48.

[89] 'De Dheasca an Úis . . ./Because of Usury', *SP/TD* p. 60.

[90] 'Faoiseamh'/Respite, *D* p. 77.

[91] Kavanagh, 'Memory of Brother Michael', in Muldoon (ed.), *The Faber Book of Contemporary Irish Poetry*, 70–1.

[92] See Ó hEithir (ed.), *An Aran Reader*, 101, 112, and 220–6.

[93] 'Mo Mhairg an Ghlac'/Alas the Leadership, *D* p. 75.

[94] 'Nuair a bhéas fíor-stair na hÉireann dá scríobh feicfear gur sna blianta tar éis 1930 a tharla Ré Dhorcha na hÉireann'/When the true history of Ireland is written, the years after 1930 will be seen as the Dark Age of Ireland. See Houlihan, C., 'An Gearrscéal—agus rudaí eile', *Comhar* (November 1968), 11–18 (p. 17). See also Ó hAnluain, E., 'Nóta

While Ó Direáin's early poem 'Stoite/Uprooted' (*SP/TD* p. 12) spoke of rootless individuals at a loose end in the city, by the time he wrote 'Blianta an Chogaidh'/The War Years,[95] he presents this uprooted class as entirely cut off from their ancestors, their people, their country, and even from their true selves. Having deviated from the road of their fathers' fathers, they have become for Ó Direáin an incarnation of Thomas Davis's sad prophesy that 'if we live influenced by wind, and sun, and tree, and not by the passions and deeds of the Past, we are a thriftless and hopeless people.'[96] If you remove the 'tree' (a positive symbol for Ó Direáin despite the fact that Aran is famed for its lack of them[97]) from the above quotation, you are left with a common Aran phrase of reassurance in which the speaker swears that he does *not* 'take after the sun or wind' but is his father's son and, therefore, will not do violence to the family tradition.[98] Violence to the family tradition was, in Ó Direáin's view, responsible for the years of stagnation from the 1930s to the 1950s during which national and cultural aspirations were far from realized. On the language issue alone, for example, one commentator found that 'the Department of Education had failed the Irish test which had been set by the state'.[99]

However, it is worth noting at this point that the traditionalist Ó Direáin (who wanted the high tide of tradition to return) and the anti-Revivalist Kavanagh (who wanted puddles of the past to dry up) *both* saw 1950s Ireland as benighted by what the latter called 'the victory of mediocrity'. For Kavanagh, the fruits of this victory were provincialism and censorship. He viewed the whole period, in fact, as one in which a 'wake' was in progress for 'the corpse of 1916, the Gaelic Language, the inferiority complex . . .'[100] Ó Direáin's poetry, up to and including the

faoi Bhlianta an Chogaidh le Máirtín Ó Direáin', *Scríobh 2* (Dublin: An Clóchomhar Tta., 1975), 21–9 (p. 26).

[95] There are two versions of this poem about the 'war years'. The first appeared in *Comhar*, August 1953, and the second (with a revised ending) in *Ó Mórna*, 1957; see *D* p. 78. For both, see *Scríobh 2* (1975), 21–9 (pp. 22–4).

[96] See Molony, J. N., *A Soul Came Into Ireland: Thomas Davis, 1814–1845: A Biography* (Dublin: Geography Publications, 1995), 144.

[97] Flaherty, R. J., 'Man of Aran', in Ó hEithir (ed.), *An Aran Reader*, 209–11 (p. 209).

[98] O'Flaherty, T., *Aranmen All*, 86.

[99] McCartney, Donal, 'Education and Language, 1938–1951', in K. B. Nowlan and T. D. Williams (eds.), *Ireland in the War Years and After: 1939–1951* (Dublin: Gill and Macmillan Ltd., 1969), 93.

[100] Patrick Kavanagh, quoted in Keogh, D., *Twentieth-Century Ireland: Nation and State* (Dublin: Gill and Macmillan, 1994), 222.

Ó Mórna collection, certainly provided some of the 'bright candles' for this wake but he increasingly felt that these were candles in the wind, illumining only the full extent of the darkness ahead:

> Ach mar chuaigh an choinneal go dtí seo,
> Téadh an t-orlach ina bhfuil romhainn amach.
>
> *But as the candle has wasted till now*
> *Let the last inch waste in the time to come.*[101]

Was the wake to go on forever or were the Finnegans to begin again anew?

3.2 *ÁR RÉ DHEARÓIL* (1962)

There is a mode of vital experience—experience of space and time, of the self and others, of life's possibilities and perils—that is shared by men and women all over the world today. I will call this body of experience 'modernity'. To be modern is to find ourselves in an environment that promises us adventure, power, joy, growth, transformation of ourselves and the world—and, at the same time, that threatens to destroy everything we have, everything we know, everything we are. [. . .] People who find themselves in the midst of this maelstrom are apt to feel that they are the first ones, and maybe the only ones, to be going through it; this feeling has engendered numerous nostalgic myths of pre-modern Paradise Lost. In fact, however, great and ever-increasing numbers of people have been going through it for close to five hundred years. Although most of these people have probably experienced modernity as a radical threat to all their history and traditions, it has, in the course of five centuries, developed a rich history and a plenitude of traditions of its own.[102]

Ó Direáin's *Ár Ré Dhearóil*/Our Wretched Era volume appeared in the 1960s, an era in which the nature of modernism, 'based on attitudes to modern life as a whole', was hotly disputed.[103] Thought on modernity was divided into three main tendencies: affirmative, negative, and withdrawn. For example, one very influential early twentieth century 'No!' to modernity came from Max Weber who saw the modern economic order as an 'iron cage' determining the lives of his prisoner-like contemporaries. Weber described these contemporaries as 'specialists without spirit, sensualists without heart' and bemoaned that 'this

---

[101] 'Mar Chaitheamar an Choinneal/How We Wasted the Candle', *SP/TD* pp. 98–9.
[102] Berman, *All That Is Solid Melts Into Air*, 15–36 (pp. 15–16).
[103] Ibid. 29.

nullity is caught in the delusion that it has achieved a level of development never before attained by mankind.'[104]

Much further to the right of, but still sharing, Weber's neo-Olympian perspective were Spengler and Eliot[105] whose dual influence on Ó Direáin cannot be overestimated.[106] Consequently, of the two sterile antitheses of modernolatry and cultural despair into which twentieth century thought on modernity has been polarized,[107] Ó Direáin veered towards despair. He saw himself in the modern city as a 'cime mar chách'/a prisoner like all, and believed that if he as an individual stood out from the crowd in any way, it was as a mourner placing his 'cloichín ar charn na sean/pebble on the ancestral cairn'.[108] While even Eliot turned from despair to 'rejoice, having to construct something/Upon which to rejoice',[109] Ó Direáin, sadly, was resigned to burying what was not, in fact, dead: namely, the growing Gaelic branch on the flowering tree of Irish culture as a whole.

Yet, the poet can be excused to some extent for seeing nothing but the end in sight. The 1950s were, indeed, a dark decade for Ireland from both the modernolator's and the traditionalist's point of view.[110] Population and native language use were both in decline; towns and cities offered some work but minimal possibilities for citizens wishing to conduct their business, cultural, and social affairs through the medium of Irish. The bright new wave of enthusiasm for the Irish language was not in evidence during the period 1957 to 1962 when the poems of *Ár Ré Dhearóil* were being written. In fact the actual presence, power, and potential of the language weren't fully appreciated until the seventies and now:

---

[104] Ibid. 27.   [105] Ibid. 28.

[106] In almost all of his public pronouncements on poetry, for example, Ó Direáin supports his arguments with quotes from Eliot; while Spengler's shadow over what many critics see as Ó Direáin's two finest collections, *Ó Mórna* and *Ár Ré Dhearóil*, has already been noted (*SP/TD* p. xii). See also Ó Tuathail, 'Cloichín ar Charn', in *CMC*, p. 125; and Ó Direáin, 'Mise agus an Fhilíocht', *D* pp. 215–17 (p. 216).

[107] Berman, *All That Is Solid Melts Into Air*, 164–71 (p. 169).

[108] 'Ár Ré Dhearóil/Our Wretched Era', *SP/TD* pp. 66–75, and 'Mar Chaitheamar an Choinneal/How We Wasted the Candle', *SP/TD* p. 99.

[109] Eliot, 'Ash-Wednesday—1930', *Collected Poems 1909–1962*, 2nd edn. (London: Faber and Faber, 1974), 93–105 (p. 95).

[110] 'It is generally held that Irish society had to await the end of the de Valera era to awake from its nostalgic slumbers. With revisionist hindsight, 1959 is taken as the annus mirabilis of modern Ireland, the year in which God said 'Let Lemass be!'—and there was light, dispelling the mists of traditionalism which had obscured the path to progress and industrialization.' See Gibbons, L., *Transformations in Irish Culture* (Cork: Cork University Press, 1996), 82.

Many modernisms of the past have found themselves by forgetting; the modernists of the 1970s were forced to find themselves by remembering [. . .] The new departures of the 1970s lay in attempts to recover past modes of life that were buried but not dead [. . .] At a moment when modern society seemed to lose the capacity to create a brave new future, modernism was under intense pressure to discover new sources of life through imaginative encounters with the past.[111]

Berman borrows from Bob Dylan to characterize this process (in a way that Seán Ó Ríordáin would appreciate) as *Bringing It All Back Home*. Yet, he insists that while the look toward home is a look 'back' in time, into our childhood or our society's historical past, modernism is distinguished from sentimentalism by the fact that 'modernists do not try to blend or merge themselves with the past' (in which case they might well disappear into it like Muldoon's Brownlee[112]) but to

'bring it all back' into the past, that is, to bring to bear on the past the selves they have become in the present, to bring into those old homes visions and values that may clash radically with them—and maybe to re-enact the very struggles that drove them from their homes in the first place. In other words, modernism's rapport with the past, whatever it turns out to be, will not be easy.[113]

Ó Direáin's rapport with the past becomes increasingly uneasy; he does verbally register the struggles that drove large numbers of his people from their homes but, crucially, he fails to bring the present to bear on the past. With Ó Direáin it is always the other way round: the past overbearing on the unbearable present. Therefore, he is, in Berman's sense, a 'sentimentalist' as he does wish to merge with the past in order to escape a 'wretched' present. One perceives in his work, especially *Ár Ré Dhearóil*, a 'mystificatory nostalgia' as opposed to the 'responsible expectancy' which Heidegger appreciated in the work of Hölderlin:

Heidegger cites Hölderlin's feastday hymn 'Remembrance' as a celebration

---

[111] Berman, *All That Is Solid Melts Into Air*, 329–48 (p. 332). It is interesting, in this context, to note that on the eve of the 1970s in Ireland, Thomas Kinsella published his translation of the ancient Irish epic *The Táin*, Dolmen Editions 9 (Dublin: Dolmen Press, 1969).

[112] Muldoon, P., 'Why Brownlee Left', *New Selected Poems 1968–1994* (London: Faber and Faber, 1996), 50.

[113] Berman, *All That Is Solid Melts Into Air*, 333.

which 'gathers a people together' in the common pursuit of their originality. Authentic poetry can remind a community that they have been exiled from their tradition which must be sought after anew. But if this seeking is to be a genuine 'homecoming' it must avoid the danger of a reactionary regression to some antique memory of self-possession. On the contrary, it must expose the community to an experience of uncanny dispossession (*Unheimlichkeit*) in order that it may open itself to a genuine future. If Hölderlin speaks therefore of poetry allowing us to come home, he means it, according to Heidegger, not in the sense of some triumphalistic return to a fixed past (*Heimkunft*), but rather in the sense of a futural arriving which can never finally arrive (*Heimkommen*)—an arriving which, in Heidegger's phrase, preserves itself as a perpetual advent (*Ankunft*).[114]

As a minority language writer working and more at home in the pre-colonial language of his country, Ó Direáin reminds himself and other Irish readers of our exile from a valuable tradition but he seems to believe that tradition to be dying rather than arriving and thus his work fails to grow beyond *Unheimlichkeit* and the desperate dream of *Heimkunft*. Heidegger wrote that 'just as every work is itself responsible for the awakening and formation of the generation that will set free the world hidden in that work, the growth of the work in turn must *hear ahead* to the tradition it is responsible for.'[115] Ó Direáin's contemporary cultural despair and disillusion made him listen back more than hear ahead to what he then imagined was the no-sound of the future.

However, Ó Direáin's rejection of modernity due to 'an ethic of nostalgia for origins, an ethic of archaic and natural innocence, of a purity of presence and self-presence in speech'[116] and, say, Paul de Man's rip-roaring 'zero-year' modernolatory of the new, of the future,[117] *both* merely reveal how 'forms of modernist thought and vision may congeal into dogmatic orthodoxies and become archaic'.[118] Where de Man is too modern and wants to bury the past alive, Ó Direáin is not modern enough and buries alive the present:

Machnamh an Duine Stoite

Caithimse seal in éad
Leis an dream a d'fhás

114 See Kearney, R., 'Martin Heidegger', *Modern Movements in European Philosophy* (Manchester: Manchester University Press, 1987), 28–50 (p. 40).   115 Ibid.
116 Derrida, 'Structure, Sign and Play'. See Rylance (ed.), *Debating Texts*, 123–36 (p. 134).
117 Berman, *All That Is Solid Melts Into Air*, 331–2.   118 Ibid. 171.

I dtaithí áilleacht chathartha,
Eaglais, stua, is foirgneamh ard,
Is íomhá chloiche greanta,
Saothar na bpéintéir oilte
Inár ndánlann taiscthe
Is an dréacht téadbhinn ceoil
Thugann aoibhneas ard don aigne.

Ní bhainim as na nithe seo fós
Toisc ainchleachta, iomlán taithnimh:
Is iad na nithe príomháille léir
Is fuíoll na saíochta sinseartha
A roinn mo dhaoine liom ar a dteallach,
A shuigh i gcoróin ar mo chroí óighe,
Is mó is lón do m'anam.[119]

It is indeed rare for Ó Direáin to mention, never mind 'envy', urban splendour. Drawn more to the hand-made stone walls erected by his people in Aran, he has no difficulty in justly celebrating their lasting memorials in poems such as 'Stoite/Uprooted' (*SP/TD* p. 12). In the above poem, however, he attributes his inability to appreciate fully (and celebrate?) favourable aspects of city life to 'ainchleacht/inexperience' with the urban landscape. But how could he be inexperienced with cities when he left Aran at eighteen and had already lived in Galway and mainly Dublin for thirty-three years when he first published this poem? It is more a question of failure or reluctance to engage with the city and the modern world. Consequently, Ó Direáin's custom when not censuring city life is to bury it alive as he did with this uncharacteristic but revealing poem which only appeared in one edition of the magazine *Feasta* and was not seen again until it was included among the miscellaneous and previously uncollected pieces at the end of *Dánta 1939–1979*. Written as far back as 1951, this poem's *qualified* praise for the urban landscape would have been out of place in any of Ó Direáin's full collections and thus, it appears to me, was left out.

In 1961, one year before *Ár Ré Dhearóil* was published, *Feamainn Bhealtaine* appeared. This collection of stories, essays, and anecdotes includes a discussion of the problems facing a poet writing in Irish at the time should s/he wish to depict city life: 'Is teanga í an Ghaeilge nach raibh i ngleic leis an saol sin, agus caithfear gortghlanadh is

---

[119] *D* p. 200. The poem first appeared in *Feasta*, November 1951. Translation L in Appendix.

forbairt a dhéanamh uirthi fós sula mbeidh sí i ngleic leis'.[120] Ó Direáin had two main worries: firstly, that work in Irish may be received differently from that in English and, perhaps, be ghetto-ized or ghettoed;[121] secondly, that the Irish language then lacked, in his opinion, a diversity of registers in actual use so that while the language was rich in real words spoken by real rural or island wo/men, it was as yet uncomfortable with new-fangled urban terms which, in Irish, either squeaked like new shoes or had still to be cobbled together.

The poet was concerned about how the work of a typical *'primitif'* arriving in the city and recording his personal feelings 'in his own way' would be received by sophisticated city-dwellers (*FB* p. 87). Such worries are as old as modernity itself (approximately five hundred years old according to Berman[122]) but literary history has shown that there is enthusiasm for work which reflects the battle to assert human dignity and maintain personal values in the high-speed modern tide. For example, Rousseau's *Julie, où la Nouvelle Héloïse*, an early but classic text of modernity delved into *le tourbillon social* and raised the question central to *Ár Ré Dearóil* and to Ó Direáin himself: 'how was the self to move and live in the whirlwind', to keep lit the candle of self and/or nationhood?[123]

While Louis MacNeice could rejoyce in 'the drunkenness of things being various', Rousseau's young hero (like Ó Direáin) is doused and lost in it:

I'm beginning to feel the drunkenness that this agitated tumultuous life plunges you into. With such a multitude of objects passing before my eyes, I'm getting dizzy. Of all the things that strike me, there is none that holds my heart, yet all of them together disturb my feelings, so that I forget what I am and who I belong to.[124]

[120] 'Irish is a language that has not yet struggled with that life and must be further weeded and cultivated to take it on'. See *FB* p. 86. Note that Ó Direáin's terminology prefigures that of Ní Dhomhnaill who more recently declared that both she and Seamus Heaney are engaged in 'gortghlanadh'/'clearing home fields' and 'talking to ourselves [in Irish *and* English] about the things that concern us, without having to be looking over our shoulders and telling others out there what they want to hear.' See McDiarmid and Durkan, 'Q. & A.: Nuala Ní Dhomhnaill', interview by Lucy McDiarmid and Michael Durkan, *Irish Literary Supplement* (Fall 1987), 41–3 (p. 42).
[121] These terms, in current English and American-English use, provide an example of how the English language has itself had to invent its own new-fangled words for urban experience.
[122] Berman, *All That Is Solid Melts Into Air*, 15–16.   [123] Ibid. 18.
[124] *Julie, où la Nouvelle Héloïse*, 1761, Part II, Letters 14 and 17, in the Bibliothèque de la Pléiade edition of Rousseau's *Oeuvres Complètes* (Paris: Gallimard, 1959ff.), Volume II,

The motor driving this agitation and turbulence/'gaoth aduaidh' is capitalism which draws people to cities in the first place and revolutionizes social life:

All fixed, fast-frozen relations, with their train of ancient and venerable prejudices and opinions, are swept away, all new-formed ones become antiquated before they can ossify. All that is solid melts into air, all that is holy is profaned, and men at last are forced to face . . . the real conditions of their lives and their relations with their fellow men.[125]

Marx, a revolutionist, admired this process as the undisguised glee of his prose (above) illustrates; however, for a cultural nationalist like Ó Direáin such movement or 'progress' was tantamount to driving and following one's country's entire stock of sacred cows over a cliff and into the abyss which Eliot once described as 'what few ever see, and what those cannot bear to look at for long'.[126] What Ó Direáin foresaw on the road before him was the dying of the light and he raged against it. Feeling that his self and his culture were being smothered or buried alive, and apparently considering the real conditions of modern lives and relationships to be unbearably wretched, empty, and deceitful, Ó Direáin, in the Ireland of his day, lacked the air to breathe or believe in any future for what's often disparagingly termed 'Irish' Ireland.

Ó Direáin's vision of mid-twentieth-century Ireland could be summed up in two words: destruction and desecration.[127] For him, romantic Ireland seemed dead and gone, in the grave with Pearse and Connolly, and the grave overrun with mice (modern politicians) champing on the Host or Eucharist fallen from the hands of the brave martyrs who gave body and blood for Ireland's freedom.[128] The former underlings who came to power and prominence (apart from de Valera[129]) in the Republic of Ireland, he generally denounced as

pp. 231–6, pp. 255–6. Excerpt translated by Berman, in *All That Is Solid Melts Into Air*, 17–18.

[125] Marx and Engels, *Manifesto of the Communist Party*, adapted from the Samuel Moore version of 1888. See Berman, *All That Is Solid Melts Into Air*, 21. See also *Clár na Comharsheilbhe: Forógra Pháirtí na gCumannach* (Dublin and Belfast: Páirtí Cumannach na hÉireann, 1986), 10.

[126] Helen Gardner, *The Art of T. S. Eliot* (London: The Cresset Press, 1949, repr. 1968), 79.

[127] 'An Milleadh'/Destruction, *D* p. 105, and 'Éire ina bhFuil Romhainn/To Ireland in the Coming Times', *SP/TD* pp. 96–7.

[128] 'Ár Laochra'/Our Warriors [or Heroes], *D* pp. 94–5.

[129] See 'Éamon de Valera', *CMC* pp. 48–51.

[. . .] daor ag faire daoir eile   *one slave intent on another*
Is gach daor mar dhea ina mháistir.   *and therefore every slave a master.*

                         ('Daordháil'/Thraldom, *D* p. 104)

Ó Direáin adopts a Yeatsian view of his country's new leaders and bour-
geoisie whom he portrays as fumbling in greasy tills only to sell out their
country and the old nationalist ideals for profit.[130]

Such Ó Direáin poems give expression to an experience of modernity which Marshall Berman associates more with Russia than with most
Western societies: the 'modernism of underdevelopment' which

is forced to be shrill, uncouth and inchoate. It turns in on itself and tortures
itself for its inability to singlehandedly make history—or else throws itself into
extravagant attempts to take on itself the whole burden of history. It whips itself
into frenzies of self-loathing, and preserves itself only through vast reserves of
self-irony. But the bizarre reality from which this modernism grows, and the
unbearable pressures under which it moves and lives—social and political pressures as well as spiritual ones—infuse it with a desperate incandescence that
Western modernism, so much more at home in its world, can rarely hope to
match.[131]

A similarly desperate incandescence flares up in Ó Direáin's *zeitgeist*
poem 'to Ireland in the coming times':

       Éire ina bhFuil Romhainn

       An té a nocht a chlaíomh go hard
       I do pháirt um Cháisc na lasrach,
       Má shíl gur shaor tú ón iomad náire
       Nach cuma, óir ní raibh ann ach fear saonta
       Is file laochta nár cruinníodh leis stór,
       Is nár fhág ina dhiaidh ach glóir;
       Cuirfear iallach ort a ghlóir a dhíol,
       Faoi mar ab éigean duit roimh a theacht
       A bheith i do thráill ag gach bodach anall,
       Is má thugtar meas méirdrí arís ort
       Bí i do mhéirdrigh mhóir dáiríre,

---

[130] Yeats, of course, was a major influence on Ó Direáin. Here, I am highlighting the
similarities between Yeats's two poems 'Under Ben Bulben' and 'September 1913',
Collected Poems, p. 343 and p. 102, and Ó Direáin's 'Éire ina bhFuil Romhainn', *SP/TD*
pp. 96–7 and 'Ceannaithe/Merchants', *SP/TD* pp. 88–9.

[131] Berman, *All That Is Solid Melts Into Air*, 229–32 (p. 232). Berman's comments
regarding the 'modernism of underdevelopment' are equally applicable to the
modernism of a decolonizing nation such as that in Ireland.

Is díol a ghlóir is tabhair a sháith
Do gach bodach aniar chun éilimh,
Reic fós a mhian is beir i do threo
Céile nua is a stór chun leapan,
Mar ní tú feasta céile Choinn ná Eoghain,
Céile an Phiarsaigh ná rún na laoch,
Ach más éigean an cumann a chur i gcrích
Agraím thú a shearc na bhFiann,
Gan ceangal leo gan raidhse dollar.[132]

This poem touches a nerve that runs deeper than the old-style nationalist rhetoric at its surface. Berman writes that

modernists today no longer insist, as the modernists of yesterday so often did, that we cease to be Jewish, or black, or Italian, or anything, in order to be modern. If whole societies can be said to learn anything, the modern societies of the 1970s seem to have learned that ethnic identity—not only one's own but everyone's—was essential to the depth and fullness of self that modern life opens up and promises to all.[133]

Similarly, what Ó Direáin opposes is the extreme of characterless modernolatry which seeks to dispose of *national* identity as unnecessary baggage, which seeks to bury aspects of Irish culture still alive in him (and in others) under its latest grey high-rise block. Basing his satire on Yeats's famous poem, 'To Ireland in the Coming Times',[134] Ó Direáin suggests that Yeats's 'angelic' Irish clan has mightily fallen, that the red-rose-bordered-hem has climbed way above the knee in the decade of the mini-skirt, that Time's candles have burnt down to an all-time low, that the bartered gaze has turned back to a solicitous wink, and that the Druid land and tune are now on sale and going cheap; worst of all, it is the Irish themselves, and he includes himself as always, who are to blame. The natives, in this view, had as much 'post-'colonial confidence in their national identity and true colour as Michael Jackson.

Increasingly, Ó Direáin appears in his poems to have felt out of step with the times, world-weary, short of breath and wanting to give up the ghost.[135] The bright affirmative candles of his first volumes are trans-

---

[132] *SP/TD* p. 96. For another version, see Translation M in Appendix.
[133] Berman, *All That Is Solid Melts Into Air*, 287–348 (p. 333).
[134] Yeats, *Collected Poems*, ed. Augustine Martin, 46.
[135] 'Mar Chaitheamar an Choinneal/How We Wasted the Candle', *SP/TD* p. 98. Interestingly, the conceit of this poem is based on the proverbial expression and image for 'taking the candle as the inch is taken—spending the whole when it is broken into'.

formed in the middle and later poetry into a cruel image of the dying light of selfhood and nationhood. On the positive side, the poet may have illumined some of the flaws and contradictions of modernity:

> Déan do mhachnamh a chathair fhallsa
> Is bíodh a fhios agat dá éis,
> Nach é an té a char an lasair
> A thógfaidh an t-ár ina dhóid
> Le scaoileadh anuas ort lá an léin.

> *Think it over, deceitful city,*
> *and be assured therefore*
> *that it isn't the freedom-fighter*
> *who will raise his destroyer's hand*
> *to you on demolition day.* (*D* p. 90)

However, the tone of most poems is crushingly negative, entirely lacking in faith that future moderns might realize that renewal from within is better than macadamizing the past in the mistaken belief that Ireland or any country 'could overcome its inner contradictions simply by driving away from them'.[136] This lesson is, of course, still being learnt today.

Rejecting his country's new leaders and untraditional values, Anglo-American customs, the whole cruel modern age which seemed to him to be deflecting Ireland like a river from its course, Ó Direáin remained faithful to his own language and tradition which still, he said, had 'neart inti fós is teagar'.[137] Ó Direáin, throughout his work, clings to the 'strength and substance' of his 'rock-like absolute of integrity',[138] stands by and for the tradition and language which he feels are increasingly subject to, at worst, disdain and, at best, suspicion:

Aodh de Blacam, in *Gaelic Literature Surveyed*, shows how this idea was previously used in poetry by Maolmhuire Ó hUiginn who died around 1591: 'Tig saoirse i ndiaidh ró-bhruide/tar eis dubhaidh tig soineann; fuilngeam feadh an órlaigh-se/mar do caitheadh an choinneal.' De Blacam translates: 'Freedom cometh after dire oppression,/as after gloom the sunshine comes;/let us endure while the inch is burning,/even as the candle was burnt.' There is certainly more solace in Ó hUiginn's early reworking of the image than in Ó Direáin's version.

136 Berman, *All That Is Solid Melts Into Air*, 328.

137 'Strength in it yet, and substance', with a slight pun on [Celtic] 'tiger', 'Dúshlán'/Challenge, *D* p. 110.

138 Milner-Gulland, Robin, and Peter Levi, S.J., (eds.), Introduction, *Yevgeny Yevtushenko: Selected Poems*, 6.

Cúram	Duty
Garda i mbun a chúraim	*A guard doing his duty*
Féachann i mo dhiaidh	*looks back at me*
Is an t-amhras ina shúil;	*doubtfully.*
Leas an phobail gnó an gharda	*The public is his concern,*
Mo ghnósa leas an dáin	*mine—poetry,*
Is focalbhrat a fháil	*finding a mantle of words*
Do gharlaigh m'intinne,	*for my brainchild,*
Gnó ar leor a dhua	*a job that's hard enough*
Seach ceannairc is gleo	*without all the fuss*
A shéideadh ina theannta suas,	*and fighting about it,*
Ach ní thógaim ar an ngarda	*but I don't blame the guard*
An t-amhras ina shúil,	*for being suspicious.*
Mar cá bhfios nach treise	*Who knows? One might yet*
Duine ná daoine fós,	*be stronger than the many,*
Is é ar a mharana	*quietly walking the road,*
Go ciúin sa ród.	*deep in thought.* (*D* p. 100)

The poet walks his own ground, his feet on Dublin pavement, his mind on 'cloch, carraig is trá'/stone, rock and strand from where he sends out the bottled messages and sometimes molotov cocktails of his poems. A necessary voice of opposition or an annoying 'rough-tongued bell' of doom,[139] Ó Direáin's lamentations outnumber his celebrations in *Ár Ré Dhearóil*/Our Wretched Era (1962) but his poems still highlight an area of experience and emotion which might otherwise be missing from Irish poetry in either of its present languages.

In this sense, as with Blok, Ó Searcaigh, and the Galway lamplighter whom he eulogized in 'Fear Lasta Lampaí—Gaillimh 1928' (*D* p. 97), Ó Direáin was on the side of light.[140] His poems stand like Ó Ríordáin's 'poblacht solais'/republic of light not just as sentences 'to fight off the death-sentence'[141] but as a direct challenge against 'the forces that would consign their art to oblivion' (*SP/TD* p. xx). However, a poet, like the flame from a candle, suffocates (as Blok said of Pushkin) for lack of air: 'the poet dies because there is nothing left for him to breathe; life has

---

[139] Philip Larkin, likewise famed for his morbidity, refers to the 'rough-tongued bell' of Art in 'Reasons for Attendance', *Collected Poems*, 80.

[140] See Forsyth, J., *Listening to the Wind: an Introduction to Alexander Blok* (Oxford: Seacourt Press Ltd., 1977), 126; and Cathal Ó Searcaigh, 'Do Isaac Rosenberg', *Out in the Open*, 240–3.

[141] See Ó Ríordáin, 'Claustrophobia', *Brosna*, 13; and Ó Coileáin, *Seán Ó Ríordáin*, 3.

lost its meaning.'[142] A stranger in his own land with his 'allegiance to the older vision' of Aran as much as to that of early twentieth-century Irish nationalism (*SP/TD* p. xix), Ó Direáin begins to feel himself and his nation to be burnt out in poems such as 'Mar Chaitheamar an Choinneal/How We Wasted the Candle' (*SP/TD* p. 98). His response may, at times, be one of defiance and savage indignation but all too often he makes a bitterly despairing gesture resigned to its, and his own, eventual negation.[143]

Alternatively, Ó Direáin either buries his disillusioned head in the sand or props it up on a pillow of idealized, comforting memories.[144] However, the more he does so, the more apparent become his own inner flaws, contradictions, and divisions. For example, in 'Ár Ré Dhearóil/Our Wretched Era' (*SP/TD* p. 66), he claims to be 'a prisoner like everyone else' in the low tide of modern city life 'since another tradition usurped the true one'.[145] In fact, he was inclined to view any place as a prison. *Feamainn Bhealtaine* contains this revealing admission:

My secret homeland was never narrow. It never is for boys [children]. When I go home now and the weather happens to be bad, I mostly imagine the place as a prison. A prison in the middle of the sea, and the very sea that used to spellbind me so much once [upon a time], is a big green monster or dragon foaming at the mouth, keeping me prisoner. (*FB* pp. 21–2)

The poet maintains his child-like, imaginative vision of a dragon in the sea around Aran (*FB* p. 35) but now, in adulthood, the image turns sinister as the monster keeps him prisoner. Similarly, while in his earlier poetry Ó Direáin advocated keeping a good solid grip or sustaining hold on one's own resources, in later poems such as 'Fuaire/Coldness' and 'Ár Ré Dhearóil/Our Wretched Era', this hold or grip turns chillingly cold.[146] A previously positive image, concept, or idea, when upheld for too long, seems to turn crushingly negative.

What these poems—and the admission above—reveal is that Ó Direáin *was* a prisoner, increasingly condemned or condemning himself

[142] Blok quoted by Forsyth, in *Listening to the Wind*, 118.
[143] See 'Sláinte na hAthbhliana'/New Year's Toast. *D* p. 105.
[144] 'Do Easnamh'/A Lack or Want, *D* p. 116; 'Taibhsí'/Ghosts, *D* p. 141.
[145] 'Ó chuaigh cleacht eile/Lastuas dá gcleacht dílis.' From 'Dán an Tí'/The House's Poem, *D* p. 87.
[146] See 'Cranna Foirtil/Stout Oars', *SP/TD* p. 54; 'Fuaire/Coldness', *SP/TD* p. 94; and 'Ár Ré Dhearóil/Our Wretched Era', *SP/TD* p. 72, respectively.

to a form of solitary confinement in what could have been the open opportunity of the city crowd. His poetry moves from the 'dúthaigh dearóil'/wretched ancestral homeland of his people into what he and many others perceived as a 'ré dhearóil'/wretched era of 'dí-lárú'/ displacement, dislocation, or de-centring, causing the bitter distrust and disillusionment of by far the majority of poems in this collection.[147] The poet emerges as a man painfully divided from his past home, from his country's present and from other individuals and groups.[148] Eoghan Ó hAnluain wrote that Aran values remained 'the yardstick by which the poet could gauge life and which he used as a barrier between himself and the "rat-race of the street" ' (*D* p. 13); Ó Direáin certainly shook this yard-stick at the sort now growing up but it also seems, according to his poems, that there was many a modernolator, 'cruel' youth, critic or scornful woman with daggers drawn for him.[149]

A number of poems show Ó Direáin as smarting from criticism. A group of younger, more pro-modern poetry enthusiasts are alleged to have complained to the editors of *Comhar* about the readiness and frequency with which Ó Direáin's work was published. Many of the younger generation viewed this work as too conservative and traditional.[150] Ó Direáin responded by labelling these 'conspirators' as eunuchs envying the man with rocks/balls.[151] What he termed uncomprehending disparagement of his or anyone else's achieved poetry left Ó Direáin feeling like

> . . . fear a mbeadh a ghrá   . . . *a man whose love*
> Ina hábhar gráisce   *is the subject of dirty talk*
> I mbéal na bréine féin.   *in the mouth of filth itself.*
>
>   (*D* p. 93)

Therefore, for Ó Direáin, even poetry could sometimes turn into a troublesome burden, a chore attracting spite from others and rewarding its practitioner with nothing but loneliness.[152] Yet, poetry was necessary

---

[147] *Ár Ré Dhearóil* (1962). See, for example, *D* pp. 104–5 and *SP/TD* xix–xx.

[148] 'Aisteoir Tuatach'/An Uppity Actor, and 'Mothú Feirge'/A Feeling of Anger, *D* p. 96.

[149] See 'Comhrac'/Encounter [or Fight], *D* p. 107; and 'An Ghoin'/The Wound, *D* p. 109.

[150] See *CMC* p. 118. Ironically, Ó Direáin had earlier been a prominent defender of Ó Ríordáin when the latter was charged by a different group of critics with not being traditional enough. See Ó Coileáin, *Seán Ó Ríordáin*, 241 and 248–50.

[151] 'Na Coillteáin/The Eunuchs', *SP/TD* p. 86.

[152] See 'Comhairle'/Advice, *D* p. 108, and 'An Duais'/The Reward, *D* p. 106.

for him not just because contact with Irish meant contact with his past, with his centre (as he saw it) of origin, but because the language continued to be an essential part of his identity, his medium for interpreting the world and life itself.

Repeatedly, however, Ó Direáin sanctifies not only his former Aran community and culture but also the (inter)nationalist ideals of Pearse, Connolly, and others which he felt had fallen like the Holy Eucharist to mice[153] or into what Baudelaire termed '*la fange du macadam*/the mire of the macadam'.[154] Taking a disdaining view of the contemporary metropolitan crowd (and of his own position in it), Ó Direáin refuses to '*épouser la foule*'/to *willingly* marry or become one flesh with the crowd as Baudelaire advocated for any 'Painter of Modern Life';[155] instead, Ó Direáin feels that modern life and the city make him a 'cime mar chách'/prisoner like everyone else when, in fact, he is a prisoner of cultural despair like Eliot.[156]

Ó Direáin's response is to model oneself on a tree and cleave to traditional roots, to stand one's ground in what Eliot had already convinced him, however, was the 'stony rubbish' of the city.[157] Meanwhile, at his back he always hears 'the sound of horns and motors',[158] a moving chaos of traffic. In the confusion, Ó Direáin's gods or ideals each seem to lose their 'halo' or sacred aura. While Baudelaire believed that the modern poet was literally and metaphorically enlightened by such a loss,[159] Ó Direáin is even more disillusioned and feels as if he is being kicked and laughed off the street:

---

[153] 'Ár Laochra'/Our Warriors [or Heroes], *D* p. 95.

[154] 'Well, just now as I was crossing the boulevard in a great hurry, splashing through the mud, in the midst of a moving chaos, with death galloping at me from every side, I made a sudden move, and my halo slipped off my head and fell into the mire of the macadam.' See Baudelaire, 'The Loss of a Halo'; translation by Berman, 155–6. For Marx *and* Baudelaire, 'one of the crucial experiences endemic to modern life, and one of the central themes for modern art and thought, is *desanctification*.' Berman, 155–64 (p. 157).

[155] Baudelaire, *The Painter of Modern Life and Other Essays*, ed. Jonathan Mayne (London: Phaidon, 1965). See Berman, 145.

[156] 'To perceive "reality" as dingy or unattractive is itself an imaginative act [. . .], but an ironic act, an irony deepened by the fact that other modes of perception are equally possible [. . .] and there can be no question of accepting only one as true.' Frye, N., 'The Realistic Oriole: A Study of Wallace Stevens', in *Fables of Identity*, 238–55 (p. 244).

[157] See Ó Direáin , 'Bí i do Chrann'/Be a Tree, *D* p. 128; and Eliot, 'The Waste Land' (1922), *Collected Poems*, 61–86 (p. 63).　　　　[158] Eliot, *Collected Poems*, 70.

[159] ' "Loss of a Halo" is about how Baudelaire's own God fails.' See Berman, 156; and 160.

Déithe Bréige	*False Gods*
Maise a sheanpháiste	*Well then, you dotard*
A chuir déithe in airde,	*Who set up gods,*
Ná tóg ar na déithe	*Don't blame the gods*
Má léimeadar anuas	*If they leaped down*
Faoi do chosa,	*Right at your feet,*
Is má chaith gach dia	*And each god hurled*
A choróin leat aniar	*His crown at your back,*
Is an fhonóid ina diaidh	*Derisive laughter following*
Sna sála ort.	*Hard on your heels.*

(*SP/TD* p. 80)

What has happened is that Ó Direáin has fallen not so much into the mire of the macadam as the poetic mispractice of the 'bad poets' named X and Z in Baudelaire's prose-poem 'Loss of a Halo'. X and Z fail to realize that

the aura of artistic purity and sanctity is only incidental, not essential, to art, and that poetry can thrive just as well, and maybe even better, on the other side of the boulevard, in those low, 'unpoetic' places ... If he [the poet] throws himself into the moving chaos of everyday life in the modern world—a life of which the new traffic is the primary symbol—he can appropriate this life for art. The 'bad poet' in this world is the poet who hopes to keep his purity intact by keeping off the streets, free from the risks of traffic. Baudelaire wants works of art that will be born in the midst of the traffic, that will spring from its anarchic energy, from the incessant danger and terror of being there, from the precarious pride and exhilaration of the man who has survived so far.[160]

Whenever Ó Direáin does confront the modern world, it is only to chastise rather than appropriate it; to be fair, he does, in his poetry, sometimes venture out on to the street, setting his precarious pride *vis à vis* the risks and terrors of traffic to make art out of the exchange but he is generally overwhelmed by the crowds, horns, and motors, and displays none of Baudelaire's, or Berman's, energy, enthusiasm, and exhilaration.[161] From their viewpoint, it seems that to survive the moving chaos of modern capitalist advancement, a poet or any heroic citizen of the modern world is compelled to meet all traffic and change with the same courage, skill, and flexibility with which, say, an Aran man in his currach meets the waves: 'he must become adept at *soubresauts* and *mouvements brusques*, at sudden, abrupt, jagged twists and shifts—and not only with

---

160 See Berman, *All That Is Solid Melts Into Air*, 155–64 (p. 160).
161 Ibid. 162–3.

his legs and his body, but with his mind and his sensibility as well.'[162] In Berman's terms, the modernist makes him/herself at home in his/her environment, whereas the anti-modern 'searches the streets for a way out'.[163] Ó Direáin's anti-modern stance renders him spiritually homeless and leaves him in line for direct confrontation with the traffic of modern life whose moving chaos he aggravates[164] by stopping to assert his dignity, or rather his *steadfastness*, in its midst:

> Achasán éigin i ngarbhghlór
> A chaith dailtín i mo threo
> De dhroim ghluaisrothair:
> D'imigh na focail le gaoth,
> Is an bhail chéanna a ghuím
> Ar a dtiocfaidh eile uaidh.
>
> Mhionnóin go raibh aige féin
> Teastas an léinn ó scoil éigin,
> Ach geallaimse dósan gan bhréag
> Gur chaitheas-sa seal de mo laetha
> I dteannta daoine uaisle gan 'léann',
> Gan focal dá theanga ina mbéal.
>
> Teastas ní raibh acu ná a dhath
> Ach lámh ar an bpeann is a marc,
> Ach cheapas a gcaint i mo líon
> Mar ba thrua í ligean le gaoth:
> Trua eile nár cheapas tuilleadh di.[165]

What I imagine to be the Mod who found the Aran-rocker Ó Direáin in his road no doubt scootered off in a cloud of smoke as fleeting as his words. The poet's reply, on the other hand, is paradoxical. His defence of his kind (a form of self-defence against the youth's insult) and loyalty to his language and culture are admirable. He deftly captures some of that language in the fine 'net' of this poem and preserves it unlike the Mod's insult (in English) which, he proudly states, is not worth preserving. But what does Ó Direáin have to say beyond the usual old fogey's reproach of impatient youth, the Yeatsian scorn for 'the sort now growing up'?

---

[162] Ibid. 159.   [163] Ibid. 162.   [164] Ibid. 163.
[165] 'Achasán'/Insult, *D* p. 154. Translation N in Appendix. This poem comes from a later volume, *Crainn is Cairde* (1970), and is revealing in terms of Ó Direáin's general attitude to the city in his writing.

He convinces the reader, I believe, of the worth, potential, and dignity of *his* language but also, I am afraid, that—despite the achievement of this poem itself—his own store of the language is running out, melting into air: 'trua nár cheapas tuilleadh di/pity I didn't catch more of it'. It also becomes apparent, especially in Ó Direáin's later collections, that his store of language, images, and ideas, is grounded mostly in the distant past, centred on his island of origin. Ultimately, therefore, Ó Direáin lacks Baudelaire's *dual* vision of modernity, the 'will to wrestle to the end of his energy with modern life's complexities and contradictions, to find and create himself in the midst of the anguish and beauty of its moving chaos'.[166]

It is important to acknowledge, however, the main reason why Ó Direáin refused to *épouser la foule*, to become socially, culturally, or politically 'flexible', to find and re-create himself again and again. The Aran poet was more concerned with preserving his original cultural and ideological self-construct, with remaining loyal, for example, to the principles of cultural nationalism. To deviate from that position was, in his view, betrayal or treachery: 'Coigil aithinne d'aislinge,/Scaradh léi is éag duit.'[167] The sub-text of Ó Direáin's 'Comhairle Don Fhile Óg'/Advice to a Young Poet, for example, is that one should sooner die than be disloyal as that would mean, in effect, to cease to be one's self anyway:

Creimeadh tusa an abhlann	*Gnaw on the Eucharist*
Más leat a bheith ar barra,	*if you're to get ahead,*
Is an méid nach bhfónann duit salaigh	*and desecrate the bits*
Is abair nuair is caothúil	*you don't want.*
Gur díth na céille an galar	*Say, when it suits you,*
A bhí ar na móir atá marbh,	*that the great ones, now dead,*
Anois nuair nach mairid	*suffered from a lack of sense.*
Ní heagal duit a n-agairt,	*Since they're no longer living,*
Ná leon ar bith	*you don't have to fear*
Tríd an gcré dhubh	*threat or reproach from them*
Aníos chugat ag bagairt.	*or any hero in the ground.*
	Concentrate your efforts
Caitheadh tusa do dhúthracht	*on getting the top-notch job,*
Ar thóir an ríphoist,	*and pledge your loyalty*

---

[166] Berman, *All That Is Solid Melts Into Air*, 170.
[167] 'Keep alight the coal of your vision;/To part with that is death.' See 'Cranna Foirtil/Stout Oars', *SP/TD* pp. 54–5.

Is tabhair tairise don mhodh
Don ghnás don ardú gradaim.

Ach fág a mhic fós
Cion ag an dán agraím,
Mar measaim gur mhór an feall
Nach mbeadh lá éigin feasta
Cuid iontais i do dhiaidh
Ag ollaimh is lucht sanais.

*to proper procedures,
the norm, and the promotion.
But keep some consideration,
please, for the poem,
because it would be too bad,
I think, if you left nothing
behind for the professors
and chattering classes
to marvel at.* (D p. 92)

Even if it means repeating himself, Ó Direáin continually insists that the dead are the great, heroic and dignified, while his generation, living in a 'wretched era', are either the disappointed, disillusioned inheritors of a broken Communion or else have degenerated into

an liacht eile
Atá ar na lucha
A chreimeann an abhlann
A thit as bhur lámha;
Loitiméireacht is obair dá laethe.

Ach libh féin bhur nglóir
Bhur gceart bhur gcóir
Libh go deo ár mbeannacht.

*the other horde
among the mice
who gnaw the Eucharist
that fell from your [the heroes'] hands;
destruction is their days' work.*

*But to you your glory,
your right, your due,
on you our blessing forever.*[168]

For Ó Direáin, 'áit' or 'slí na *fírinne*'/the place or way of *truth* is associated always with the past, the dead and, therefore, even the *next* world but rarely with this world, the living, changing present, summed up in his phrase as 'slí na bréige'/the path or way of deceit.[169]

CONCLUSION

Ó Direáin's entire poetic oeuvre insists that in a life of constant erosion like that between shore and sea, there are some things worth holding on to, worth getting to know before they and/or we melt into air. One of these things is home, the place where we are born or live and grow into

[168] 'Ár Laochra'/Our Warriors [Heroes], *D* pp. 94–5. See also 'Mac an Aitis'/The Strange or Happy Boy, *D* pp. 88–90.
[169] Ó Direáin seems to take to its logical conclusion the idiomatic expression in Irish: 'tá sé in áit na fírinne anois'/he is 'in the place of truth now', i.e. gone to his judgement, dead. In other words, if the next world is the proverbial 'place of truth', this world must be the way of 'untruth'. See 'Reilig/Cemetery', *SP/TD* pp. 82–3, and also Ó Dónail, *Foclóir Gaeilge-Béarla/Irish–English Dictionary* (Dublin: Oifig an tSoláthair, 1977), 550.

the people we become. In such a case, Ó Direáin believed that to throw out the baby with the bathwater of past experience (your own and your people's) would be to lose yourself, to lose your beginning and, therefore, your way.

His Aran exile's view of the modern city does at times appear blinkered and reactionary, while his fixation with his island home and its values (his 'ethic of nostalgia for origins, an ethic of archaic and natural innocence, of a purity of presence and self-presence in speech'[170]) may seem naive, sentimental, and even utopian,[171] but far more objective witnesses have been drawn back time and time again to the same shinglebanks as Ó Direáin: 'the ocean encircles Aran like the rim of a magnifying glass, focusing attention to the point of obsession.'[172]

Ó Direáin's obsession was with the old world of his youth in Aran whose ways, language, and values seemed to him to be dying. Even so, he was not like Kavanagh's 'Brother Michael' who actively *sought* decay, and believed that 'it would never be spring, always autumn'. On the contrary, Ó Direáin felt that spring, summer, and autumn were over (for himself and soon, probably, his culture), and so he mourned these past glorious seasons in what he believed to be winter and therefore 'deireadh'/the end. Thus, he was not 'wintering out' in Heaney's sense (that is, of hibernation) but wintering over and out.

'Is Máirtín Ó Direáin a great poet?', Liam O'Flaherty was once asked.[173] He might have been a greater one if he had known O'Flaherty's secret that in winter all things die but that finally winter dies. Surely that was the bird's lesson/'ceacht an éin':

The larks rose with the bleak dawn, stammering as they leaped from the earth, as if their music, frozen by winter, was being melted in their throats by the joyous light. Their voices rang clear and defiant as they soared high over Inverara. The heralds of spring and life, they sounded the reveille to the earth below.

---

[170] Derrida, 'Structure, Sign and Play', in Rylance (ed.), *Debating Texts*, 134.

[171] Fay Weldon reminds us that 'Utopia comes from the Greek [. . .] and means a Nowhere Place, not a Good Place, as many people think.' See Weldon, 'The City of Invention', *Letters to Alice: On First Reading Jane Austen* (London: Sceptre, 1993), 7–21 (p. 19).

[172] Robinson, *Stones of Aran*, p. 10. See also Synge: 'In this ocean alone is there not every symbol of the cosmos?', quoted in Agostini, R., 'J. M. Synge's "Celestial Peasants"', in *Rural Ireland, Real Ireland?*, ed. Jacqueline Genet, Irish Literary Studies, 49 (Gerrards Cross: Colin Smythe, 1996), 159–73 (p. 160).

[173] Ó Tuathail, 'Cloichín ar Charn', *CMC* pp. 105–26 (p. 109).

'Spring has come. Up, you luggards. Your sleep is o'er.'[174]

To be fair to Ó Direáin, he may personally have been sounding the last post rather than the reveille but he was ready for a change of tune from other voices, should they arise. He may not have learnt the bird's lesson but he had learnt Eliot's:

> For last year's words belong
> To last year's language.
> And next year's words await
> Another voice.[175]

New generations, *INNTI* and after, have arrived to add *their* bricks not to the 'carn' or burial-mound of poetry in Irish but to the latest wing or extension in the Alhambra of Irish art in general.[176] Ó Direáin had been working on the growing Irish language section of this Alhambra all along, even though it mostly appeared to him as a mausoleum. My final image of the man is, therefore, as a restorer and sculptor who, working closely at the rock face, extends and decorates the Alhambra without seeing all of it at once, apart from the occasional glimpse:

Tarlaíonn . . . i gcás na filíochta agus ealaíona nach í, go mbraitheann an déan-tóir féin ní hea amháin gur cheart dó buinne nua a chur ar an gcaiseal a thóg an mhuintir a chuaigh roimhe ach go gcaithfidh sé é a dhéanamh ar mhódh sainiúil, módh a léireoidh nach aon ghiolla aithrise orthusan é . . . Rud eile dhe, beidh a chuid léitheoirí an chuid is tuisceanaí agus is beoga orthu, ag súil le malairt poirt uaidh.[177]

Ó Direáin had sung what *he* had to sing and now it was someone else's turn to try to set the temple of Irish 'ag teilgean a paidre in iomlán a nirt'/ringing out its prayer in full force,[178] someone like Nuala Ní Dhomhnaill:

---

[174] Compare the excerpts from Liam O'Flaherty's *The Black Soul* and *Thy Neighbour's Wife*, in Ó hEithir (eds.), *An Aran Reader*, 140 and 147, respectively. Although Ó Direáin entitled his 1979 volume *Ceacht an Éin*/The Bird's Lesson, it seems that it was Ó Flaherty and not Ó Direáin who learnt the lesson from the birds.

[175] See *CMC* p. 125. [176] See Introduction.

[177] 'It happens . . . in poetry and other arts that the maker feels not only that he ought to add another brick in the wall built by the people before him but that he must do it in an individual style, a way that shows he is no slavish copier . . . Another thing, his readers, the most discerning and zestful ones, will expect a change of tune from him.' Ó Direáin, *CMC* p. 125.

[178] Ó Ríordáin, Introduction, *Eireaball Spideoige*, 9–25 (p. 25).

'Los Cantigas de Sancta Maria' ón Spáinn sa tríú céad déag.
Is léir an bhuntsraith Múrach leis na haeranna.
Tá ceol 'arabesque' an lae inniu féin
is seanmaí fada na n-Arabach
le clos laistiar de, cé nach móide go dtaitneodh
smaoineamh dá leithéid leis an Rí Alfonsó a Deich
a thiomsaigh iad is ba chúis lena mbailiú.
Is cuma; fiú agus an seicteachas abú
maireann an ceol agus tugann sé leis an lá.

'Los Cantigas de Sancta Maria'—Spain, thirteenth century.
There's no mistaking the Moorish undercurrent.
And you can hear in the background the 'arabesque' of today
not to mention the long drawn-out melodies the Arabs have,
not that that thought would please the likes of King Alphonso the 10th
who kept them and had others collect them for him.
Never mind; even with everlasting sectarianism,
music lasts, and wins the day.[179]

---

[179] From Ní Dhomhnaill's 'Ceol/Music', *H.U.* (*The Honest Ulsterman*), Issue 102 (Autumn 1996), 88–9.

CHAPTER 4

Nuala Ní Dhomhnaill: Journeying to the Shrine

Nuair a thaibhsigh sí ar dtúis
ar an láthair bheannaithe
gan cíos, cás ná cathú uirthi
is gan cead nó míchead ó éinne,
bhraith sí an sioscadh is an cogarmogar;
míogadaíl ceart i measc na ndaoine.

Chuala sí ag caint le chéile iad
ar fónanna póca,
ag fiafraí don Té a bhí i gceannas
cad sa diabhal ba chóir dóibh
a dhéanamh léi.

'Lig di,' a chuala sí é ag rá thar n-ais.
'Ach níl eolas na slí aici ná fios ar fhaid an turais
ná aon chur amach dá laghad ar ord na ngnás.'
'Scaoil léi', an freagra neamhleisciúil
uaidh siúd. 'Is file í, tar éis an tsaoil
is bíonn eolas rúnda acu siúd go léir
ar cad is cóir a dhéanamh nuair a bhíonn an scéal doiléir.
Ní bhéadh aon iontas orm mura mbeadh macasamhail na scríne
tógtha cheana féin istigh inti.'[1]

INTRODUCTION

Nuala Ní Dhomhnaill was born in Lancashire, England in 1952 and brought up speaking Irish there, in the west Kerry Gaeltacht, and in Tipperary. She studied literature and Irish at Cork University and then

---

[1] Ní Dhomhnaill, N., from 'Turas na Scríne', *Cead Aighnis* (An Daingean: An Sagart, 1998). This volume was published *after* this chapter was written. However, the poet kindly gave me a preview of some of the poems. See Translation O in Appendix.

spent seven years abroad in Holland and Turkey, returning to Ireland in 1980. To date, she has published three full collections in Irish: *An Dealg Droighin* (1981), *Féar Suaithinseach* (1984) and *Feis* (1991);[2] and three bilingual selections with facing translations in English: *Selected Poems / Rogha Dánta* (1988), *Pharaoh's Daughter* (1990) and *The Astrakhan Cloak* (1993). These volumes have been hugely successful, each running into several editions and earning Ní Dhomhnaill a leading place among contemporary Irish poets of either language or gender. Ní Dhomhnaill's bilingual selections of poems have, moreover, found a ready audience abroad including, crucially, countries such as Wales and Scotland where the nature of her success has implications for Celtic-language writers there.[3]

Ní Dhomhnaill's rise coincided with that of two major cultural movements to which she naturally belonged: the women's movement; and the 'bright new wave' of Irish language writers[4] who produced or, at least, contributed to the magazine *INNTI*. The declared aim of the *INNTI* group was to breathe new life into the apparently moribund body of Irish-language literature, to put the language itself to the test and prove that it could swim rather than sink in the much maligned modern tide:

let us not harp on too much about the past; the eighties lie ahead and might well make for a resurgence of poetry in Irish. *INNTI* is determined to make poetry years out of them in any case [. . .] One of the main barriers, I think, that come between the writer and this new flowering is the despondency about the state of Irish, about the lack of reading public. If we were to accept these negative, off-putting views voiced of late, we might as well give up the ghost entirely, and say to hell with poetry in Irish, that you'd be as well taking up Latin [. . .] *INNTI* says the complete opposite.[5]

Therefore, instead of writing off literature in Irish, the *INNTI* generation of writers, including Ó Searcaigh and Ní Dhomhnaill, ensured that it was written up, written large as life.

---

[2] Since the writing of this chapter, a further volume has been published. See Note 1.

[3] Welsh poet Menna Elfyn recently informed me that she followed Ní Dhomhnaill's bilingual example for her collection *Cell Angel* (Newcastle: Bloodaxe, 1997).

[4] See Bolger, D. and G. Fitzmaurice (eds.), *An Tonn Gheal/The Bright New Wave* (Dublin: Raven Arts Press, 1986). *INNTI* was founded as a poetry broadsheet by students at UCC in March 1970 and relaunched as a journal by Michael Davitt, a founding editor, in 1980.

[5] Michael Davitt, Editorial, *INNTI*, 4 (Feabhra 1980), 6. My translation.

A similar impulse prompted Ní Dhomhnaill to call Irish 'the corpse that sits up and talks back'[6] and also to produce the recent poem 'Oscailt an Tuama/The Exhumation' in which a long-dead foremother comically sits up in her grave and places a 'bond' on her descendants that compels them to perform yearly 'gurning [crying] games' by way of not-so-solemn commemoration.[7] Far from indulging in 'gurning games' for what is not really dead, Ní Dhomhnaill strongly believes that the acid test of any language or writing is whether it is 'alive, alive-oh'.[8]

Among the first books Ní Dhomhnaill ever read was a lively series entitled *Myths and Legends of the World*.[9] These certainly fired the imagination of the then ten-year-old girl and have continued to influence and broaden her work. Just as important in her development, however, is her absorption in and/or of béaloideas[10] and living Gaelic speech: there is, she says, 'this wonderful interaction'.[11] Such an interaction or transgressive mixing and merging of sources and forms both animates and characterizes her poetry.

For example, the poem which Ní Dhomhnaill selected for the anthology *Rogha an Fhile/The Poet's Choice*[12] was 'Eitleán/Flight' (*DD* p. 23). She chose this particular poem because it highlighted two essential and interdependent elements in her work: firstly, 'an ionspioráid phearsanta'/personal inspiration (with a suggestion, in the context, of personal circumstance or predicament) and, secondly, béaloideas. 'Tá nascadh mar sin,' she wrote, 'idir mo thrioblóid féin agus gach a thagann anuas chugam trí mheán na teanga agus trí mheán an bhéaloidis.'[13]

The poem's central metaphor and image comes from an old Irish riddle which enabled the poet to articulate a grief that might otherwise have left her 'balbh le brón'/dumb with sorrow, or frozen. Through such

---

[6] Ní Dhomhnaill, N., 'Why I Choose to Write in Irish: The Corpse that Sits Up and Talks Back', *The New York Times Book Review* (1 August 1995), 3 and 27–8.

[7] See Translation P in Appendix.

[8] Ní Dhomhnaill, 'The English for Irish', *Irish Review*, 4 (1988), 116–18 (p. 117).

[9] Ní Cheallaigh, P., 'An Nuala Rua is Dual . . .', *Comhar* (May 1992), 211–13 (p. 211).

[10] The word 'béaloideas' literally means 'oral medicine' and refers to a broad combination of folklore, mythology, and legend retained in memory, recited in prose and, where appropriate, in verse.

[11] McDiarmid, L. and M. Durkan, 'Q. & A.: Nuala Ní Dhomhnaill', *Irish Literary Supplement* (Fall 1987), 41–3 (p. 43).

[12] Ó Tuairisc, E. (ed.), *Rogha an Fhile/The Poet's Choice*.

[13] 'There is a bond between my own situation and everything that comes down to me through the language and béaloideas.' Ibid. 57–8.

articulations, finding in béaloideas objective co-relatives to express her own modern concerns, the poet hoped from early on in her career to achieve what she has described as 'forbairt ar an traidisiúin trína phearsanú, agus saibhriú an duine trí mheán an traidisiún'.[14] She uses béaloideas, then, as other writers use myth: 'every telling of a myth is part of that myth',[15] keeping it alive while enhancing the lives of teller and hearers with 'meat of the tongue'.[16]

Moreover, in a decolonizing country such as Ireland, Ní Dhomhnaill's forays into a wounded language and tradition have the additional and salutary effect of rescuing from discredit and disuse, pearls of the Irish people's language and past, Whitman-like tokens of their ancestors and themselves.[17] Ní Dhomhnaill's poetic practice is to surface like a modern-day mermaid whose songs lend some truth to Marina Warner's optimistic claim that 'from submersion, from engulf-ment, the images can return, the drowned can rise, the devoured be pieced together and the cannibalised past be heard, telling its stories'.[18] These stories, moreover, do not refer solely to the past but open vistas to alternative present and future possibilities for development and fulfil-ment, equality and healing. In the meantime, retelling folk-type tales allows for articulation, offers a mode of expression for the otherwise inexpressible or, perhaps, unspeakable.

Ní Dhomhnaill mines the rich ore of béaloideas not only because folklore can be described as 'contemporary prehistory'[19] but also because she wants to carry over some of the sheer vibrancy, luminosity, and memorability of the tales into her poetry. In many cases, these tales provide a language and imagery for psychic traumas and human predicaments no less urgent today than when the tales themselves were first created. While such tales may often contain archetypes merging

---

[14] 'Development of the tradition through personalisation, and enrichment of the person through tradition.' Ibid.

[15] Warner, M., *Managing Monsters: Six Myths of Our Time*, The 1994 Reith Lectures (London: Vintage, 1994), 8.

[16] See Warner, M., *From the Beast to the Blonde: On Fairy Tales and Their Tellers* (London: Chatto and Windus, 1994), xi.

[17] Whitman, 'Song of Myself.' See Hall, D. (ed.), *A Choice of Whitman's Verse* (London: Faber and Faber, 1968) 23–83 (pp. 53–4).

[18] Warner, *Managing Monsters*, 79.

[19] Roffole Corso's definition. See Ó Drisceoil, P., 'À la Carte Paganism?', *Poetry Ireland*, 34 (Spring 1992), 121–4 (p. 121).

into stereotypes,[20] and assign gender and other roles, the fact that they are constantly re-told or written anew by artists such as Ní Dhomhnaill and Tsvetaeva[21] reveals not only feminism's but the creative imagination's refusal to accept closure or the predetermination of relative positions for female and male, for example, or for aggressor and victim, master and slave. On the contrary, Ní Dhomhnaill views the re-interpretation of béaloideas (and of dreams emanating from the subconscious) as the *lapis alexir* or cure for such traps and divisions in the psyche and in society.

For Ní Dhomhnaill, the past is always alive and has something to say which people today can interpret in various ways to broaden and expand the range of present and future possibilities made narrow by outdated but still extant orthodoxies such as patriarchy, colonialism, religion, rationalism, etc. It is these constructs which, in her view, have become fixed, static, and restrictive, and *not* the suppressed, native and/or feminine 'stones of the past' out of which she, as a modern poet, creates 'new myths', spectrums and possibilities.[22]

Finally, Ní Dhomhnaill's poetry is so wide-ranging in its subject matter, style, and technique, that I have decided—for the purposes of this chapter—to concentrate on her two most important, organic and original volumes of poetry to date, *Féar Suaithinseach* and *Feis*, and on one fundamental aspect or essential element of her writing: the modernization of tradition, what she calls 'development of the tradition through personalization, and enrichment of the person through tradition'.[23]

---

[20] This danger is noted and discussed by Pádraic de Paor in 'Idir Aircitíp is Steiréitíp', Chapter 1, *Tionscnamh Filíochta Nuala Ní Dhomhnaill* (Dublin: An Clóchomhar Tta, 1997), 1–72.

[21] Marina Tsvetaeva, 1892–1941. Her biographer Schweitzer writes:

And—most important for a poet—Tsvetaeva's ear was opened to [. . .] another variety of Russian: not the bookish, literary, poetic Russian she had known from her earliest days but the Russian spoken by the common people [. . .] This encounter awakened her interest in Russian folklore, and prompted her to write 'Russian' poems of her own. The new linguistic element transformed Tsvetaeva's diction and her metre, and remained with her to the last.

See Viktoria Schweitzer, *Tsvetaeva* (London: Harvill Press, 1993), 167.

[22] See O'Connor, M., 'Lashings of the Mother Tongue: Nuala Ní Dhomhnaill's Anarchic Laughter', in T. O'Connor (ed.) *The Comic Tradition in Irish Women Writers* (Gainesville: University Press of Florida, 1996), 149–70 (p. 156).

[23] 'Forbairt ar an traidisiún trína phearsanú, agus saibhriú an duine trí mheán an traidisiúin'. Ó Tuairisc, E. (ed.), *Rogha an Fhile/The Poet's Choice*, 57–8.

4.1 *FÉAR SUAITHINSEACH* (1984)[24]

The first poem of Ní Dhomhnaill's *Féar Suaithinseach* is 'Mise an Fia/I am a Deer' which tells of a shrewd and daring rescue of a 'sister' from the lios or fairy-fort. The story is based on folklore[25] but is retold or translated into a poem-tale which is open-ended and suggestive:

> Ansan teascfaidh an gaiscíoch an ceann den tseanachailleach
> lena lann leadartha líofa
> go bhfuil faobhar, fadhairt, is fulag inti
> is slánóidh sé tú le buille dá shlaitín draíochta.
>
> *Then the hero chops her [the old hag's] head off*
> *with his smiting, polished blade,*
> *with his sharp, tempered punishing blade*
> *and saves you with a tap of the magic wand.* (*SP/RD* pp. 18–23)

The hero or male presence in the poem is 'a brother' with jet-black hair unlike the fairness of his sister but 'thairis sin is maith an té a d'aithneodh thar a chéile [iad]'/apart from that, it would take some doing to tell them apart. This dashing young blade, in fact, combines the archetypal roles of brother/lover/and other half of the psyche[26] who saves the (male–female) individual by balancing the apparent polarities of hardness and softness, cunning and credulity. The tale suggests that such a combination of seemingly opposite qualities is necessary to survive certain challenges and dangers in life, certain monstrous aspects of one's own psyche such as the poem's Freddy Kruger-like Hag or Tooth-and-Nail Mother.

'Mise an Fia/I am a Deer', like the excerpt from béaloideas that precedes it, points back to and counterbalances the earlier béaloideas foreword to Ní Dhomhnaill's first volume, *An Dealg Droighin*. There, a female character suffered dismemberment at the hands of a 'brother' whom she cursed, then healed, after her own rescue by the Virgin Mary.

---

[24] 'Amazing Grass'—title of a poem and of Ní Dhomhnaill's 1984 collection, this is variously translated as 'marvellous' (*SP/RD* p. 75) and 'miraculous' (*PD* p. 33) grass.

[25] See Ní Dhuibhne, E., ' "The Old Woman as Hare": Structure and Meaning in an Irish Legend', *Folklore*, Vol. 104, Nos. 1–2 (1993), 77–85.

[26] For example, in another context, Juliet Mitchell describes the relationship of Heathcliff to Cathy in *Wuthering Heights* as that of a 'brother/lover': 'Each is the bisexual possibility of the other one, evoking a notion of oneness which is the reverse side of the coin of diverse heterogeneity.' See Mitchell, 'Femininity, Narrative and Psychoanalysis', in M. Eagleton (ed.), *Feminist Literary Theory: A Reader* (Cambridge MA and Oxford UK: Blackwell, 1986; repr. 1994), 100–3 (p. 103).

Here, in the foreword and opening poem of *Féar Suaithinseach*, a female character is restored by male intervention on her behalf.
Male–female relations, as presented in Ní Dhomhnaill's work, can,
therefore, be damaging and destructive *or* nourishing and creative. The
outcome may depend upon whether the masculine and feminine
elements are 'too far separated by sexual fear and loathing, segregated by
contempt for the prescribed domestic realm for female, and above all by
exaggerated insistence on aggression as the defining characteristic of
heroism and power'[27] or whether they co-exist in some non-patriarchal
interdependency, union, or harmony. This is true of societies, couples,
and even individuals for, as Louise Bourgeois said, 'we are all vulnerable
in some way, and we are all male–female.'[28] Admitting such facts could,
feminist criticism alleges, bring real strength and the potential to escape
by transgressing dangerous divisions and purist, elitist limits which
spawn 'monsters of machismo' and, in return, hags and tooth mothers.[29] Failure to face up to or face down, to acknowledge, and if not
unmake then manage, these inner monsters or demons,[30] is to let loose
the sexism, class division, racism, and colonialism that have truly bedevilled human history. V. G. Kiernan, for example, has written that the
ultimate causes of modern imperialism and war 'are to be found less in
tangible material wants than in the uneasy tensions of societies distorted
by class division, with their reflection in distorted ideas in men's
minds'.[31]

Repeatedly, Ní Dhomhnaill's poetry suggests that these distortions
began with the Christian concept of the Fall when it was thought, as in
Ó Ríordáin's version, that

. . . thuirling eolas buile	*knowledge dealt a blow*
A scoilt an mhaidin álainn	*that split the beautiful morning*
'Na fireann is 'na baineann	*into male and female . . .*[32]

Ní Dhomhnaill sheds some light on distorted, divisive, and destructive
ideas in *Irish* men's minds when she notes that the head was the 'central

[27] Warner, *Managing Monsters*, 30.
[28] Morgan, S., 'Louise Bourgeois: Nature Study' (London: Arts Council of Great
Britain, 1985), 2.
[29] Warner, *Managing Monsters*, 30–1. [30] Ibid. 31.
[31] Quoted by Said, E., *Culture and Imperialism* (London: Chatto and Windus, 1993),
11.
[32] Ó Ríordáin, 'Oilithreacht Fám Anam'/Pilgrimage through My Soul, *Eireaball
Spideoige*, 71.

icon of the Celts' and suggests that consequently 'our ancestors were severely cut off from what the French feminist literary theorists call the "language of the body" '.[33] However, the Celts, at least, had various and variable (male, female, and animal) gods and goddesses of everything from death to fertility. Christianity seems to have compounded the patriarchal breach with nature and the body when after the Fall (Eve's fault anyway), the sword of knowledge dealt the death-blow which Ó Ríordáin describes above, cutting goddesses down to (at best) saints; and women, in some cases, to the position of chattel-brides. Ní Dhomhnaill writes:

without wishing to exonerate established Christianity from an unmistakably patriarchal bias it may be that the death-dealing propensities of our head-hunting Celtic forebears had a role to play in perverting the basically moderately life-enhancing qualities of the message of Christ into the particularly virulent life-denying force that has come to be Irish Catholicism.[34]

In her reclamations, reinterpretations, and retellings of béaloideas, Ní Dhomhnaill offers an alternative myth: for example, the remarkable tale of 'Mis and Dubh Ruis' from a tradition that dates back to the 'pre-Celtic strata of Mother-Goddess worshippers' or further back to when the builders of Newgrange could worship Earth-Mother and Sky-God jointly. Ní Dhomhnaill views such a tale as a deeply symbolic gift from the subconscious with layers of meaning that have deep significance for the present.[35] She believes, in fact, that while an 'underlying mythic drama (such as those contained in béaloideas and folkloric tales) is kept from conscious evaluation', it will consequently have to be 'literally acted out'—even violently.[36] Alternatively, she calls for a re-negotiation of the terms; for a new, more mutually acceptable treaty much needed to affect, for example, 'the inner conversion which must be made in face of the imminent destruction of this planet'.[37]

These quotations come from Ní Dhomhnaill's essay 'Mis and Dubh Ruis: A Parable of Psychic Transformation' where she suggests that re-union or harmony is possible between apparently opposing elements such as male and female. Through love (with an emphasis on sex and the body) and music, rather than war and argument, the poet's ancient

[33] Ní Dhomhnaill, 'Mis and Dubh Ruis: A Parable of Psychic Transformation', in *Irish Writers and Religion*, ed. by Robert Welch, Irish Literary Studies, 37 (Gerrards Cross: Colin Smythe Ltd., 1992), 194–201 (p. 198). [34] Ibid. 198.
[35] Ibid. 199. [36] Ibid. 196. [37] Ibid. 198.

sovereignty tale of Mis shows how wounded and destructive 'hag' or cailleach energy can be turned into the nurturing power of the 'goddess' or spéirbhean. The transformative vision or 'fís' that Ní Dhomhnaill offers is that of a new, more equal marriage of apparent opposites which could, she believes, temper the negative extremes of both genders, say, and healthily meet the psychic and physical needs of each. Importantly, what for her is true of pairs of individuals, such as Mis and Dubh Ruis, is also true of different parts of the psyche, of tribes within a nation, and of one nation's relationship with others.

Yet, Ní Dhomhnaill, as a poet, is more than a teller of timeless tales or activist for the equal rights of deities and/or humans, as the title-poem 'Féar Suaithinseach'/Amazing Grass (*SP/RD* p. 74) reveals. This poem is based on the introductory excerpt from béaloideas in which a girl contracts a mysterious illness which a poor wandering scholar finally attributes to her having dropped her First Holy Communion or Encharist long before. Ní Dhomhnaill's diagnosis is different. She blames the male priest for dropping the 'holy communion' that could have made the now 'anorexic' girl well.[38] His own sexual discomfort with the girl's female image or form has made the girl create a false or negative self-image of her own. She can, however, be healed:

> Tagadh an sagart is lena mhéireanna
> beireadh sé go haiclí ar an gcomaoine naofa
> is tugtar chugham í, ar mo theanga
> leáfaidh sí, is éireod aniar sa leaba
> chomh slán folláin is a bhíos is mé i mo leanbh.
>
> *Let the priest come and with his fingers*
> *take dextrously the sacred host.*
> *And it's given to me: on my tongue*
> *it will melt and I will sit up in the bed*
> *as healthy as I was when young.* (*SP/RD* p. 74)

The poem's transgressive (cannibalistic/sexual) imagery may seem shocking but teases the reader into acknowledging that it is all based on core tenets of Christian doctrine.[39]

---

[38] In *Féar Suaithinseach* (1984) the title-poem appears with the subtitle 'Fianaise an chailín i ngreim "Anorexia" '/Evidence [or Testimony] of the Girl in the Grips of Anorexia.

[39] See Warner, 'Cannibal Tales: The Hunger for Conquest', in *Managing Monsters*, 68–70.

Another poem, 'An Leanbh Gan Baiste'/The Unbaptized Child (*FS* p. 45), revisits and expands upon the earlier béaloideas foreword in *An Dealg Droighin* (1981). In this poem, a female character does not let her son be baptized for seven years until she can tell her own story before priest and family. What apparently has happened to her is remarkable: blamed for the killing of a pup, a mare, and the destruction of an apple-tree by the real culprit (her sister-in-law), the woman is 'punished' by her married brother who cuts off her arms and breasts.[40] Left to die, she was finally rescued by 'Our Lord' and, having finally confessed as much, she can now have her son baptized.

Ní Dhomhnaill tempts the reader to tease out some possible meanings from this béaloideas tale, magic realist or fantastic 'gift from the subconscious'. What was the *married* woman's motive in destroying the mare, pup, and tree, and then blaming her sister-in-law?[41] As in 'An Crann/The Tree' (*SP/RD* p. 92), there is a suggestion that she was reacting to the fact that her husband may have slept with the 'other woman', in this case, apparently, his own sister. He, meanwhile, is only too glad to punish his sister, remove her harmful and sexual parts which (presumably, he would allege) tempted him to fall.[42] However, following the female victim's miraculous restoration, a child is born who can only finally be baptized—which requires naming him and/or the father—whenever his mother decides it is safe or time, a full seven years on.

Ní Dhomhnaill gives the tale another twist in the final stanza by introducing an apparently modern-day first-person omniscient narrator. This narrator wonders where she can find an unbaptized child to whom she can divulge *her* 'secret'. The nature of this secret is left open. What is clear, however, is that she, a modern woman, identifies with the female victim's sense that she has been abused, blamed, and punished by others perhaps as carnally knowledgeable—if such is her 'secret'—as her but less understanding of some (taboo) aspects of human sexuality.

The history of psychology (and criminology) shows that the body— and particularly that of women—has been the battle-ground for '*la guerre*

---

[40] In the béaloideas version, he cuts off the arms only, see *DD* p. 5.

[41] Representing, perhaps, the woman, her child and the husband's penis.

[42] Compare to Louise Bourgeois's feminist sculpture 'Harmless Woman' whose head, arms and legs are removed to leave only her sexual and reproductive parts exposed: the proverbial 'sex object'.

à tout sentiment, à toute sensation.[43] For example, the man-made injuries on the body of the woman in Ní Dhomhnaill's poem are mirrored in the 'Renata case' of Dr L. Schnyder, although the metaphorical knife that 'unsexed' *his* patient was anorexia.[44] As in Ní Dhomhnaill's poem, however, the woman was restored; afterwards renaming herself 'Renata', the reborn. It is interesting to note that Renata's 'hysteria' was triggered by the all-too-fleshy spectacle of the 'promiscuity of sexes on a crowded beach'.[45] Renata came from a strict upper-middle-class Swiss Catholic family and her brother, a Catholic priest, was also diagnosed as an hysteric and treated by Dr Schnyder at the same time.

Cases like these, and the interest in them, show how the unruly subconscious with repressions, inversions, and eruptions, continually fascinates. Ní Dhomhnaill has written: 'I find myself increasingly impatient of any kind of writing, prose or poetry, which does not bring with it the coiled energy, the dark tincture of the unconscious.'[46] It is precisely to release some of this coiled energy (Eastern mystics would call this *kundalini* or *sakti*) that Ní Dhomhnaill mines the mysterious ore of the unconscious which, she then finds, can be revealed or expressed through a combination of béaloideas with personal, real, and dream experience: 'poetry is bringing stuff from that other world into this world. Anything that comes from there will be imbued with an extraordinary charge, a luminous quality that will make it jump off the page.'[47] However, is there a danger that Ní Dhomhnaill's practice could make her a modern-day Faust conjuring devils, monsters?

The above quotation comes from a collection of 'conversations with Scottish and Irish Women Poets' called *Sleeping with Monsters*, published in 1990. Four years later, Marina Warner became only the second woman ever to deliver the BBC Reith Lectures. She gave her lectures the title: *Managing Monsters: Six Myths of Our Time*, preceding them with part of a poem by Suniti Namjoshi which sheds much light also on Ní Dhomhnaill's exploration of the unconscious:

---

[43] Peter Stallybrass and Allon White, *The Politics and Poetics of Transgression* (London: Methuen, 1986), 185.

[44] Ibid. 184. [45] Ibid. 180.

[46] See O'Driscoll, D. (ed.), 'Findings', *Poetry Ireland*, 36 (Autumn 1992), 123–8 (p. 126).

[47] See Somerville Aryat, G. and R. E. Wilson (eds.), *Sleeping with Monsters: Conversations with Scottish and Irish Women Poets* (Edinburgh: Polygon, 1990), 148–56 (p. 150).

> And all the monsters said in a chorus:
> You must kiss us.
> What! You who are evil,
> Ugly and uncivil.
> You who are cruel,
> Afraid and needy,
> Uncouth and seedy.
> Yes, moody and greedy.
> Yes, you must bless us.
> But the evil you do,
> The endless ado.
> Why bless you?
> You are composed of such shameful stuff.
> Because, said the monsters, beginning to laugh,
> Because, they said, cheering up.
> You might as well. You are part of us.[48]

And we are part of you, the monsters might as well add, like those parts of the body and their functions famously repressed and demonized throughout the history of psychology and now celebrated and flaunted, in order to be healthily re-integrated, by the carnivalesque or grotesque transgressions of modern Rabelaisian-style art. Ní Dhomhnaill's work, famously *and traditionally* frank and sometimes humorous about sexuality and the body, clearly belongs in this category.[49]

Even so, monsters *are* monsters, and whether they are asleep or we sleep with them, there is no guarantee that we can 'unmake' or 'manage' them. In 'Sceimhle/Paranoia', the monsters of the speaker's unconscious will not let her sleep (*PD* p. 56). If she sleeps at all, it is with a 'brass candle-stick'/'Mo Choinnleoir Práis' under her pillow for protection (*FS* p. 43). In 'Sa Suanlios'/In the Fairy-fort (*FS* p. 55), she is at the mercy and service of a wolf-headed giant in the woods—although she uses her stay of execution actively to plan an escape. Most tellingly, in 'Don nGaiscíoch Istigh Ionainn'/To the Daring in Us, Ní Dhomhnaill suggests that 'you'[50] might get away with killing up to three male giants

---

[48] See Warner, *Managing Monsters*, vii.

[49] Compare to Stallybrass and White, *The Politics and Poetics of Transgression*, 11–12 and 186–7.

[50] Here, the second person singular is used, I believe, to represent the *male* ego which is finally going to 'snuff it'. See Ní Dhomhnaill's account of her two 'favourite poems' in MacMonagle, N. (ed.), *Lifelines: Letters From Famous People About Their Favourite Poem*, 2nd edn. (Dublin: Town House and Country House, 1992, repr. 1995), 146.

and a single female monster 'a shúfadh isteach i bpollaíocha a sróna tú'/who could suck you in through her nostrils, but you will not live happily ever after because the mother of the brood must and will have her revenge. Final defeat and execution is seen as inevitable in this poem:

> Nuair a thagann sí i láthair
> ná caill do cheann. Faoi mar a bheadh
> gloine fíona ceangailte do do rúitín
> siúil go réidh, a chroí, siúil go réidh.
> Bain míotóg as do cheathrú,
> más gá; cogain t'fhiacla, tóg trí anáil
> dhoimhin, cruinnigh do mheabhair go maith
> is ar do bhás, ná geit.
>
> *When she comes for you,*
> *don't lose your head. Just as if*
> *there was a glass of wine tied*
> *to your ankle, tread softly, love.*
> *Clench your buttocks, if you must;*
> *and also your teeth, take three*
> *deep breaths, collect your thoughts*
> *and on your death, don't scream.* (FS p. 58)

You will not go Scot-free it seems because you have not made peace with the Negative Mother Archetype but instead killed her sons and ripped out the *tongue* of her butchered daughter. In this poem, Ní Dhomhnaill dramatizes what she thinks happens in Derek Mahon's 'Antarctica': 'the bouncing common-sense ego on which our civilization is built [. . .] the more-than-faintly-ridiculous heroic male ego finally snuffs it.'[51] As in the tale of 'Mis and Dubh Ruis', Ní Dhomhnaill has more faith in the vulnerable man with his harp and gaming-stick than in 'any of the conquering heroes'.[52] It is the vulnerable music-and-love-maker, she believes, who is more likely to overcome by 'kissing the monster', loving and thereby transforming the archetypal hag or cailleach into spéirbhean or Primavera.[53]

All of these poems, stories, folk/fairy/fantastic tales belong to the wide and international genre of béaloideas, literally meaning oral lore or teaching but also 'prescription', as in recipe or remedy, what a Kenyan seanchaí/storyteller might call 'meat of the tongue':

---

[51] Ibid.   [52] Ní Dhomhnaill, 'Mis and Dubh Ruis', 199.   [53] Ibid. 201.

the tongue meats that the poor man feeds the women are not material, of course. They are fairy tales, stories, jokes, songs; he nourishes them on talk, he wraps them in language; he banishes melancholy by refusing silence. Storytelling makes women thrive—and not exclusively women, the Kenyan fable implies, but other sorts of people, too, even sultans.[54]

All literature, as Brodski noted, owes its origin to the spoken word,[55] to the human need to tell or hear real, dreamt, or imagined stories, the felt need to self-express, to witness and/or embellish the world, the show-man's or shaman's desire to weave and unweave (like the 'magic rings' of a clown or magician) word from world and world from word. Marina Warner has explained that even the Greek word *myth* 'means a form of speech' and that ' "epos" [epic] in its origin means, and in truth is, the spoken word.'[56] But what has all this saying got to say?

Artists do not take 'being' for granted. They recognize that existence and potential development or fulfilment come under threat from 'monsters' within and without. Art often becomes for artists the 'weapon of the weaponless',[57] the black-hafted knife/'scian na coise duibhe' with which they can carve the names and the things which they wish either to bless and preserve, or curse and remove. 'Deamhan a rá, sin deamhan a chloí'/to name a devil is to defeat a devil, wrote Seán Ó Ríordáin,[58] and Louise Bourgeois, whose personal *bête noir* is fear, has stated:

I am saying in my sculpture today what I could not make out in the past. It was fear that kept me from understanding [. . .] It paralyzes you. My sculpture allows me to re-experience the fear, to give it a physicality so I am able to hack away at it. Fear becomes a manageable reality. [. . .] Fear is a passive state. The goal is to be active and take control.[59]

Ní Dhomhnaill, like Bourgeois, tries to survive, I would say, as much as 'manage' the fears and monsters of her unconscious. In her poetry,

---

[54] Warner, *From the Beast to the Blonde*, xi.

[55] 'Literature started with poetry, with the song of a nomad that predates the scrib-blings of a settler.' Josef Brodski, 'How to Read a Book', *The Times*, Monday 21 October 1996, 17.

[56] See Warner, *Managing Monsters*, 19 and *From the Beast to the Blonde*, 418.

[57] See Warner, *From the Beast to the Blonde*, 412; and Burkman, K. H. (ed.), *Myth and Ritual in the Plays of Samuel Beckett* (Mississauga: Associated University Presses, 1987), 15.

[58] Ó Ríordáin, 'Oilithreacht Fám Anam', *Eireaball Spideoige*, 73.

[59] See Meyer-Thoss, C., *Louise Bourgeois: Designing for Free Fall* (Zurich: Ammann, 1992), 195.

she names and gives a physicality to the inner and outer demons that inhibit her, in an attempt to get around as much as 'overcome' them. Therefore, her journey or progress is circuitous, long and winding: 'an timpeall chun an teampaill'. Setting and solving the devilishly difficult riddles of art-production, finding what Marie Cardinal calls 'the words to say it',[60] Ní Dhomhnaill frees herself in the breathing-space of verse from the freezing paralysis of emotions such as fear, disgust or anger in order, like the sculptor Bourgeois, 'to be active and take control'.

However, this respite or victory is only ever temporary; Bourgeois writes that 'the devil is always lurking' and that the process must be started again and again after each successful negotiation or accomplishment. This for her is 'the real tragedy of the artist'.[61] An indicator of the nature of this 'tragedy' is the weary note on which the volume *Féar Suaithinseach* ends, finally giving way to a caoineadh or lament, the poet 'ar fóraoil/go huile is go hiomlán, fiú ós na haircitípeanna coitianta'.[62] In this poem, 'Maidin sa Domhan Toir'/Morning in the Eastern World (*FS* p. 113), the poet/speaker is still *looking*, at least, for her salvation, for a way through or past the vengeful and unappeased 'ainmhithe an fhochonsiasa'/animals of the subconscious, for the cheering sight of a robin ('Ó Súilleabháin') red-breast or any other reminder of her homeland whose neglected traditions, beliefs, and rituals might yet enrich the individual, enhance her or his life and scope.

Indeed, Ní Dhomhnaill's poetic method suggests that an active exploration, interrogation, retelling and expansion of the tradition really could combat some late twentieth-century ills affecting body and soul with 'meat of the [Irish] tongue'. She wrote, remember, that there is a strong link between her own trouble, condition, or situation and everything that comes down to her through tradition.[63] Her work suggests that there is more than a link: language and tradition (béaloideas) may provide the 'remedy', the *lapis alexir*, alchemical 'comaoin naofa'/holy communion or good medicine, sought or promised throughout the volume.[64]

For example, in 'Maidin sa Domhan Toir'/Morning in the Eastern

---

60 See Stallybrass and White, *The Politics and Poetics of Transgression*, 181.

61 See Meyer-Thoss, *Louise Bourgeois*, 129

62 'In a bad way/totally and utterly, even from the usual archetypes', from 'Maidin sa Domhan Toir'/Morning in the Eastern World, *FS* pp. 113–14.

63 Ó Tuairisc, E. (ed.), *Rogha an Fhile/The Poet's Choice*, 57–8.

64 Literally from the *Foreword* to the back cover.

World, the possibility is raised that if Ní Dhomhnaill had known to choose the 'small loaf' instead of the big one, she would have received a blessing rather than a curse; or fed the 'burnt end of the black bread' to the 'lion-footed hound', she might have appeased those animals of her subconscious (*FS* p. 114). Perhaps making the pilgrimage to Cathleen's Temple to perform seven clockwise mandala rounds, would (as she claims) appease the goddess, connect the poet with her 'lost *tuath*',[65] provide 'protection from malevolent forces', and reward her with a bouquet of 'courage and noble spirit'.[66]

These possibilities, rich and imaginative as they may be, could seem preposterous to some but so too did Ní Dhomhnaill's description in childhood of 'men on white horses' in a box in the living-room called a television.[67] However, Ní Dhomhnaill is making the point that performing these rituals and folk-practices can help one to survive, creates a 'pattern' or stability and may even invoke a supernatural blessing that allows people to '*get through* their days'.[68] Rituals, then, can be as colourful, useful and necessary as storytelling—that 'meat of the tongue' which is essential for the well-being of tellers and hearers.

For Ní Dhomhnaill, one of the boons of Irish language and tradition (including rituals), is their openness to the Otherworld, 'An Saol Eile which English, on the other hand, reduces to mere "superstition" or "Pisroguery" and fairies-at-the-bottom-of-the-garden'.[69] Since Irish (luckily, in Ní Dhomhnaill's view) escaped being 'industrialized and patriarchalized', it would seem the perfect language to resurrect not just great grandma's 'seananathanna/old saws [sayings]' that may or may not be relevant to our lives now,[70] but to activate or enact a form of carnivalesque inversion similar to that which Mikhail Bakhtin identified in his study of Rabelais.[71]

---

[65] McDiarmid and Durkan, 'Q. & A.: Nuala Ní Dhomhnaill', 43. 'Tuath' refers to the poet's 'tribal stomping ground' and to the tribe itself. See Somerville Aryat and Wilson (eds.), *Sleeping with Monsters*, 153–4.

[66] References here are to the trilogy of poems 'Mandala', 'Turas Chaitlíona' and 'An Turas', *FS* pp. 77–81.

[67] McDiarmid and Durkan, 'Q. & A.: Nuala Ní Dhomhnaill', 41.

[68] Rosette Lamont, for example, notes that Beckett's characters enact 'ritual routines that allow them to get through their days'. See Burkman, (ed.), *Myth and Ritual in the Plays of Samuel Beckett*, 15.

[69] Ní Dhomhnaill, 'Mis and Dubh Ruis', 199.

[70] See 'Dinnéar na Nollag/Christmas Dinner', *SP/RD* pp. 66–9.

[71] Bakhtin, M., *Rabelais and his World*, trans. Hélène Iswolsky (Bloomington: Indiana University Press, 1984).

For example, Terry Eagleton finds that *Rabelais and his World* pits against the 'official, formalistic and logical authoritarianism whose unspoken name is Stalinism the explosive politics of the body, the erotic, the licentious and semiotic'.[72] Similarly, other critics have noted that the most convincing attempts 'to apply Bakhtin *tout court* focus [. . .] upon literatures produced in a colonial or neo-colonial context where the political difference between the dominant and subordinate culture is particularly charged'.[73] Stallybrass and White, for example, single out for special praise Régine Robin's 'La Littérature Yiddish Soviétique' which

nicely applies Bakhtin's use of the polyphonic 'multi-voicedness' of Yiddish (arguably in itself already a 'carnivalesque' language), the language of the oppressed Jewish minority. The rightness of this is underwritten by Bakhtin's championing of the humorous resistance of the 'folk' through the darkest period of Stalinist terror.[74]

Ní Dhomhnaill makes similar claims for the polyphonic multi-voicedness of carnivalesque Irish and of women's writing in general. Indeed, she equates the two: 'Irish in the Irish context is the language of the Mothers, because everything that has been done to women has been done to Irish. It has been marginalized, its status has been taken from it.'[75] She rests her hope on the power or potential of language and literature (béaloideas/oral medicine) to turn, pacify or re-balance the patriarchal tide: 'a certain water-level in Ireland will roll toward Irish, and if it doesn't, damn it all, what can I do?'[76] In the meantime, she waits like her 'mermaid' on dry land, or mouse-girl 'on a lonely quay-side', waiting for the tide to turn.[77] If it does and 'the girl who was a mouse' makes it across to the 'king's house', uses her compensatory talents, cunning, and humour, to break the fairy-woman's curse (itself the result of a prior male curse), then she will be restored, transformed back to her full estate, glory, and honour as 'woman', *post*-colonial Irish woman no longer dispossessed due to her gender, nationality, or language. Such tales, parables, allegories, dreams constantly remind us

---

[72] See Stallybrass and White, *The Politics and Poetics of Transgression*, 11–12.
[73] Ibid.   [74] Ibid.
[75] Somerville Aryat and Wilson (eds.), *Sleeping with Monsters*, 154.
[76] McDiarmid and Durkan, 'Q. & A.: Nuala Ní Dhomhnaill', 42.
[77] 'An Mhaighdean Mhara/The Mermaid', *SP/RD* pp. 52–5, and 'An Cailín a Bhí Ina Luch'/The Girl Who Was a Mouse, *FS* pp. 67–9.

of the possibility of change[78] or, at least, that in adversity we should keep our eyes and minds open for alternatives, improvements, and transformations: 'the faculty of wonder, like curiosity, can make things happen; it is time for wishful thinking to have its due.'[79]

The poem that I have been referring to above, 'An Cailín a Bhí ina Luch'/The Girl Who Was a Mouse (*FS* p. 67), highlights a myth that is central to Ní Dhomhnaill's 'vision' as a poet. You could call it her version of the Fall and what is to be done about it. The girl's father banishes a fairy woman from his land under threat of violence because he sees her as an archetypal Eve-il woman. His harsh treatment of her redounds, however, on his own daughter when the 'bean an leasa'/fairy-woman curses the girl seven times more than she herself has been cursed by the father. To protect the daughter, her father locks her up at home[80] but she crosses the threshold of his power (literally transgresses, steps beyond), only to fall under the fairy woman's spell.[81] The girl's reduction to a 'wee, sleekit, cow'rin', tim'rous beastie'[82] seems to mirror what Ní Dhomhnaill sees as the position of women in a patriarchal society which is out of touch or at war with the 'deep feminine'.[83]

The mouse-girl in the poem (a good example of the transgressive, transformative nature of Ní Dhomhnaill's work) actively sets about her own inner development towards self-fulfilment. This seems to involve a wooing back of the male, represented by the king and particularly his son whom she aims to marry for the sovereignty perhaps but, ultimately, her goal is equality, the re-attainment of her full human 'dignity' as a woman.[84] This union of the younger generation, it is hinted, will repair the breach that existed between male (the father) and female (bean an leasa), promoting nurturing virtues for the common good

---

[78] See Warner, *From the Beast to the Blonde*, xvi–xvii.

[79] Ibid. 418.   [80] Ibid. 334.

[81] See Watt's discussion of Beckett's liminal characters for whom 'new status is never easily attained' and who move 'betwixt and between the categories of ordinary social life'. Watt, S., 'Beckett by way of Baudrillard', in K. Burkman (ed.), *Myth and Ritual in the Plays of Samuel Beckett*, 103–23 (p. 104).

[82] Burns, R., 'To a Mouse', *Selected Poems* (London: Penguin Classics, 1996), 109–110.

[83] Ní Dhomhnaill, 'Mis and Dubh Ruis', 198. Note also that she reads Plath's work as 'expressions of women's emotions in a society that frustrates the self-fulfilment of women'. See MacMonagle, N. (ed.), *Lifelines*, 144.

[84] Compare to feminist readings of Cinderella in the 1970s: 'an oppressor's script for female domestication—the prince's castle as a girl's ultimate goal', quoted by Warner, *From the Beast to the Blonde*, xiv.

rather than continued conflict, war, and curses. Yet, such a positive, perhaps utopian, resolution is still not assured in the poem:

Ach táim anseo ar an gcé uaigneach	*But I'm here on the lonely quay*
is gan eolas agam cur chuige,	*not knowing how to proceed,*
tá na báid bheaga iompaithe béal faoi	*the small boats are overturned*
is mé ag feitheamh leis an uain farraige.	*and I'm waiting for the tide.*
Seo libh, cabhraíg' liom.	*Here now, help me.* (FS p. 69)

A happy ending is only possible with 'help' from outside, from the *other* side whether it is the male, the reader of the poem or the hearer of the poem-tale in an imaginative and transformative bond with the teller. The female image in the poem has made her move and now it is up to the deep masculine to catch up and on like Dubh Ruis. Ní Dhomhnaill herself writes: 'I'm still working on that inner Harper in all his powerful dream manifestations as Enemy, Sea-Horse, or Minotaur, Bull of the Mothers. But there does seem to be a way forward, and I live in hope.'[85] Once again, the poet places her hope on the water, symbolizing a journey or immram through time, space, language, and, of course, the mind. Ní Dhomhnaill's post-modern immrama are like those of Beckett who uses the quest motif to parallel 'psychological searches, metaphysical struggles, and linguistic voyages', voluntary pilgrimages 'chosen in hopes of a miraculous transformation'.[86] Ní Dhomhnaill travels through her own mind's and life's labyrinth towards the centre (if there can ever be one) of her own identity, to unravel the knot, solve the riddle of self-hood. The journey towards spiritual knowledge and peace is, however, mirrored in (and can only be discussed in terms of) the physical outside world and the carnal. This partly explains Ní Dhomhnaill's fascination with the Annunciation and her apparent solution to the division (from self as well as each other) visited upon humankind ever since the Fall: to journey back to the tree of knowledge for another, curative taste of the apple from the tree of knowledge.[87]

Even if this taste proves poisonous (and Ní Dhomhnaill always acknowledges that possibility), she lives in hope that the poison will, according to ancient wisdom and ritual, provide relief:

---

[85] Ní Dhomhnaill, 'Mis and Dubh Ruis', 200.

[86] See Burkman, (ed.), *Myth and Ritual in the Plays of Samuel Beckett*, 15 and 28–9.

[87] See 'Cuireadh'/Invitation, *FS* p. 109. Similarly, Louise Bourgeois has commented: 'What I want is the forbidden fruit.' See Meyer-Thoss, *Louise Bourgeois*, 141.

| Ní mór nimh a chur | *Poison is the cure* |
| ag coimheascar nimhe. | *for the poisoned mind.* |

(*SP/RD* pp. 104–5)

If, however, the poison proves deadly, it may still prove to be sweeter than 'Spanish wine, Greek honey, or Viking beer' (*SP/RD* p. 140). The sweetness of such a potion (apple, kiss, or drink) comes from its Medb-like, intoxicating potential for miraculous transformation[88] but also from its danger. Ní Dhomhnaill's poetry shares the same erotics of 'release and restraint'[89] that operate in the sculpture of Bourgeois:

The fear of sex and death is the same. Attraction and fear move back and forth. Which is the cause and which is the effect? It's important to know.

Turenne was standing by his horse ready to go to battle. He said to his horse, which was really his unconscious, 'You tremble, carcass, but you would tremble even more if you knew where I am going to take you.'

It is at this moment, the thrill of danger, that the erotic impulse is activated. The thrill is an erotic presence, that all-or-nothing feeling. You either resist or let go. If it terrorises you, it means the resistance is too much. There is the refusal to go to battle with the unconscious. I become paralyzed by the fear.[90]

That paralysis, the state of being frozen or silenced by fear is passivity, death; to survive, Bourgeois writes, considering her own sculpturing of the emotions, that 'you take the event in hand and actively manipulate it'.[91] In béaloideas or literary terms, this means you tell the tale to live; and in life terms, you live to tell the tale.[92]

Such sculpting and saying or telling is necessary because even though male–female relations are sometimes acknowledged as highly desirable and potentially enjoyable in *Féar Suaithinseach*,[93] it still seems that individuals cannot escape for long 'feachtaí borba an tsaoil'/the rough currents of life (*FS* p. 107). Ní Dhomhnaill seems to believe Marlow's dictum in *Heart of Darkness* that, at a profound level, 'we live as we dream, alone'.[94] Dropped into the world like the questor in Ní Dhomhnaill's recent poem 'Turas na Scríne'/Journey to the Shrine,

---

[88] See Ní Dhomhnaill, 'Mis and Dubh Ruis', 201 and 'Réamhrá', *Feis*, 7.

[89] Meyer-Thoss, *Louise Bourgeois*, 60.

[90] Ibid. 196.   [91] Ibid. 197.

[92] See Brienza's discussion of Winnie's verbal shield and 'journey' in Beckett's play *Happy Days*. Brienza, S. D., 'Perilous Journeys on Beckett's Stages', in Burkman (ed.), *Myth and Ritual in the Plays of Samuel Beckett*, 28–49 (pp. 40–1).

[93] See, for example, 'Mo Ghrá-sa (Idir Lúibíní)'/My Love (In Brackets), *FS* p. 29. Translation Q in Appendix.

[94] See Conrad, J., *Heart of Darkness* (Harmondsworth: Penguin, 1982).

individuals appear to plough through their own course to their own end with only limited or temporary 'communion' along the way. Each 'báidín guagach'/rocky boat (*FS* p. 107) may pull in to banks or islands but is often under a 'geasa'/bond to sail on:

> Má chuirim aon lámh ar an dtearmann beannaithe,
> má thógaim droichead thar an abhainn,
> gach a mbíonn tógtha isló ages na ceardaithe
> bíonn sé leagtha ar maidin romham.
>
> *If I put my hand on holy ground*
> *if I built a river bridge*
> *all built by day by the craftsmen*
> *is felled on me by morning.* (*SP/RD* p. 64)

Even in marriage, it seems that the morning can bring destruction, the crushing necessity of 'having to put up with whatever the day/blows our way', including estrangement.[95] For example, Pádraig de Paor interprets the bean an leasa/fairy-woman figure in 'Fuadach'/Abduction (*FS* p. 65) as a representation of the estrangement (even from themselves) that married women can feel under patriarchy.[96] In this reading of the poem, the woman loses herself, her sanity, in adopting the conventional woman's role although, it seems, she can then only be restored by 'the male principle, the sword of light'—a resolution which de Paor finds disturbingly phallic and violent in the context. For him, such a resolution merely represents a modern 'biorán suain'/sleeping charm or pacifying illusion. In actual fact, Ní Dhomhnaill, like Louise Bourgeois, is an artist who is 'interested in the *erotic process* as an *aesthetic solution*'.[97]

The violence, with its sexual overtones, done to the fairy-woman or impostor in 'Fuadach/Abduction' is paradoxically indicative of a real desire for wholeness.[98] Ní Dhomhnaill represents the (married) woman

---

[95] 'Glacadh le pé rud a sheolfaidh/an lá inniu an tslí', from 'Aubade', *PD* p. 148.
[96] See de Paor, P., *Tionscnamh Filíochta Nuala Ní Dhomhnaill*, 144–6.
[97] Meyer-Thoss, *Louise Bourgeois*, 59. My emphasis.
[98] Ibid. 132–3. Louise Bourgeois has stated that
the theme of the woman cut in half is a theme of the passive state. It reminds me of the women, the lavandières in France, whom I used to see as a child. When they washed tapestries in the river, these girls knelt inside little boxes. You couldn't see their lower bodies; they looked as if they were cut in two. That gave me a fantastic pleasure, because I myself wanted to cut them in two. I wanted to move from the passive to the active, since I experienced myself as cut in two. I have always applied this aggression to women. It has been an unfulfilled wish, of course, but whenever it is made conscious there is an explosion of pleasure. Yet I am ashamed of the violence [. . .] It's very unreasonable, but I wanted to be whole.

as someone divided, 'cut in two', whose imposed self-image becomes—
for her real self—an object of fear and loathing. Alternatively, this or
any real woman (questor or artist) who wants to see and restore her true
image must take the tools of what seems to be a male trade (since patriarchy buried her alive in the first place) and, moving from the position
of passive abductee to active mover and shaker, 'hack away' at her fear,
at the false image into which she has fallen or, rather, been plunged.
Working from a similar vantage point, Bourgeois writes that 'exorcism
is healthy. Cauterization, to burn in order to heal. It's like pruning trees.
That's my art. I'm good at it.'[99]

Ní Dhomhnaill's identification of the assumption of control (the
hacking away) with the 'male', phallic 'sword of light', may be worrying
to modern, sometimes politically correct readers but such a reading of
the poem is too literal. The entire episode is a fantasy dreamt up in the
volcanic and unruly unconscious of an individual, a poet who, like
everyone else, is 'vulnerable [. . .] male–female', as Bourgeois reminds
us.[100] In this one poem, Ní Dhomhnaill highlights a way out of the
proverbial woods, or the fairy-fort, using another version of the
béaloideas 'scian na coise duibhe'/black-hafted knife available to all: this
time, 'an claidheamh solais'/the sword of light. The entire poem, therefore, could be read as an example of the casting and playing of
(béaloideas) roles, the verbal sculpture or personification of diverse,
shared, overlapping, and transgressive male–female aspects of the
psyche into a 'manageable reality', a state of selfhood that can then,
through action ('cauterization', burning in order to heal), move from
the passive to the active: 'you take the event in hand and actively manipulate it in order to survive. You turn the passive into active, the Freudian
identification with the aggressor. You have to be able to do that. There
is a constant desire to manipulate instead of being manipulated.'[101]

The unconscious is, in reality, a mysterious, non-'p.c.', amoral area
whose monsters and goddesses we all have to bear and 'manage', by any
means possible.[102] The aesthetic solution of Ní Dhomhnaill's
'Fuadach'/Abduction is comparable to the voodoo-like exorcisms of

99 Meyer-Thoss, *Louise Bourgeois*, 194.
100 See Morgan, 'Louise Bourgeois: Nature Study', 2.
101 Meyer-Thoss, *Louise Bourgeois*, 197.
102 'The unconscious is something which is volcanic in tone and yet you cannot do
anything about it. You had better be its friend, or accept it, or love it if you can, because
it might get the better of you. You never know.' Ibid. 68–9.

Bourgeois's sculpture, more emotional catharsis than analysis or intellectual process. Incidentally, and importantly, the voodoo doll can be male or female, and the sword of light (as of old) wielded by 'maidens' as well as knights:

Once when we were sitting together at the dining table, I took white bread, mixed it with spit, and molded a figure of my father. When the figure was done, I started cutting off the limbs with a knife. I see this as my first sculptural solution. It was right for the moment and it helped me. It was an important experience and certainly determined my future direction.[103]

The king or the father must also die by the sword in Ní Dhomhnaill's interpretation of 'Mis and Dubh Ruis' before a new, more vulnerable but productive, male energy can display itself in the unconscious, unite with and dilute the negative female energy present and so bring forth 'the conscious reality of the Goddess, as spéirbhean'.[104]

Ní Dhomhnaill, therefore, offers an optimistic, transformative vision for the good of the psyche, the individual, the nations, and even of the planet.[105] If too long a sacrifice has turned a woman, for example, to stone, Ní Dhomhnaill's answer is to chip away at the stone (like certain African sculptors) to free the female image or 'soul' trapped within it. In *Féar Suaithinseach*, she refashions images of women's past so that she and her 'sisters' may live more freely and actively in the present. Alicia Ostriker writes that

old stories are changed, changed utterly, by female knowledge of female experience, so that they can no longer stand as foundations of collective male fantasy. Instead, they are [when rewritten *by* women] corrections; they are representations of what women find divine and demonic in themselves; they are retrieved images of what women have collectively and historically suffered; in some cases they are instructions for survival.[106]

For similar reasons, Ní Dhomhnaill 'gives voice' to the Morrígán or 'Great Queen' who dares to chide no less a male icon than Cú Chulainn, and to 'berate the Badhbh'. The poet also invokes the ancient Irish, but time-traversing, figure of Queen Medb to declare war on modern twenty-pint heroes who would infringe upon her—and any

---

[103] Ibid. 53.
[104] Ní Dhomhnaill, 'Mis and Dubh Ruis', 200.
[105] Ibid. 196; see also 'An Ollmháthair Mhór/Great Mother', (*SP/RD* pp. 58–9).
[106] Quoted in O'Connor, M., 'Lashings of the Mother Tongue', 162.

woman's—person or dignity.[107] Significantly, the war which Medb declares in Ní Dhomhnaill's poem is more defensive than aggressive. She has no urge to be conquering all she sees[108] but instead wants to recover her *stolen* dignity, her *right* to equality, her freedom to be and to be let be. Hers is 'not a cry of power but a rising up from powerlessness'.[109]

True to ancient Celtic dualism and, indeed, pluralism, the lashings of Ní Dhomhnaill's 'anarchic' Mother Tongue are also 'lashings' in the sense of 'helpings' designed to restore the fallen or dropped, imbalanced or unequal communion between male and female both in the psyche and in society:

> Labhrann an Mhór-Ríon
> *Mo shlánú*
>
> Mise an tseanbhean
> a thagann it 'fhianaise.
> Táim ar leathcheann,
> leathshúil, leathchois.
> Bleáim bó
> ar a bhfuil trí shine.
> Iarrann tú
> deoch bhainne orm.
> Tugaim duit bolgam.
> Ólann tú siar é.
> 'Beannacht Dé is aindé ort.'
> Imíonn an phian
> a bhí ag ciapadh m'easnaíocha,
> an trálach ó mo lámh,
> an ghoin ó mo chois,
> leis an tríú bolgam leamhnachta
> téarnaíonn agus is slán mo leathrosc.
>
> Toisc gur tú a ghoin ar dtúis mé
> le ladhar do choise,
> le do chrann tabhaill,
> ní raibh i ndán dom
> feabhsú i t'éagmais,
> cé gur de do dhearg-ainneoin
> a thugas uait an leigheas [. . .]

[107] See *SP/RD* pp. 116–25.
[108] McDiarmid and Durkan, 'Q. & A.: Nuala Ní Dhomhnaill', 42.
[109] O'Connor, M., 'Lashings of the Mother Tongue', 163.

de dheasca tarta,
tagaim slán ó do ghoin
de bhíthin t'íocshláinte.[110]

The other side of this sibyl's tongue, however, carries a warning that to ditch the mythical, mystical 'communion' that restores and unites, to reject that binding exchange of bodily fluids (*SP/RD* pp. 116–25), is to erect a mutually destructive 'Fál go hAer'/Sky-High Partition (*FS* p. 48) between co-existing and co-dependent elements such as male and female, I and Other, East and West, North and South, science and nature, etc. Such a false partition always, it seems, unleashes negative, predatory male and female archetypes from 'Masculus Giganticus Hibernicus' (*SP/RD* p. 78) to the Badhbh, and even a vengeful Great Earth Mother/'An Ollmháthair Mhór' herself (*SP/RD* p. 58).

That just such a partition has been allowed to grow all the way up to the sky (the gods) and become permanent is Ní Dhomhnaill's great fear and worry throughout *Féar Suaithinseach*. Her response is to dig down and in (like Heaney) to the self, to Ireland and its traditions, to mythical and psychological archetypes on a quest to 'develop the tradition through personalization, and enrich the person or self through tradition' since each belongs to the other.[111] Finding herself in a society which, she feels, frustrates the self-fulfilment of women, Ní Dhomhnaill word-journeys back to the sources of the dichotomous dualism of the patriarchal system to transgress, step beyond, its strict hierarchical limits into 'hybridity, impurity, intermingling, the transformation that comes from new and unexpected combinations of human beings, cultures, ideas, politics'.[112]

This sounds to me like sound artistic practice with boundless potential for poets, in particular, who have traditionally sought unusual correspondences of imagery and fresh conjugations of words. Nowadays known as 'transgression', Foucault wrote, in 1977, of this activity that

perhaps one day it will seem as decisive for our culture, as much a part of its soil, as the experience of contradiction was at an earlier time for dialectical thought. But in spite of so many scattered signs, the language in which

---

[110] 'The Great Queen Speaks', *SP/RD* p. 120. Translation R in Appendix.

[111] 'Forbairt ar an traidisiúin trína phearsanú, agus saibhriú an duine trí mheán an traidisiúin.' Ó Tuairisc (ed.), *Rogha an Fhile/The Poet's Choice*, 57–8.

[112] Salman Rushdie quoted by O'Connor, T. (ed.), *The Comic Tradition in Irish Women Writers*, 6.

transgression will find its space and the illumination of its being lies almost entirely in the future.[113]

On the contrary, Ní Dhomhnaill points out in her own time-honoured and transgressive language that such 'illumination' is at least as old as Newgrange.

4.2 *FEIS* (1991)

Ní Dhomhnaill's third individual volume of poems, *Feis*, is divided into four sections: Cailleach/Hag, An Leannán Sí/the Fairy (or Demon) Lover, Feis[114] and Spéirbhean/Sky-Woman. These divisions follow the four-part pattern of development which the poet highlighted in her essay 'Mis and Dubh Ruis'. Ní Dhomhnaill's parable tells of Mis who, having been turned into a negative female archetype/cailleach or hag-figure, encounters her lover/'leannán', plays 'the game of the stick'—an early example of 'feis'—and is then transformed into a beautiful and creative princess/goddess or 'spéirbhean'. The progress charted in such a tale is a form of Jungian development towards individuation[115] which ranges, in Ní Dhomhnaill's account, from 'the darkness of "An Cailleach" to the light of self-fulfilment as "An Spéirbhean" '.[116]

In terms of Ní Dhomhnaill's own creative odyssey, however, even by the time she had written 'Primavera', placed in the Spéirbhean section of *Feis* (*F* p. 114), she remarked that

having long been acquainted with the 'Cailleach' as an inner reality, I have to admit that I have not yet personally met the Spéirbhean. I'm still working on that inner Harper in all his powerful dream manifestations as Enemy, Sea-Horse or Minotaur, Bull of the Mothers. But there does seem to be a way forward, and I live in hope.[117]

This way forward, this hope accounts for the fact that even though the 'cailleach', hag, or negative mother archetype may dominate or

---

[113] See Stallybrass and White, *The Politics and Poetics of Transgression*, 200.

[114] The word 'feis' can be interpreted as meaning 'carnival', combining both the 'carnal' and the 'carnivalesque' (Muldoon), *AC* pp. 10–19; festival, festivity, or celebration; and (more literally, as verbal noun of the Old Irish *fo-aid*) 'to spend the night with'.

[115] This refers to the process or state that allows the whole personality to blend and balance the various aspects of the psyche in order to be true to the real or whole self.

[116] Referring to the first and last sections of *Feis*. See Ó Drisceoil, P., 'À la carte Paganism?', 123.

[117] Ní Dhomhnaill, 'Mis and Dubh Ruis', 200.

overshadow the first, and by far the largest, section of *Feis*, she is *not* allowed to have the last word. That is left until the final Spéirbhean/Sky-woman section of the volume where the poet (under the positive influence, or in expectation, of the Spéirbhean) sounds more optimistic and confidently asserts that music, song, and poetry *can* help even the most harried and put-upon woman to 'see through the dark mist all around her', to have 'courage and sense'.[118] There may, by the end of *Feis*, be no complete transformation into 'spéirbhean' but a '*window* in the sky' has, at least, been located which lets in light, and poetry.[119]

4.2.1 Cailleach

Feis begins, like Ní Dhomhnaill's early volume *An Dealg Droighin*, with images of Autumn, the fall into darker, colder weather, the 'good going out of the year', with omens of death and doubt about the likelihood of resurrection in Spring. This marks a natural, objectively co-related 'turning', falling down and inward to the lios or subconscious—a dark, un-p.c. realm of violence and fear, of entrapment and its accompanying desperation to escape. For example, although the first poem, 'An Casadh'/The Turning (*PD* pp. 113) looks forward to a 'turning in' to home and hearth for shelter, warmth, and entertainment (including story-telling to 'ward off the bad and welcome the good into the family'), it is soon apparent that the seanchas which Ní Dhomhnaill has lined up—in the poems that follow—is characterized by the horror and fascination of fairy-tales and mythology, combined with the wonder of modern experience itself, all coloured with her favourite dye: 'the dark tincture of the subconscious'.[120]

According to Pádraig de Paor, the poem 'An Bhatráil/The Battering' (*AC* p. 24), for example, tells of a woman who has fallen under the spell of bean an leasa/the fairy-woman[121] and appears to have become possessed by a negative mother archetype. This woman's story could be read as a béaloideas-style interpretation of post-natal depression and

---

[118] 'Féachfaidh an bhean aníos as an gceo modardhorcha/atá ar foluain ina timpeall, is glacfaidh sí misneach is ciall.' From 'Éirigh, a Éinín', *PD* pp. 28–31 (p. 30).
[119] See Ní Dhomhnaill, 'An Fhilíocht á Cumadh: Ceardlann Filíochta', in P. Ó Fiannachta (ed.), *Léachtaí Cholm Cille XVII: An Nuafhilíocht* (Maigh Nuad: An Sagart, 1986), 147–79 (p. 149).
[120] See O'Driscoll, D. (ed.), 'Findings', 126.
[121] de Paor, P., *Tionscnamh Filíochta Nuala Ní Dhomhnaill*, 22.

child abuse and/but there is also evidence that the poet herself, initially and in part at least, has interpreted the poem as representing a female poet's raid on the unconscious, an attempt to smuggle something of the live 'being' of a poem past the male muse at great risk to the self as well as to the poem or 'child', that is, 'the potential, the image for the new or future dispensation'.[122] One of the boons of Ní Dhomhnaill's poetry is its ability to work on several levels. For me, this poem highlights the psychological violence of this poet's methods although they appear to be designed to spare more or worse violence, even death:

> Nuair a tháinig an fear caol dubh romham
> ag doras an leasa
> dúrt leis an áit a fhágaint láithreach
> nó go sáfainn é.
> Thugas faobhar na scine coise duibhe
> don sceach a bhí sa tslí
> romham is a dhá cheann i dtalamh aige.
>
> *When a tall, dark stranger barred my way*
> *at the door of the fort*
> *I told him to get off-side fast*
> *or I'd run him through.*
> *The next obstacle was a briar,*
> *both ends of which were planted in the ground:*
> *I cut it with my trusty black-handled knife.*
>
> (*AC* p. 24)

Ní Dhomhnaill's view is that unless you face and, if necessary, fight the 'dark strangers' of the unconscious, you can either fall prey to their violence or become an agent of it, as in the domestic and, likewise, historical cycles of violence mentioned in 'Hotline' (*PD* p. 100).

Increasingly, the Cailleach section of *Feis* faces the apparent *inevitability* of the dark, wintry side of life that may extinguish but also lets there be light[123] or, at least, awareness of the two and of the difference.[124] For example, Ní Dhomhnaill invokes Persephone, the Goddess Durga or Snow Queen, An Coiste Bodhar or the Death-Coach, and even the common household freezer to focus on life's various rites of passage, all as natural and inescapable for each one of us as night, day

---

[122] Somerville Aryat and Wilson (eds.), *Sleeping with Monsters*, 150–1.
[123] See Ó Searcaigh, 'Johnny Appleseed', *Out in the Open*, 184–7.
[124] de Paor, P., *Tionscnamh Filíochta Nuala Ní Dhomhnaill*, 65.

and the seasons. The cold and dark of inner and outer 'tundra' are, when possible, resisted by many of the poet's personae who refuse to be *prematurely* cast into various deadly states of paralysis, symbolized by entombment in quicksand, clay, ice, or stone:

> Samhlaigh duit féin cloch ag dúiseacht gach lá is ar éirí as an leaba,
> ag searradh a charraig-ghuailne
> is ag bogadh a theanga sall is anall mar leac
> ag iarraidh labhairt.
> Bhuel, b'shin agaibh mise.

> *Imagine a stone waking up every day and getting out of bed,*
> *shrugging its shoulder-boulders,*
> *and moving its tongue from side to side like a paving stone*
> *and trying to speak.*
> *Well, there you have it: that was me.* ('Aois na Cloiche', *F* p. 24)

This tale from the 'Stone Age', narrated in the past tense, suggests that those days have, at least for now, passed and that the speaker has, inspiringly, lived to tell the tale. It also infers that, in the present, such tales can be told to cheer on what Gramsci would call the optimism of the will in overcoming the pessimism of the intellect and other such obstructions. Indeed, while many of Ní Dhomhnaill's poems speak of a deep-freeze,[125] their very ability to do so marks and celebrates the miracle, and possibility, of defrostation.

For example, in poems such as 'Lá Chéad Chomaoineach/First Communion' (*AC* p. 32) and 'An Poll sa Staighre/The Crack in the Stairs' (*AC* p. 32), Ní Dhomhnaill transforms a diet of specific fears, one at a time, with (ironically) lashings of a language which some, for centuries, have been declaring 'marbh agus cruaidh is chomh fuar leis an uaigh'/dead and hard and cold as the grave[126] but which, on the contrary, keeps *this poet* going, as she keeps it going, with fresh or defrosted 'meat of the tongue', béaloideas—developing the tradition through personalization, and enriching the person through tradition. Yet, 'keeping going', as in Heaney's poem by that name, no less than in Kristeva's feminist theory, is a daily undertaking.[127]

---

[125] For example, the female speaker of 'Banríon an tSneachta'/The Snow Queen compares herself to the keening women of ancient Babylon 'ach amháin nach deora a shileann ó mo cheann/ach dánta is dréachta is iad reoite ag an bhfuacht'/except that it isn't tears I shed but poems and drafts—frozen solid (*F* p. 21).

[126] See 'Dípfríos/Deep-freeze', *AC* pp. 36–7.

[127] Heaney, 'Keeping Going', *The Spirit Level*, 10–12; for Kristeva, see O'Connor, M., 'Lashings of the Mother Tongue', 169.

Notably, the Cailleach section of *Feis* culminates with a series of encounters with negative mother archetypes from Caitlín Ní hUalacháin, The Poor Old Woman, to what Philip O'Leary calls the 'earth mother gone wrong' of 'Cailleach/Hag' (*PD* p. 134).[128] In these encounters, the poet's response ranges from humouring to humorous riposte and raillery, from caution to helpless and hopeless anxiety—the latter producing, in the personae of the poems, symptoms of anorexia and paranoia. Ní Dhomhnaill, therefore, appears in some ways to be a contemporary 'file faoi sceimhle'/a poet in even more terror than Ó Rathaille and Ó Ríordáin.[129]

For Ní Dhomhnaill, problems in the individual's spirit or psyche are interconnected with flaws in familial and other relationships throughout society (*PD* p. 150). Too often, these relationships seem to be characterized by injustice, neglect, and the loss of traditional warmth, tribal 'communion', and customs with their potentially 'healing balm' (*SP/RD* p. 120). For example, the speaker's unrequited love in 'Leasmháthair'/ Stepmother (*F* p. 34) leads to anorexia[130] while the great grandmother of 'Na Trí Shraoth/The Three Sneezes' is left defenceless against the dark forces of the Otherworld because of her own family's preoccupation with this world. Their failure to bless and protect her with proverbial words and rituals has apparently left the great grandmother vulnerable and exposed:

'Is mo mhallacht ar an airgead	*And I curse the money*
is ar an éirí in airde,	*and one-up-manship,*
ar an tsaint is ar an saoltacht	*the greed and worldliness*
ná coinníonn daoine san airdeall	*that makes people drop*
go bhfuil fórsaí na doircheachta	*their guard on the dark forces*
dár n-ionsaí go deo	*always attacking us*
is gurb é teas ár gcine	*since it is the warmth of our kind*
a choinníonn sinn beo.'	*that keeps us going.* (*AC* p. 54)

The 'Cailleach' section of *Feis* finally ends with the appearance, in her own section, of the now familiar Bean an Leasa. As in *Féar*

---

[128] O'Leary, P., 'A Night with Nuala', *Irish Literary Supplement* (Spring 1990), 22–3.

[129] O Tuama, *Filí Faoi Sceimhle: Seán Ó Ríordáin agus Aogán Ó Rathaille* (1978).

[130] See de Paor, P., *Tionscnamh Filíochta Nuala Ní Dhomhnaill*, 25–6. Note also that the psychic states and struggles depicted in Ní Dhomhnaill's poetry increasingly refer to the experience of women in general, caught up in a society bedevilled by patriarchy and also by the 'false love' of negative mother archetypes, such as this 'stepmother'.

Suaithinseach, the fairy woman is a law unto herself with power over men and beasts. In 'An Slad'/The Slaughter (*F* p. 47), she incites some men to sacrifice a dun-coloured lamb in a manner that recalls *The Táin*.[131] Philip O'Leary finds that Ní Dhomhnaill's antiquated phrasing, including 'cosair easair'/a trummelled mire, 'encapsulates the gory battlefield of the heroic literature' and that such economy of allusion and evocation 'is among the chief satisfactions of Ní Dhomhnaill's work, at its best'.[132]

I agree but it is important to stress that modern readers are chiefly satisfied not just with the nods to and borrowings from earlier literature but by their remarkable and daring forward projection into the present. The same Bean an Leasa who incites an old-style raid also incites a modern poem-speaker's husband, in 'Bean an Leasa mar Shíobshiúlóir'/The Fairy Woman as a Hitch-hiker, to be

> . . . ag gabháilt timpeall
> na tíre i dteainc mór groí,
> na mionnaí beaga is na mionnaí móra
> á stealladh aige deas is clé,
> ag rá i measc rudaí eile go maróidh sé
> mé féin, is na leanaí is a Dhaid
> is Uachtarán na Mac Léinn.
>
> . . . *going round the country*
> *in a great big tank*
> *cursing left*
> *right and centre*
> *saying, among other things, that he'll kill*
> *me, the kids, his Da*
> *and the President of the Students' Union.*
> (*F* p. 49)

Surprisingly, Bean an Leasa's final appearance in *Feis* is relatively benign. Although she and her comrades are out to blast a French grape harvest with a taste of frost, one fairy woman is presented as assisting the poet-speaker:

> is thug [sí] comhairle dom i dtaobh na bhfíonta ab fhearr
> sa taobh seo dúthaigh.

---

[131] See Thomas Kinsella, trans., *The Táin*, Dolmen Editions 9 (Dublin: Dolmen Press, 1969).

[132] O'Leary, P., 'A Night with Nuala', 23.

Ghlacas a comhairle, cheannaíos mo dhóthain
is aililiú
sa deireadh, gan éinne ag cur chugham nó uaim,
d'éirigh liom dosaen go leith buidéal den Phinot Noir
is fearr,
a thabhairt thar na fir chustaim

and [she] advised me that the best bargains in wine
were to be had in this neighbourhood.
I took her advice and snapped up all I could
and Glory be!
if I didn't smuggle a case and a half
of a superlative Pinot Noir
right past the noses of Her Majesty's customs.

(*PD* pp. 146–7)

Muldoon, a truly Northern mischief-maker or trickster, inserts Her Majesty's Customs where Ní Dhomhnaill's favoured obstacle is simply custom's *men*. In any case, Ní Dhomhnaill is smuggling across the red wine of poetry,[133] aided and abetted by her now credited, duplicitous Muse—Bean an Leasa.

4.2.2 *An Leannán Sí*

Pádraig de Paor writes that most of the poems in the 'An Leannán Sí'/Fairy Lover section of *Feis* can be read in three main, interconnecting ways: 'as poems about love for a man (or some failure in matters of love with a man); about the poet's *animus* and personal development towards individuation; about the muse of poetry, the source of inspir-ation and the spark of creativity'.[134] It is indeed the case that the male presence of the 'An Leannán Sí' section appears as either lover and/or animus and/or muse, and that in each poem some sort of negotiation between the 'two' psychic principles (male and female) takes place. The ideal resolution of these negotiations would appear to be a new, more equal and mutually beneficial relationship but the poems are testimony to the fact that such an ideal is, so far, rarely attained.

In 'An Coilichín Márta'/The March Cock, a ship's captain wants to

---

[133] 'Fíon rua/na filíochta'. Mac Lochlainn, G., 'Amhrán Leamhain', *Babylon Gaeilgeoir* (Belfast: An Clochán, 1997), 48.

[134] de Paor, P., *Tionscnamh Filíochta Nuala Ní Dhomhnaill*, 72. My translation.

barter for the female speaker's eponymous hero who, along with God, protects her and hers from foul weather and evil in general:

'Ó díol liom é', a deir sé. 'Ní dhíolfad ná mé!
Cuirimse mo bhotháinín faoi chumraí Dé
is mo choilichín Mhárta. An sonas isteach
is an donas amach!' Bhailibh sé leis
is a theanga ina phluic.

Is má thagann sé aríst chugam
tá's agam a chleas.
Má ghaibheann sé bog is cruaidh orm
ní dhéanfaidh sé an bheart.
Mar ní dhíolfadsa mo choilichín Márta le haon chaptaen loinge,
—dá bhreátha é!

'O sell me it', says he. 'No way, José!
My wee cabin's in the hands of God
and my coilichín Márta. Good in,
bad out!' That stuck
his tongue back in his gob.

And if he comes back,
I know what he's about.
He can play hard and soft all he wants,
but he won't get what he's after.
I wouldn't sell my coilichín Márta to any ship's captain
—even one so handsome! (F p. 55)

Apart from the comic sexual innuendo, the 'coilichín Márta' represents the poet's or speaker's last defence and, in the case of the poet, her very poetry which, like the animal in question, raises a cry against the elements. The poem recalls Ní Dhomhnaill's account of her poet-fore-mother Liadán who 'refused to marry her one great love, the poet Cuirithir, in case he stole her poetry, and she was dead right'.[135]

The poem 'An Coilichín Márta' also employs some of the seanchaí techniques that Ní Dhomhnaill was so delighted to find in Ciarán Carson's *The Irish For No*: 'the long seemingly haphazard, spoken line, the miraculous non-sequiturs; the additive rather than subordinate clauses, the repetition of the just said, the transitions due to memory and association rather than due to any formal or linear logic, the vast repertoire of a good seanchaí, captured once and for all, permanently,

---

[135] McDiarmid and Durkan, 'Q. & A.: Nuala Ní Dhomhnaill', 43.

on the printed page'.[136] Many of these features account for the pleasures of Ní Dhomhnaill's own poetry:

> D'iarr sé orm ar bhraitheas aon ní as an tslí.
> Dúrtsa nár mhothaíos cóch gaoithe ná fuaim báistí,
> nár ghíosc an doras is nár chrith frámaí
> na bhfuinneog ach timpeall a dó dhéag
> gur éirigh an coileach is gur lig sé seacht nglaoch.
>
> *He asked me if I'd sensed anything untoward.*
> *I told him not even a squall of wind or sound of rain,*
> *the door didn't creak or the window-frames*
> *shake, except for about twelve o'clock midnight*
> *when the cock got up and crowed seven times.* (*F* p. 55)

The captain may be 'fine' but the female speaker of this poem won't give too much of herself or her *coilichín Márta* away. What is the meaning of this strange parable?

'Loves riddles are,' wrote John Donne, and as for the heart, 'if thou canst give it, then thou never gavest it'. Like Donne, Ní Dhomhnaill (throughout her work) wishes and calls for the two psychic principles, or the male and female, to find

> a way more liberall,
> Than changing hearts, to *joyne* them, so wee shall
> *Be one*, and one another's All.[137]

Ní Dhomhnaill's ear for and attention to language in the lover/animus/muse poems is remarkable. In 'Filleadh na Béithe'/Return of the Muse (*F* p. 56), she effectively lapses into the 'patois', or Béarlachas (Englishism) of Dublin City Gaelic schools to tell one of the gods of poetry to 'Féach anseo, tusa, faigh as!' (*literally*, word for word, 'look here, you; get out of it!'). The god comes under attack because s/he is blamed for the absence of the muse/lover/animus; an absence depicted in, for example, 'Chomh Leochaileach le Sliogán/As Fragile as a Shell' (*PD* p. 84). Ní Dhomhnaill has spoken of such an absence as 'a particular constellation that creates poetry. If I were meant to be a happy person it would be requited love all the way.'[138] Her statement

---

[136] Ní Dhomhnaill, 'The English for Irish', 116–17.
[137] Donne, 'Lovers Infinitenesse', *Selected Poems of John Donne*, ed. by James Reeves, 7th edn. (London: Heinemann, 1969), 9. My emphasis.
[138] McDiarmid and Durkan, 'Q. & A.: Nuala Ní Dhomhnaill', 43.

recalls Meyer-Thoss's definition of poetry as 'a longing for remote intimacy'.[139]

To restore this intimacy or, at least, re-collect it, Ní Dhomhnaill takes a 'léim caorach'/sheep's leap[140] into language and/or béaloideas and/or poetry to send her and our 'imagination hop, skip and *bucléip-ing*/over the sky of materialism'.[141] Poetry, traditionally symbolized by the 'wingèd horse', transgresses the subject–object, I–Other boundary, bridging gaps, bearing artist, audience, reader, or addressee across in an act of translation. Ní Dhomhnaill, a markedly transgressive artist is more inclined, however, to hitch a lift on the grotesque 'griffin' than on the classical Pegasus:

> Is éirigh, a ghriffin, a éin mhóir ghroí fhiain
> na filíochta is cuir aniar ar do dhrom ort mé [. . .]
> is ní thiocfam abhaile go n-aimseod mo leannán
> is go bhfaighead mar leath leapan é.
>
> *And rise, griffin, enormous strange, wild bird*
> *of poetry and put me on your back [. . .]*
> *and I won't come home until I find my love*
> *and get him back in the conjugal bed.* (*F* p. 61)

At a recent conference on transgressive aspects of visual and literary art, the sculptor Lloyd Gibson declared that 'power lies at the interface between separate identities', that (paraphrasing the anthropologist Edmund Leach) binary polarizations of 'I' and 'Other' are transgressed and dissolve, for example, in the sexual embrace; likewise distinctions between devotee and deity during religious worship which is itself designed to transcend the border between life and death. For Gibson, new trends in art reflect an implosion of the two-term, binary system as, increasingly, a 'synchronic' vision emerges.[142] New art is often characterized, therefore, by what he calls 'conjugation' or, in musical terms, a fusion. This conjugation or fusion—particularly in its sexual connotation, an example of erotic process as aesthetic solution—is apparent,

---

[139] Meyer-Thoss, *Louise Bourgeois*, 67.

[140] 'Léim caorach'. See Ní Dhomhnaill, 'An Fhilíocht á Cumadh', 147.

[141] 'Samhlaíocht ag dul de hop, scip, cosabacóid/thar spéir na hearraíochta'. 'Clingeann na Clog', *F* p. 60.

[142] Gibson, Lloyd, 'Pleasures of the Interface', paper given at the conference *Fabulous Transgressions: Defining the Grotesque in Contemporary Literary and Visual Culture* (University of Sunderland, 11 September 1997).

I believe, in the work of Ní Dhomhnaill, and is evidently responsible for the flowering of sensuous poems such as 'Blodewedd':

> Oiread is barra do mhéire a bhualadh orm
> is bláthaím,
> cumraíocht ceimice mo cholainne
> claochlaíonn.
> Is móinéar féir mé ag cathráil
> faoin ngréin
> aibíonn faoi thadhall do láimhe
> is osclaíonn
> mo luibheanna uile [. . .]

> *At the least touch of your fingertips*
> *I break into blossom,*
> *my whole chemical composition*
> *transformed.*
> *I sprawl like a grassy meadow*
> *fragrant in the sun;*
> *at the brush of your palm, my herbs*
> *and spices spill open.* (*PD* p. 116)

Nevertheless, the ancient notion that after coitus every animal is sad is often illustrated in Ní Dhomhnaill's work by the painful separations to which a poet's necessary honesty makes her bear witness:

> Ach níl in aon ní ach seal:
> i gcionn leathuaire
> pógfaidh tú mé ar bharr m' éadain
> is cásfaidh tú orm do dhrom,
> is fágfar mé ar mo thaobh féin
> don leaba dhúbailte
> ag cuimhneamh faoi scáth do ghuailne
> ná tiocfaidh orm bás riamh roimh am.

> *But nothing lasts forever:*
> *in half an hour*
> *you'll kiss my forehead*
> *and turn your back on me,*
> *leaving me alone*
> *on my side of the double-bed*
> *reminded under your shoulder's shadow*
> *that death will never come to me too soon.*
> ('Dún/Stronghold', *F* p. 69)

Inspiration may be, for Ní Dhomhnaill, impregnation by the divine but 'he', like a mortal being, can prove to be an inconstant, absent, or unfaithful lover, muse or animus who may only be reached or contacted at a high cost to the self: 'smut de mo cheathrú is smut eile de mo chliathán/mar lón bídh ar an aistear [duit]'.[143]

Worse than inconstant or unfaithful, the male muse, in particular, can be 'ferociously dangerous',[144] a terminally unavailable Prince of Darkness who mercilessly exacts the price which Nietzsche said had to be paid for writing any 'real' book: namely, blood ('Stigmata', *F* p. 73). Such grotesque images and ideas, borrowed in part from the horror genre, are a feature of Ní Dhomhnaill's transgressive work. However, while earlier patriarchy viewed the female imagination as itself monstrous, Ní Dhomhnaill demonstrates that the male muse and even patriarchal thinking itself may be the real 'monster'.

Marsha Meskimmon argues that women artists in general, once seen as marginal and therefore monstrous in the sights of the male canon, have increasingly used the power and potential of the grotesque, of otherness, in a feminist form of canonical transgression.[145] This transgression, she believes, demands a strategy central to which is the use of the grotesque and/or monstrous in a process of 'perpetual becoming', of articulation, of assuming and asserting an identity that outgrows the traditional, male-prescribed role or limits for women.

Meskimmon points out, for example, that the two great mothers of classical tradition are Jocasta and Mary—both mothers of sons, of the heralded male genesis. These potentially powerful women/goddesses are, according to Meskimmon, reduced to empty vessels for the father-figure's lineage. In her view, modern women artists question and challenge these male-dominated histories with work such as Valerie Reardon's 'Madonna of Chernobyl' (1988) and by exploring the more blurred, less strictly delimited relationship of mother and daughter through, for example, re-experiencing and re-negotiating the mythical Demeter-Persephone pairing.

It is interesting that Meskimmon chooses to highlight Reardon's veiled introduction of her pubescent daughter into her three-part series

---

[143] 'A chunk of thigh and another of my flank/for fuel on your [the griffin's] journey.' From 'An Ghríobh Ingneach'/The Griffin, *F* p. 61.

[144] Somerville Aryat and Wilson (eds.), *Sleeping with Monsters*, 150.

[145] Marsha Meskimmon, 'The Grotesque as a Feminist Visual Strategy', conference paper. See Note 142.

of paintings, 'Persephone's Journey'; Ní Dhomhnaill just as readily and naturally incorporates and assimilates *her* experiences as a child-bearer and rearer into her own oeuvre, with her own Persephone-like daughter appearing in 'An Prionsa Dubh'/The Dark Prince (*F* p. 74) and with an utterly unpredictable 'hairy' baby girl arriving in the fabulously transgressive poem 'Mac Airt' (*PD* p. 78). While there is no telling the precise ingredients of the mysterious alchemy or confluence of courses leading up to any (artistic or other) incarnation (*DD* p. 85), it is clear that Ní Dhomhnaill is a woman artist who does use transgression as a strategy in the process of becoming master/mistress of her self, life, and work; of taking over the driver's seat—'tar éis an tsaoil, is liomsa an carr'.[146]

4.2.3   Feis

The Feis section of the volume *Feis* is divided into three consecutive sections for three poems which are themselves divided internally into various parts: 'Immram/The Voyage' (*AC* p. 72), 'Feis/Carnival' (*AC* p. 10) and 'Toircheas'/Pregnancy, Broodiness or Expectation (*F* p. 105).

In 'Immram', Ní Dhomhnaill follows the traditional route of some of her people (including St Brendan and, Muldoon's precursor, Mael Dúin), setting off on 'a night-journey by sea', referring more clearly in her case to a trip into the psyche or subconscious.[147] The envisioned destination is Hy-Brazil, an Atlantis of true-selfhood, a part-Pagan, part-Christian buried land where contraries combine and polarities pull together.[148] The poet is very aware that such a journey towards 'individuation' may sound Jungian and out of date, or utopian and naïve; that such an island could appear as sheer fantasy or illusion. However, she plays on these apparent weaknesses in her 'vision' by stressing their repetition and variation throughout the ages among various peoples. In her view, other more rationalist notions of 'progress', for example, have merely led the human race to the hells of the Holocaust and Cambodia, and 'brought us no closer to Mount Sion'. For Ní Dhomhnaill, therefore, it follows that other forms of knowledge (pre-, trans-, non-rational), including native or tribal lore and 'meat of the tongue', can or may

---

[146] 'After all, it's my car.' See 'Mise ag Tiomáint'/I'm Doing the Driving, *PD* p. 102.
[147] This symbolism recalls Ó Ríordáin's poem 'Múscail do Mhisneach', *Brosna*, 19.
[148] de Paor, P., *Tionscnamh Filíochta Nuala Ní Dhomhnaill*, 94.

offer humanity a better path to travel through the woods of existence and of the mind:

> Seo thíos uainn an crosaire,
> crosaire na gceithre rianta. Tá an bóthar ar chlé ag dul
> go Cathair na nGairdíní. Tógaimis an bóthar ar dheis
> go Cé na mBád.
>
> *You see where the four roads meet there down below?*
> *The left goes to the Garden City. The right takes us to the ferry*
> (*AC* p. 74)

The 'right' road may well be the one not to the 'gardens' but to Cé na mBád/The Boat Quay from which one enters the dangerous but compelling and unavoidable waters of the unconscious.

The poem repeatedly contrasts different types of knowledge: that which can be formulated and pinpointed, wriggling on a wall or chart like Eliot's Prufrock, and a more intuitive, instinctive lore of the tribe that tells you, for example, that the relative proximity of Hy-Brazil is 'a sure sign of rain'. These two types of knowledge (like this world and the next) are brought ever closer together—if not shown to overlap—in Ní Dhomhnaill's poetry. For example, while she associates men with the world of 'everyday consciousness and action', and women with 'the other world, other levels of consciousness native to their gender and outside patriarchal law',[149] she generally seeks to combine and balance these 'worlds' or world-views which, taken singly, seem insufficient.

For example, Ní Dhomhnaill criticizes masculinist imbalances in the psyche and in society when she associates men, in her poetry, with the dry, non-mouth-watering, 'proper Irish' of politicians (*AC* p. 84), or with the thankless O'Sheas more interested in oilskin than female skin (*AC* p. 100), or, worst of all, with what Louise Bourgeois might call the 'no-marcher' of 'Beirt Fhear/Two Men' (*AC* p. 102) whose negativity and hot temper sparks a 'hullabaloo' that ultimately makes the boat miss the island, and the island miss the boat—and, therefore, this world the other world—forever.[150] Men are mocked and cajoled throughout 'Immram/The Voyage' for their talk about paramilitary 'Boys being Boys'/'gaiscíocht pharaimíleatach' (*AC* p. 74), their poor taste in words (*AC* p. 92) and even poetry: preferring, for example, a stuffed and

---

[149] Ibid. 96.
[150] Ní Dhomhnaill, 'A Ghostly Alhambra', in T. Hayden (ed.), *Irish Hunger: Personal Reflections on the Legacy of the Famine* (Dublin: Wolfhound Press, 1997), 68–78 (p. 78).

clichéd yellow bittern (*AC* p. 94) to perhaps something more fantastic and imaginative such as a griffin.

Even past masters like Ó Ríordáin and Ó Direáin receive a tweak on the beak. Ní Dhomhnaill's trees, for example, in 'Coco-de-Mer' are nothing like Ó Direáin's 'crainn seasta'/stalwart, still-standing trees, and her island is populated by male *and female* trees none of which are as ascetic as those in Ó Ríordáin's 'Oileán agus Oileán Eile'/One Island and Another:

> Ach de réir an scéil oíche amháin sa bhliain
> craitear cré de sheanphréamhacha nuair a éiríonn na crainn,
> gluaiseann i bhfochair a chéile
> is téann i mbun gnímh.
>
> *One night in the year, however,*
> *they shake the mud off their roots and veer*
> *towards each other*
> *for a bit of how's your father.* (*AC* pp. 90–1)

This poem alone typifies how Ní Dhomhnaill's 'island' (and word-journey) with its folkloric rituals, cross-fertilizations, linguistic daring and humour, transgressive, panoramic, and multitudinous perspectives is a more enjoyable and imaginative destination than that offered by her more repressed (mostly male) predecessors.

The Feis section continues with the title-poem: an eleven-part poem of love and loss that tells explicitly of the attainment of communion or intercourse between traditionally masculine (sky or air) and feminine ('mother'-earth) realms, but also of what Bourgeois sees as the non-durability of fulfilment, the transient nature of the mechanism of seduction.[151] Sublunary love is, according to these artists, passionate in both the pleasurable and painful sense. In 'Feis', for example, to convey the intensity of the speaker's suffering and endurance, Ní Dhomhnaill takes recourse, in sections *vi* and *vii*, to the repetition and triplism of the ancient Celtic triad for its magical and sacred power:

> Leagaim síos trí bhrat id fhianaise: *I lay down three robes for you:*
> brat deora,   *a mantle of tears,*
> brat allais,   *a coat of sweat,*
> brat fola.   *a gown of blood.* (*AC* p. 14)

---

[151] Meyer-Thoss, *Louise Bourgeois*, 127 and 129.

Miranda J. Greene writes that for the Celts, triple repetition symbolized not only intensity but also totality in either time (past, present, and future) or space (behind, before, and here, or else sky, earth, and underworld).[152] In 'Feis', it is the female presence who loves/worships the male wholly and completely, while his commitment is to another. This leaves the female speaker quite literally unfulfilled, and the poem itself seeming—deliberately—incomplete:

Nuair a d'fhágas tú	*When I left you*
ar an gcé anocht	*at the quay tonight*
d'oscail trinse ábhalmhór	*an enormous trench opened up*
istigh im ucht	*in my core*
chomh doimhin sin	*so profound*
ná líonfar	*it would not be filled*
fiú dá ndáilfí	*even if you were to pour*
as aon tsoitheach	*from one utensil*
Sruth na Maoile, Muir Éireann	*the streams of the Mull of Kintyre*
agus Muir nIocht.	*and the Irish Sea and the English Channel.*[153]

In 'Toircheas',[154] the final part of the Feis section, we find that (unknown at first to the speaker) a seed has been planted and that some kind of birth or off-spring is imminent. The poem spans a somewhat surreal and uncertain incubation period in which plant and animal imagery designating life is juxtaposed with contrasting images of death in a way that recalls—including for Ní Dhomhnaill—her 'chéad ghiotaí filíochta'/first pieces of poetry such as 'Sabhaircíní i Samhain/ Primroses in November' (*DD* p. 11).

The first and last sections of 'Toircheas', for example, contain the detail of some ducks which have escaped the guns of male hunters. The flight of the ducks marks the arrival of Spring, the season of new birth. What is borne and, indeed, beginning to be born in this poem is, in Ní Dhomhnaill's metaphorical terms, the child or new birth, 'the

---

[152] Greene, Miranda J., *Dictionary of Celtic Myth and Legend* (London: Thames and Hudson Ltd., 1992), 214.

[153] See *AC* p. 18–19. My sense of the poem as formally, and deliberately, incomplete is based on the fact that it contains eleven and not twelve stanzas which would, being a multiple of three, better satisfy a Celt, echo the many twelves of the Bible, including Stations of the Cross, the apostles; and recall the number of signs of the zodiac, the months, etc.

[154] The word 'toircheas' suggests, in English, conception, pregnancy, broodiness, expectation, burden, fruit of the womb, foetus, offspring, progeny, etc.

potential, the image for the new or future dispensation'.[155] This could refer to the gift of art from the unconscious and/or to the development of the poet or individual, transforming cailleach or hag energy (following the visitation, in the poem 'Feis' of 'an leannán sí'/the faery lover) into that of 'an spéirbhean' or the goddess (sky or air-borne woman), the name given to the ultimate section of the volume as a whole.

4.2.4 Spéirbhean

Transition to An Spéirbhean/the goddess section of *Feis*, and to the state or condition associated with the 'skywoman' (in Jungian terms, individuation) is marked by a slow psychic transformation presented in natural, classical images of Winter turning into Spring: for example, it is 'only with the arrival of softer Spring weather' or 'Venus' herself that birds, plants, and poet-speaker are finally coaxed out of their shells, as in the poem 'Primavera'.[156]

Pádraig de Paor reads this seasonal transition or resurrection motif in Ní Dhomhnaill's poetry as a clear instance of the growing influence of Jung's theories on her vision and work:

Is dán é seo ['Primavera'] a chuireann síos ar shaolú an anama, ar fhuascailt an anama ó ghréim an ábhair, agus dá réir, ó ghréim an bháis. Tugtar an tsíoraíocht ar an réimse sin taobh amuigh den am líneach a shamhlaítear an bás agus an t-ábhar léi. De réir an smaointeoireachta Jungaí seo, agus de réir an rómánsachais go ginearálta, is gné de chuid an tsaoil seo, an saol daonna gnáthlaethúil, an tsíoraíocht; ní chuirtear an bhéim ar shíoraíocht an tsaoil iarbháis.[157]

Ní Dhomhnaill's vision may be Jungian and Romantic in some ways but it is also closely related to earlier and continuing (Celtic, Latin, and other) world-views of, for example, non-linear time and of life-cycles which incorporate the seasonal and yearly turns of 'rotha mór an tsaoil'/the great

---

[155] Somerville Aryat and Wilson (eds.), *Sleeping with Monsters*, 151.

[156] See Ní Dhomhnaill, 'Mis and Dubh Ruis', 201.

[157] '["Primavera"] is a poem that describes the birth of the soul, the release of the soul from materiality and death. Eternity is the name given to the realm outside of linear time associated with death and materialism. According to this Jungian thought, and Romanticism in general, eternity is an aspect of this everyday human world; eternity after death is not stressed at all.' See de Paor, P., *Tionscnamh Filíochta Nuala Ní Dhomhnaill*, 116.

wheel of life. 'What happens in poetry', according to the Polish poet Jan Polkowski, is 'the original rotational force of this earth.'[158] Similarly, following her own real-life experience of seeing an imperious-looking eagle overhead, reminding her in turn of an earlier sighting of seven white pelicans which appeared to her immediately as a flock of pterodactyls, Ní Dhomhnaill writes in 'Heracleia' that 'three hundred million years can pass/in the blink of an eye (no thanks to Einstein/i bhfáiteadh na súl imíonn trí chéad milliún bliain thar bráid, gan buíochas d'Einstein' (*F* p. 127).

Among Ní Dhomhnaill's finest achievements as a poet is her ability to stand 'behind a million pair of eyes' and show us how she sees[159] things such as three hundred million years go by at a blink, and to bring these past and other (magical and divine, subconscious and imaginative) worlds and possibilities to our attention.[160] Often, her poetry, like a good béaloideas tale, leaves the reader feeling like the children in 'Loch a' Dúin':

> Ní raibh aon ghá a thuilleadh a bheith ag cumadh scéil dóibh,
> rith a samhlaíocht thar cuimse.
> Bhí fathaigh, manaigh, lucht na Craoibhe Rua
> acu suite ar aon bhinse.
>
> *There was no longer any need for my story-telling art*
> *now that their own imaginations ran riot*
> *and giants, monks, and the Knights of the Red Branch*
> *jostled each other on one bench.* (*AC* pp. 68–9)

One may wonder if the poet's children really do tell her (in so many words) *not* to 'ceil orainn ár ndúchas féinig, na treabhchaisí a tháinig romhainn/gloss over our heritage [. . .] draw a veil over those who were our forefathers' (*AC* p. 64), but she certainly feeds their—and her readers'—great hunger for 'meat of the tongue' which she continues to serve up with more natural relish and imaginative sauce than even the great 'Chef Yeats' his 'celebrated Anglo-Irish stew'.[161]

Nietzsche wrote that

---

[158] Pirie, D. (ed.), *Young Poets of a New Poland: an Anthology* (London: Forest Books, 1993), 76.

[159] I am paraphrasing David Bowie, 'Song for Bob Dylan', *Hunky Dory* (London: RCA Records, 1971).

[160] See, for example, 'An Sceach Gheal/The Whitethorn Bush' (*AC* p. 58), 'An Bád Sí/The Fairy Boat' and 'Loch a' Dúin' (*AC* pp. 60–71).

[161] Michael Hartnett, 'A Farewell to English', *A Farewell to English*, 30–5 (p. 32).

Man today, stripped of myth, stands famished among all his pasts and must dig frantically for roots, be it among the most remote antiquities. What does our great historical hunger signify . . . if not the loss of myth, of a mythic home, the mythic womb.[162]

Are Ní Dhomhnaill's motherly attempts to quell that hunger Romantic, as de Paor occasionally suspects,[163] or 'romantic' in the general sense? I feel that while Ní Dhomhnaill's work contains elements of Romanticism in, for example, its rejection of rationalism and recourse to dreams, the unconscious and various aboriginal or tribal perspectives, it also displays a hard-earned, hard-nosed realism. Even in a short, relatively optimistic poem such as 'Caora Fíniúna'/Grapeseed Wine,[164] she echoes Ó Ríordáin's grim acceptance that a half-mind grinds nothing and that human life in its entirety demands (as in Plath's poetry) painful, alchemical grinding and transformation in order to survive and make the best wine out of life or art. This idea found its clearest expression in Ní Dhomhnaill's more recent poem 'Epithalamium':

> Ach cuimhním ansan nach cuing ach gur soitheach í an pósadh
> ina gcuirtear na mothúcháin faoi theannasaí is brú
> is mura bpléascann sé go gclaochlaítear an dá phearsain
> mar chloch éibhir, atá deacair le hídiú.
>
> *But then I remember that marriage isn't a chain but a vessel*
> *in which feelings are put under strain and pressure,*
> *and if it doesn't go bust, the two people are changed*
> *like a granite-stone that's hard to do away with.*[165]

It is also important to note that Ní Dhomhnaill does not necessarily 'romanticize' the past either. In 'Béaloideas III', she highlights an earlier and unacceptable attitude to women which she only recalls in order to condemn. She is, therefore, a truly post-modern *bricoleuse* or builder, an unapologetically *à la carte* Pagan chef who *includes* certain neglected ingredients from the past *or* present in order to produce a more whole-

---

[162] Friedrich Nietzsche, *The Birth of Tragedy, and, The Genealogy of Morals* (New York/Toronto: Doubleday Anchor Books, 1956), 137.

[163] de Paor, P., *Tionscnamh Filíochta Nuala Ní Dhomhnaill*, 280.

[164] *F* p. 113. This poem, moreover, comes from the Spéirbhean section of *Feis* where individuation, self-presence, and self-content is supposedly attained. For Ó Ríordáin, see 'A Theanga Seo Leath-Liom'/Half-With-Me Language, *Brosna*, 25.

[165] See Rumens C., *Brangle: Essays, Reviews and Poetry from N. Ireland and Beyond*, 2 (London: Brangle Publications, 1997), 46–8.

some soul-food, or poetry, than is already available. Is that necessarily a sentimental wish on the part of any artist?

Philip O'Leary worries that a note of sentimentality creeps into the final poem of *Feis*, 'Éirigh a Éinín'/Rise, Little Bird (*PD* p. 28) even though he feels that the poem's 'wary optimism' may well have been earned by the volume's overall design which reflects a difficult four-part transformation, transition, or journey towards individuation and transcendence, 'salvific light'.[166] In my view, however, there is very little chance that sentimentality could outweigh the wariness and awareness of danger, death, and depression in almost any Ní Dhomhnaill poem. For example, the little bird in the title of 'Éirigh, a Éinín' has to 'rise' precisely because s/he is 'down' in the first place; the reason that the poet-speaker sings at all is that 'cé gur mór é mo bhrón [níl] teora le ceolta an tsaoil'/although my grief is great, there is no limit to life's music; if the cows in the poem stand up to their ears in grass, they still have to face the butcher and liver-fluke; the poem's head-scarved pilgrims may be praying for a special dispensation but only because they sorely need it and, moreover, their petition involves the ritual of a struggle against the August sun and heat; most tragic of all is the plight of the depressed mother painfully out walking her handicapped child. This woman sorely needs, it is implied, the singing bird and her own laughing child to help her see through the everyday gloom to a 'fuinneog sa spéir'/window in the sky;[167] to the light (as well as dark) which one sees with 'misneach is ciall'/courage and sense in moments of vision.

Bearing 'witness to the joy *and* the pain/of living' (*PD* p. 28), Ní Dhomhnaill's work is generally saved from sentimentality because her vision is inclusive, not exclusive, admits whole, and not part, truths. Sandra Schneiders writes that

the word which has progressively come to serve as a cipher for feminist spirituality is 'interconnectedness'. [Many feminists seek] ways to reunify [that which] has been divided by the all-pervasive dichotomous dualism of the patriarchal system, to replace the win–lose, either–or, we–they, in–out, right–wrong bases of mutual destruction with a both-and inclusiveness which will both achieve and be achieved by reconnecting that which has been separated.[168]

[166] O'Leary, P., 'A Night With Nuala', 22–3 (p. 23).
[167] Ní Dhomhnaill, 'An Fhilíocht á Cumadh', 149.
[168] Quoted in O'Connor, M., 'Lashings of the Mother Tongue', 168.

Ní Dhomhnaill has likewise, throughout her work, consciously and unconsciously highlighted the union of opposites, the co-existence and interdependence of diverse elements: we are reminded in 'Cú Chulainn I' that men *and* women both 'come from wombs' (*SP/RD* p. 112); in poems such as 'Parthenogenesis' (*SP/RD* p. 132), Pagan *and* Christian myths combine; in 'An Ollmháthair Mhór/Great Mother' (*SP/RD* p. 58), the urgent need for science and nature to work *in tandem* is stressed; and in 'Caoineadh Mhoss Mháirtín/Lament for Moss Martin (*PD* p. 44), the poet declares that the best music is that which matches or follows the highs *and* lows of what happens, 'an aiteas is an phian'/the joy and the pain.

Similarly, in Ní Dhomhnaill's poetry there are often striking *combinations* of contrasting images: for example, the colourful, earthy mix of blood and honey in 'Oileán/Island' (*SP/RD* p. 70) and 'An Bhabóg Bhriste/The Broken Doll' (*SP/RD* p. 90); the sensuous, aromatic blend of eastern spices, honey, and original Irish musk in 'Venio ex Oriente' (*SP/RD* p. 26); and also the grotesque, mysterious milk-well in cow-dung dug by Suibhne in 'Muirghil ag Cáiseamh Shuibhne/Muirghil Castigates Sweeny' (*SP/RD* p. 128).

That final, resonant, earthy image stands out like many of the images and transgressive combinations of images which render Ní Dhomhnaill's poems objects 'that fascinate and enthral, not merely [. . .] edify or entertain',[169] each one a gift from the subconscious 'that can be pondered, worried over, wondered at, told over and over again, [which] because of its deeply symbolic significance [. . .] never loses anything in the telling'.[170]

CONCLUSION

Ní Dhomhnaill's work has met with an enthusiastic response at home both in the original Irish and/or in English language translation, and abroad, mostly in translation. However, two major criticisms have been made against some of the poet's working methods.

---

[169] Sontag quoted in Cole, Ian, 'Brokering Madness', n.p. Essay/programme notes for the exhibition *Louise Bourgeois: Sculpture*, 22 November to 19 December 1996 at the Museum of Modern Art Oxford. Essay ref. no. DH/g.

[170] Ní Dhomhnaill, 'Mis and Dubh Ruis', 199. Ní Dhomhnaill's description of béaloideas tales which could just as easily apply to her own poems.

In a review of *Spíonáin is Róiseanna*,[171] Gabriel Rosenstock, a fellow poet of the *INNTI* generation, questions Ní Dhomhnaill's favouring of certain Irish words over others (for example, 'greidhlic' rather than 'cabáiste faille' for 'samphire'[172]) and, in particular, her common use of béarlachas or Englishisms such as 'airtisióc'/artichoke. Worse still, he finds that she uses English itself ('grapefruit') when Irish ('seadóg') would do.[173]

Mary O'Connor, on the other hand, writes that Ní Dhomhnaill's use of language is not only representative of current macaronic usage but deliberately transgressive, simultaneously bearing and sending up the 'effects of colonization and the consequent muddying of the linguistic waters' in true Irish comic tradition.[174] One must also add that Ní Dhomhnaill's diction also largely stems from the fact that she is very much a *sound* poet for whom the rhythm and music of words and lines form as integral a part of a poem as the sense, and often come first.[175] To establish this fact, one need only listen to her recording of 'Ag Tiomáint Siar'/Driving West or even 'Éirigh, a Éinín'/Rise, Little Bird where 'grapefruit' and not 'seadóg' is mentioned.[176] In the latter example, both words have two syllables and may appear interchangeable, especially to a speaker of Ulster Irish who would stress the first syllable in both cases. Ní Dhomhnaill chooses to use the loan-word 'grapefruit', however, because she would stress the -óg in seadóg, which would (if used) upset the rhythm of her line. In addition, she evidently wanted to play the 'g' and 'gr' sounds of 'grapefruit' off the 'c' and 'cr' sounds of 'cíocha . . . córach . . . cruinn' and even 'cíor gruaige' in the next line. The word 'grapefruit' may also, I suspect, be preferred by Ní Dhomhnaill because, in her terms, it is as tasty a word as 'greidhlic'— not merely because of its sound (*AC* p. 92) but mainly due to the fact that it is an agglutination of two mouth-watering words and images: grape and fruit.

The other most significant criticism levelled at Ní Dhomhnaill to

---

[171] Ní Dhomhnaill, *Spíonáin is Róiseanna*, a cassette and booklet of selected poems (Indreabhán: Cló Iar-Chonnachta, 1993).
[172] See 'Greidhlic/Samphire', Part 10 of 'Immram', *AC* p. 92.
[173] See 'Gabriel Rosenstock Reviews Nuala Ní Dhomhnaill', *Poetry Ireland*, 39 (Autumn 1993), 102–9 (p. 104).
[174] O'Connor, M., 'Lashings of the Mother Tongue', 153.
[175] Ní Dhomhnaill, 'An Fhilíocht á Cumadh', 164 and 177.
[176] Ní Dhomhnaill, *Spíonáin is Róiseanna*.

date is Seán Ó Tuama's comment that none of the poems dealing with primordial images from the subconscious through the use of story-telling or narrative devices have made a deep impression on him.[177] Ó Tuama appears to echo Ó Ríordáin's belief that narrative poetry is not really poetry at all.[178] Moreover, he asserts that Ní Dhomhnaill lacks some of the seanchaí's talents for short-cutting, speed, and manoeu-vre;[179] that she is too caught up in her Jungian 'système' or framework which he recognizes as the scaffolding behind her work which allows her to build but also as a limitation; lastly, he finds that Ní Dhomhnaill is sometimes too lax and conversational in her approach, 'imithe thar fóir ar fad le seamanna béaloidis nó [shílfeá] go raibh sí ró-mhór beag beann ar an dtuiscint gur ceard í an fhilíocht'.[180] Despite all of these reservations, however, he concludes that she has produced the 'most amazing body of work' in Irish or English of her generation.[181]

Are Ní Dhomhnaill's primordial images unmemorable? For Philip O'Leary, the 'earth mother gone wrong' in 'Cailleach/Hag' is a terrify-ing and unforgettable image.[182] For me, the Freddy Kruger-like steel-clawed hag of 'Mise an Fia/I am a Deer' (*SP/RD* p. 18), the sphinx (*SP/RD* p. 100), and the female image rising in 'Aois na Cloiche'/The Stone Age (*F* p. 24) and in 'Beihoiméit' (*F* p. 37), for example, all stand out immediately from her oeuvre, though I admit that the latter pair post-date Ó Tuama's comments.

As for Ní Dhomhnaill's story-telling ability, she is a poet foremost, one who borrows from seanchaí style and imagery but still, I feel, does so successfully as the poem 'Mise an Fia/I am a Deer' and her retelling of the 'Mis and Dubh Ruis' story indicate.[183] Her Jungian système, moreover, can hardly be seen as 'un arrêt', as Ó Tuama (in part) claims, since what characterizes her work more than anything else is movement:

---

[177] Seán Ó Tuama's essay on Ní Dhomhnaill's work is full of praise and constructive criticism but begins, curiously, with a homage to Michael Davitt without whom (Ó Tuama writes) 'Ní Dhomhnaill may not have found her voice in time, nor managed to complete her work to date'. See Ó Tuama, S., 'Filíocht Nuala Ní Dhomhnaill: "An Mháthair Ghrámhar is an Mháthair Ghránna" ina Cuid Filíochta', in P. Ó Fiannachta (ed.), *Léachtaí Cholm Cille XVII*, 95–116 (p. 96).

[178] Ó Coileáin, S., *Seán Ó Ríordáin: Beatha agus Saothar* (Dublin: An Clóchomhar Tta, 1982, 1985), 155.

[179] Ó Tuama, 'Filíocht Nuala Ní Dhomhnaill', 113–14.

[180] 'Carried away too far with bursts of béaloideas or with too little heed to the fact that poetry is a craft'. Ó Tuama, 'Filíocht Nuala Ní Dhomhnaill', 114.

[181] Ibid. 116.   [182] O'Leary, 'A Night with Nuala', 22–3.

[183] See *SP/RD* p. 18 and Ní Dhomhnaill, 'Mis and Dubh Ruis'.

even when she, or one of her many representative (female) characters or narrators, looks or falls into the colder depths of the subconscious and is 'frozen' or turned to stone, she still manages to shrug her 'rock-shoulders' and move her tongue forward and back—even if it has been turned into a block.[184]

This courage and triumph over depression in Ní Dhomhnaill's work is what makes it so 'suaithinseach'/amazing, rare and, in another sense, moving. Normally, in Irish folklore and béaloideas, on the rare occasions when a woman is rescued and returned from the lios or abyss, she is left dumb.[185] Ní Dhomhnaill, Ó Tuama concedes, far from being dumb, is prolific.[186] Consequently, it appears that her Jungian *système* is more a *foundation* than limitation.

Finally, Ó Tuama's concern that some poems lack craft or are too conversational (a concern which I previously raised once myself[187]) is a classic example of the then contemporary male critic being unprepared for the necessary and natural transgressions of a female artist's work.[188] For example, in 'Hotline' (*PD* p. 100) which seems, on the surface, to be a formally lax poem, the freer, more conversational form is actually drawn from the content and context in order to create the illusion of authenticity, to place the reader in the position of someone listening in, as the title suggests, to a telephone call. In such ways, Ní Dhomhnaill shows, time and time again, that she does pay heed to the craft of poetry by exploring the possibilities of new fusions of form and content.[189]

In another poem, 'Na Trí Shraoth/The Three Sneezes' (*AC* p. 52), one may wonder at the three unsightly longer than average lines that stick out like three sore thumbs but it appears that the poet was so taken with the natural flow of speech within them that she refused to box them into a more regular stanza shape like the 'square baby' which Plath imagines lurking in 'The Arrival of the Bee-Box'.[190] Ní Dhomhnaill could, if she wished, have shortened the lines

---

184 'Aois na Cloiche'/Stone Age, *F* p. 24.
185 O'Connor, M. 'Lashings of the Mother Tongue', 160.
186 Ó Tuama, 'Filíocht Nuala Ní Dhomhnaill', 114.
187 Frank Sewell, 'Subconscious Voyager', *Fortnight*, 316 (April 1993), 49.
188 Morgan, 'Louise Bourgeois: Nature Study', 1.
189 See Ní Dhomhnaill, 'An Fhilíocht á Cumadh', 169–73.
190 See MacMonagle, N. (ed.), *Lifelines*, 145.

> bhíodar chomh scaimhte sin chuige nár bhraitheadar
> mé ag tréigean in aghaidh lae[191]

to

> bhíodar chomh scaimhte sin
> nár bhraitheadar mé ag tréigean[192]

but she obviously did not think that such formal revision was necessary or desirable for the sake of regular form alone.

I am not sure that I would agree, in this particular case, with Ní Dhomhnaill's decision to leave in the three longer than average lines (which seem to burst out of their bounds as suddenly and unexpectedly as the great grandmother's 'three sneezes'). However, while Ní Dhomhnaill's formal transgressions may very occasionally disconcert the more conservative (usually male) critic, she has, much more importantly, continually produced, in Irish, original and stunning poetry that is, as she would wish, 'alive alive-o'.[193] Moreover, one reason why Ní Dhomhnaill's poetry is so 'beo beathúch/alive, alive-oh' is precisely *because* it flows so fluidly from conversational 'caint na ndaoine', the multivoiced carnivalesque of her people's speech.

---

[191] 'They were so self-absorbed [greedy] that they did not notice/me fading away day by day', *AC* p. 52.

[192] 'They were so self-absorbed/they did not notice me fading [declining]', *AC* p. 52.

[193] Ní Dhomhnaill, 'The English for Irish', 116–18 (p. 117).

Conclusion: A Polish Perspective

Abstract thought [. . .] returns in difficult moments (i.e., politically difficult[1]) to folk wisdom, peasant motifs proverbs, legends or songs—and even technological folk traditions. Often, it is too late, and the backbone with its marrow uniting the total sum of work in a given nation disintegrates into *remembrances of the past* and *longings for the future*.[2]

The socio-historical and aesthetic philosophy of the poet Cyprian Norwid has neither dated nor shrunk in significance in or outside his native Poland.[3] Norwid stressed the role of 'peripheries'—what we would now call the 'margins' or marginalized. These, he said, proved to be 'stumbling blocks' for the supposedly more 'advanced civilizations'.[4] Two examples which he gave were 'for America—the Negro, for England—Ireland'. Norwid, in fact, is a precursor of post-colonial theory, particularly in his belief that 'every epoch passes over something in silence, and that which remains beneath the surface, inadmissible to the consciousness of one era, becomes a motive power in the next.'[5]

Yet, the question remains: what if it is too late? What if too many people have died, been silenced, exiled, or have emigrated? What if, as a North American tribesperson once said to me, 'the hoop of the nation is broken' or, as Norwid put it, 'it is too late, and the backbone with its marrow uniting the total sum of work in a given nation disintegrates into remembrances of the past and longings for the future'?

When I began this study, it was partly to find an answer to questions such as these. I knew that Irish literature in English was in a healthy and productive condition but I wondered about literature in Irish and about how they both fitted in to a national tradition. I found that Norwid's

---

[1] Also *personally* difficult moments.

[2] Cyprian Norwid (1821–1883), a Polish emigré poet and intellectual. See Milosc, C., *The History of Polish Literature* (London: Macmillan, 1969), 266–80 (p. 274).

[3] Ibid.

[4] Once asked what he thought of 'Western civilization', Gandhi replied: 'it would be a very good idea'.

[5] Norwid. See Milosc, *The History of Polish Literature*, 273.

prophecy was coming true in that Irish language and literature, once 'passed over in silence' and 'inadmissible', were now increasingly recognized as a 'motive force' in themselves and as a positive force in terms of their confluence with Irish writing in English.

The next question was: what shape was the 'backbone' of Irish literature taking if people were adding new bones and marrow (their own, in fact[6]) to it? What kind of creature or monster were they making? An old sow that eats her farrow? Or a Great Irish Elk? Perhaps a beast with two heads, one full of 'remembrances of the past', and the other with 'longings for the future'?

I found that Irish writers were faced with a choice: to go on waking Finnegan forever, mourning 'a lost tuath',[7] or else to engage in what Derrida describes as 'free play', and Lévi-Strauss, 'bricolage'.[8] In their own individual ways, as discussed in previous chapters, poets such as Seán Ó Ríordáin, Cathal Ó Searcaigh, Máirtín Ó Direáin and Nuala Ní Dhomhnaill are literary *bricoleurs* who build *anew* from the diverse and scattered materials and resources around them (including remnants of the past), modern constructs, 'bothanna',[9] buildings,[10] (literary) monuments; modern word-sculptures in which recycled material is an obvious contemporary feature; modern stanzas or 'rooms' full of life-music.

As for 'remembrances of the past and longings for the future', all people (and, therefore, poets) live, move, and struggle between the poles of past and future; tradition and individuality or contemporaneity; self and community, etc. If one looks closely, one finds that individuals and generations zig or zag into (for them) new directions, 'away from the known point',[11] so that the developing pattern or 'backbone' of a country's literature or culture, for example, is unpredictable in its shape.

The zig-zag, meanwhile, is an appropriate image for the *movement* of a national literature in its unpredictable direction. Irish literature, for

---

[6] Ní Dhomhnaill, 'An Ghríobh Ingneach'/The Griffin, *Feis*, 61.

[7] McDiarmid, L. and Durkan, M., 'Q. & A.: Nuala Ní Dhomhnaill', *Irish Literary Supplement* (Fall 1987), 41–3 (p. 43). 'Tuath' refers to tribe and homeland.

[8] Interpreted by Derrida as 'the necessity of borrowing one's concepts from the text of a heritage which is more or less coherent *or ruined*'. See Chapter 2, Introduction.

[9] Ó Ríordáin, 'Ceol'/Music, *Eireaball Spideoige*, 76–7.

[10] See Philip Larkin, 'To put one brick upon another', *Philip Larkin: Collected Poems*, ed. Anthony Thwaite, 2nd edn. (London: Marvell Press and Faber and Faber, 1990).

[11] Yuri Tynyanov. See Rylance, R. (ed.), 'Versions of Formalism', *Debating Texts: A Reader in Twentieth-century Literary Theory and Method*, 3rd edn. (Milton Keynes: Open University Press, 1990), 31–65 (p. 34).

example, has continued to move from one language (Irish) to another (English), between these languages, and between these two and other languages. Traffic between English and Irish may not always have been smooth but what Thomas Kinsella has called 'the old dividing idiocies' have given way to 'the two-tongued Irish tradition in its late twentieth-century manifestations' with 'two linguistic entities in dynamic interaction'.[12]

This interaction takes place in a broad church, the Alhambra of Ireland's art where the nightmare of history is being conducted to possible new awakenings in what one poet has called 'The Dream-Language of Fergus':

> so one river inserted into another
> becomes a leaping, glistening, splashed
> and scattered alphabet
> jutting out from the voice,
> till what began as a dog's bark
> ends with bronze, what began
> with honey ends with ice;
> as if an aeroplane in full flight
> launched a second plane,
> the sky is stabbed by their exits
> and the mistaken meaning of each.[13]

In this poem, Medbh McGuckian registers both the pain and the potential of language shifts, 'dí-lárú'/de-centring, changes and criss-crossings. She is yet another Irish writer who is concerned with and about language, its potential and vulnerability, its freedom to play and make new but also its openness to misinterpretation and exclusion.

Previously, James Stephens wrote that 'culture is a conversation between equals';[14] more recently, McGuckian has written that

> conversation is as necessary
> among these familiar campus trees
> as the apartness of torches.[15]

[12] Quotes from Kinsella. See Philip O'Leary, 'An Agile Cormorant: Poetry in Ireland Today', *Éire-Ireland*, No. XXIV: 4 (Winter 1989), 39–53 (pp. 44–5).

[13] McGuckian, M., 'The Dream-Language of Fergus', *Selected Poems 1978–1994* (Loughcrew: Gallery, 1997), 48–9.

[14] Stephens, J., 'The Outlook for Literature with Special Reference to Ireland', 1922, in M. Storey (ed.), *Poetry and Ireland Since 1800: A Source Book* (London: Routledge, 1988), 178–88 (p. 179).   [15] McGuckian, *Selected Poems*, 48–9.

Not only conversation is necessary but careful and attentive listening so that the hyphen, for example, in the out-dated term 'Anglo-Irish' does not continue to be used as an 'either/or' linguistic and cultural barrier or minus sign but, if at all, as a 'both/and' symbol of balance and confluence between Irish literature in English and in Irish—each an essential part of one country's tradition or 'Alhambra'.

Similarly co-essential and interdependent are the seemingly opposing forces of tradition and modernity. Berman, for example, claims that 'if modernism ever managed to throw off its scraps and tatters and the uneasy joints that bind it to the past, it would lose all its weight and depth, and the maelstrom of modern life would carry it helplessly away'.[16] This potentially abstract concept was powerfully personified or brought home to me during my researches into the literature and culture of one small region of Ireland, the Aran Islands, where I discovered two stories that have stayed in my mind ever since.

The first is the fictional tale of Martin Colman Tim's stallion that could not be tamed by its owner Michael Ó Direáin but which *was* tamed by George Galvin, an Aran cowboy back from the wild west of America whose native and traditional, modern and foreign, acquired skills combined to win him control and ownership of 'the best colt on the island'.[17] The second story is a true one:

A cliffman who had spent some years in America and forgotten his native skills fell to his death here once. He was being lowered down on a rope, and clumsily let himself turn away from the cliff so that the rope caught in a crevice. The team tried to jerk it free, and it broke.[18]

The first story suggests that you can go away to an important elsewhere, learn a new (foreign) skill or technique and bring it back home;[19] the second, that if you go away or deviate, you can also forget or lose some essential (traditional) skills. To paraphrase the Aran poet Máirtín Ó Direáin, the foreign light is all right so long as it doesn't drown or put out your own.[20]

---

[16] Berman, 'Modernism in New York', *All That is Solid Melts into Air: The Experience of Modernity*, 2nd edn. (London: Verso, 1983, repr. 1995), 287–348 (p. 346).

[17] O'Flaherty, Tom, *Aranmen All* (Dublin: The Sign of the Three Candles, 1934), 17–32 (p. 32).

[18] Robinson, Tim, *Stones of Aran: Pilgrimage*, 3rd edn. (London: Penguin, 1990), 101.

[19] See Larkin, P., 'The Importance of Elsewhere', *Collected Poems*, 104. See also Berman, M., *All That Is Solid Melts Into Air*, 333.

[20] Ó Direáin, M., 'Solas'/Light, *Craobhóg Dán* (Dublin: An Clóchomhar Tta, 1986), 23.

Appendix. Translations

A. FOR DANIEL CORKERY

Rise and sing our heart-felt thanks to he
who showed the way
and woke the deer of our poetry
from forests of years.

He made his soul an attentive ear
and listened without pity
(for himself, or any versifier)
until there fell

on today's strange-made floor
sweet-mouthed Eoghan,
Aindrias Mac Craith, Seán Clárach, Aodhgán:
a rain of poets.

He placed a gentle finger on Aodhgán's pulse,
trusted its vigour
and day dawned on an old mind-set
native to us.

He followed this band of poets
up the stairway
and walked the wide roads of Munster,
himself and Eoghan Rua.

He stole from them the ear of our race,
the ear of the rover;
poems no longer laboured
but were born immaculate.

I feel him listening always,
like another conscience;
his ear controls the vigour of my verse;
the service is hard.

Irish fading out in Ireland
and night spreading softly like a tale,
he listened for the natural beat of a verse
and heard the nation's heart loud and clear.
   ('Do Dhomhnall Ó Corcora', *ES* pp. 51–2)

B. JOYCE

I sent out a search-party to find
what was left of him in my sifted mind,
he who is as much part of myself
as the alphabet and gospels,

his distinct geometry
euclidizing my brain to the degree
that he is not himself anymore:
I am he, since I swallowed him, whole.

Tripping in his wake, I'm wracked;
his Latin formalism so exact
that when I think of him, I
am not I—ego subsides.

I've struggled over words with him
as harmony, the angeldemon,
mockpriest saying a mockmass
in the mockrobes of the abyss,

preaching the religion of heresy,
teaching the ten parodies
of his vocation—a turned back,
a classical unorthodoxy made perfect.

His sorcery is obscure:
yield to the angelic word,
seek beauty in the filthy,
consecrate shit with Rabelais,

steal every trick in the books,
pull without mercy your strokes,
and be a Holy Satan
kindling excommunications.

More jest or gesture than a person,
a dictionary making grammar bound,
an imagination preying on non-imagination,
he was a mock-abbot or -clown.
   ('Joyce', *TÉB* pp. 21–2)

C. ÚDAR

Is é dúirt an t-údar so
Ná scríobhfadh focal go
mBeadh Gaeilge ar a thoil aige.

Do chaith sé a óige mhoch
Is meán a aoise amach,
Is deireadh a laethanta,
Ag tóraíocht Gaolainne.

Ansan fuair bás de gheit,
Díreach is í aige.

AUTHOR/EXPERT

There was this author who said
he wouldn't write a word
ill he'd 'the tongue' in his head
and mastered.

He flew through his youth,
burnt his middle age out,
and, on his last legs,
kept up his quest for Irish.

He found it in the end
but died as he did.

(*TÉB* p. 20)

D. THE NOOSE NEAREST THE NECK

I see the man before me,
his agony and death

but I can easily put off
his agony and death;
if I don't,
I won't last;
the pain of the man round me now
is enough.

Although I am the man out there,
he is not me yet;
and I don't care about his plight
when the me I am today
doesn't have to put up with it.

And though blood is thicker than water,
I don't feel sorry for myself,
out there:

every last me is discarded, drained;
and those to come—every me of them is strange.

Every single me
has trouble enough himself.
    ('An Gad is Giorra don Scornach', *TÉB* p. 28)

E. TAILED

She found she was a cat.
Nothing strange about that,
she'd always been a cat
—four-footed, quiet,
tail sticking out of her arse,
seeing at night, scratching,
sharp claws, miaows,
supple as a river is.

If I was a turncat,
I'd find it odd,
the scratching awkward,
the tail, the miaows . . .
I can't really imagine it.

But my hand's not strange,
I'm really into it;
and my arse is no stranger,
it's like my brain here,
it makes me an intellectual
but to be catalyzed (name and all)
is way beyond my ken.
A tail and paw
is too far out for me, man.

Maybe you'd grow into it,
if you wore it discreetly,
strand by strand until
it fitted and you were tail-
ored, catinually.

('Eireablú', *TÉB* pp. 25–6)

TRANSLATIONS FROM THE IRISH OF
CATHAL Ó SEARCAIGH (CHAPTER 2)

F. SWEENEY'S EYES

I'm drawing near the top of Bealtaine,
black-hearted as the night, climbing
sloping brows of land and mind,
pushed back by the bitter wind.

She was my treasure, my Gort a' Choirce.
I brought her from wildness to cultivation
but her natural bent is coming back to her;
there's yellow-eyed weeds in the field of love.

I see Venus above Dún Lúiche,
winking her eye, coming on and coming on;
and suspended over the black dress of sky,
the moon like a breast Mucais has cupped.

Through light and dark, Bealtaine flames,
I squeeze sideways in one mad rush.
Lights in the glen shiver before me—
under the lids of those hills: Sweeney's eyes.

('Súile Shuibhne', OO pp. 50–1)

G. PASSION

I'd rather have the boy behind the bar
whose heart warms to love's occasion,

who speaks in flames
about disappointments and poems,

his laugh as consuming
as the slit in broken turf,

his eyes firing sparks
that light my tinder passion,

than Nefertiti herself in my bed
and the wonders of the Pharaohs about the house.

('Dúil', OO p. 96)

H. THE DEEP

The deep tugs at him and the crowd wait.
All he has to do is put his foot out, spread
his arms, jump and swim into the wind,
let himself go in the welcoming currents
above Alltar. For everyone, the day is fine,
a haze rises from roofs and pools, life swells.
This is no time for death, you would think,
but growth. They look up, a crowd of strangers
and friends, the tight rope of understanding

binding them in shared pain, pushing them
unsparingly into mortal grief. All together
alone, bare and weak in their own presence,
they stare up at him, out there on the edge,
and all the time they are staring at the deep
in themselves; the deep defiantly tugging them
like a demon from within, driving them out
of their minds. Soon they all grow dizzy,
caught-up in the halter of Fate where the talk
and poise, business and bluff of their lives
is only a last-ditch defence, a wall of noise,
against the deep; the deep tugging at them.

       (from 'An Duibheagán', *OO* pp. 228–31)

I. THE PINK LILY

The force I feel to express myself in a form of words—
    the lily has no call for.
She doesn't need any verbal art to reveal or identify
    herself.
Enough for her to be as she is—secure and set, staying put
    and placid, there in her clay vase.
She speaks for herself and she does so perfectly, in her shape
    and nature, scent and silence.
If I step too near, I make her tense and tremble.
    All feeling she is—as she watches;
her pure, scarlet soul taking in and glowing with life.
    Has this flower overpowered me? Drugged or bewitched me?
No. It's not that I want to be a lily exactly, even though
    I'd be happy with that fate
in some future incarnation or afterlife before me.
    All I want now
is to be as much in tune with my humanity
    as that lily with her lily-ness.
All I want is to be as much of a man as that lily
    is a lily—the lily in the pink.

       (from 'An Lilí Bhándearg', *OO* pp. 236–9)

TRANSLATIONS FROM THE IRISH OF
MÁIRTÍN Ó DIREÁIN (CHAPTER 3)

J. THE SHORE FISHERMEN

Listen to the horn sounding
its threat of war against your custom,
East it comes from the city,
the death-knell of your custom.

Don't hanker for the sea anymore
but turn your back on her soon
and turn to the churchyard, the land,
you're not far now from your doom [literally, 'grave'].
(from 'Iascairí an Chladaigh', *D* p. 67)

K. CRY FOR YOURSELF WOMAN

It was pure bad luck
that man happened your way.
He was always a bad article,
a bad sign, anyway.

Your heart turned to stone
when he put in your ear the mite
that turned your life-milk sour
and curdled away your life.

For he is one of the dark ones
who find the night-time bright.
Night and the twisted whisper
are food and drink to his kind.

Cry for yourself now, woman!
It's your turn to weep for once.
I cried for you long ago
and now my tears are done.
('Caoin Tú Féin, a Bhean', *D* p. 54)

L. REFLECTION OF AN UPROOTED MAN

There's times I'm jealous
of the crowd that grew up
familiar with urban beauty,
cathedral, arch, tall building,
images finely carved in stone,
the work of learned painters
kept on show in our gallery,
and the sweet-stringed music
highly pleasing to the mind.

I still don't fully appreciate
these things I came to late:
all the primitive things
& the remains of ancient lore
my people shared by the fire
crowned my innocent heart
and fed my soul much more.

    ('Machnamh an Duine Stoite', *D* p. 200)

M. TO IRELAND IN THE COMING TIMES

He who bared his sword so high
for you in the Rising would be surprised—
to find he freed you from all that shame
for nothing, being an innocent man,
a warrior-poet not in it for the money,
his only reward—his sometime glory.
Soon, you'll have to sell his fame,
the way you had to before he came,
to every King Dick and Henry. . . .
Still, if you're to be known as a slapper,
make sure you do it good and proper:
sell him out and give what's his
to every dickhead out for business,
sell his prize and take to bed
some new lover by the money-belt,
for you're no longer Conn's or Eoghan's,
the love of Pearse or Óglaigh na hÉireann,
and since you are bound to do the deed,
Flower of the Fianna, I beg you, please,

don't sell yourself short in this matter:
only fuck for a fuck-load of dollars.
    ('Éire ina bhFuil Romhainn', *SP/TD* p. 96)

N. INSULT

From the back of his moped,
a smart-ass shot me
some nasty insult:
words that melted into air,
and I wish the same
on all else that comes out of him.

I'd bet you the same fella
had an education behind him
but I tell him no word of a lie
that I spent a share of my days
among decent people without 'learning'
or a word of his language.

They had no Certs., just
hand on pen and their mark
but I caught their speech in my net
because it'd be a pity to lose it;
pity I didn't catch more of it.
    ('Achasán', *D* p. 154)

TRANSLATIONS FROM THE IRISH OF
NUALA NÍ DHOMHNAILL (CHAPTER 4)

O. JOURNEY TO THE SHRINE

When she first appeared
on the sacred spot
with no rent, reason or regrets,
with or without anyone's permission,
she noticed the nods and winks, the whole to-do,
the big deal people made of it.
She heard them talking to each other
on their mobile phones,

asking yer Man in charge
what the hell they were supposed
to do with her.

'Let her be,' she heard him reply.
'But she doesn't know the way; or how long the journey is;
and she hasn't got a clue how things get done around here.'
'Let her be,' the answer came back immediately.
'She's a poet and, at the end of the day,
that lot have a sixth sense
about what to do when the way is dark.
I wouldn't be a bit surprised if there was
something like the shrine already built inside her.'

(from 'Turas na Scríne', Cead Aighnis, p. 37)

P. THE EXHUMATION

When my great-grandma's tomb
that was on my aunt's land
was re-opened, the aul' doll sat up
as wide-awake and welcoming
as ever she was in her own day.

She was hail and hearty
but just not the young thing
buried there first time around
when she was tragically lost
after her third child
a hundred odd years ago.

'I've seen you looking better,'
said the oldest man among us
who knew her vaguely
from way back
when he was still a boy.

'And no wonder,'
says she, cool as you like.
'Amn't I dead and buried
this hundred years or more?
And anyway,
you're no spring chicken yourself.'

We laughed, and were so delighted
with the miracle before us

that we shared out poteen,
mince pies and apples
with the crowds that came.

The tomb was to be closed again
on the third day
and she gave us solemn instructions
to clean and scrub it
from top to bottom
and not leave so much
as a speck of dirt.

If somebody's eye or nose
was to run, or dandruff drop
from the head of any one of us
then this world would impinge
on the place
and everything inside
would rot.

So well, so good,
and when it was time
to part company,
we said our goodbyes
and shut the lid down
tight as she insisted
till she was blue in the face.

We've since carried out the commands
she laid down for us:
to sit on a hill,
let out three loud laughs
and a soft, sweet,
lingering lament,

and not let any sad bastard
be so unlucky
as to ever forget
to carry out these gurning games
every year, right up
to this very day.

'Great-Grandma's Gurning Games'
they've been called from then on,
and it's in September
that we have them.

    ('Oscailt an Tuama', *Cead Aighnis*, p. 41)

Q. 'MO GHRÁ-SA (IDIR LÚIBÍNÍ)'   *MY LOVE (IN BRACKETS)*

Níl mo ghrá-sa
mar bhláth na n-airní
a bhíonn i ngairdín
(nó ar chrann ar bith)

is má tá aon ghaol aige
le nóiní
is as a chluasa a fhásfaidh siad
(nuair a bheidh sé ocht dtroigh síos)

ní haon ghlaise cheolmhar
iad a shúile
(táid róchóngarach dá chéile
ar an gcéad dul síos)

is más slim é síoda
tá ríbí a ghruaige
(mar bhean dhubh Shakespeare)
ina WIRE deilgní.

Ach is cuma san.
Tugann sé dom
úlla
(is nuair a bhíonn sé i ndea-ghiúmar
caora fíniúna).

My love's not
like the sloe-blossom
you get in gardens
(or on any tree)

and if he's any connection
to daisies
they'll be growing out of his ears
(when he's eight foot under)

and his eyes are no
harmonious pools
(they're too close together
for a start)

and if silk is sleek
his strips of hair
(like Shakespeare's Dark Lady's)
are barbed wire.

But that's alright.
He gives me
apples
(and, when he's in good form,
grapes).

                              (*FS* p. 29)

R. THE GREAT QUEEN SPEAKS

(My salvation)

I am the old woman
who comes up to you.
My mind's half-gone.
I'm down to one eye, one leg.
I milk a cow
with three teats.
You ask me
for a drink of milk.

I give you a drink.
You take the cup and say
'Thanks and no thanks.'
The pain goes

that was wracking my ribs,
the shakes from my hand,
the gash from my leg,
with the third drink
my eye is restored.

Because it was you
who first hurt me
with the heel of your boot,
with your catapult,
I could not recover without you,
even though it was in spite
of yourself you cured me [. . .]

because of thirst,
I escape your hurt;
because of your healing balm.
    (from 'Labhrann an Mhór-Ríon', *SP/RD* p. 120)

Bibliography

SEÁN Ó RÍORDÁIN

Eireaball Spideoige (Dublin: Sáirséal agus Dill, 1952, 1986).
Brosna (Dublin: Sáirséal agus Dill, 1964, 1987).
Línte Liombó (Dublin: Sáirséal agus Dill, 1971, 1980).
Tar Éis Mo Bháis (Dublin: Sáirséal agus Dill, 1978, 1986).
Mise (Dublin: Arts Block, UCD, 1987).

CATHAL Ó SEARCAIGH

Miontraigéide Cathrach (Falcara: Cló Uí Chuireáin, 1975).
Súile Shuibhne (Dublin: Coiscéim, 1983).
Suibhne (Dublin: Coiscéim, 1987).
An Bealach 'na Bhaile/Homecoming (Indreabhán: Cló Iar-Chonnachta, 1993).
Na Buachaillí Bána (Indreabhán: Cló Iar-Chonnachta, 1996).
Out in the Open (Indreabhán: Cló Iar-Chonnachta, 1997).

MÁIRTÍN Ó DIREÁIN

Feamainn Bhealtaine (Dublin: An Clóchomhar Tta, 1961, 1971).
Dánta 1939–1979 (Dublin: An Clóchomhar Tta, 1980).
Selected Poems/Tacar Dánta (Newbridge: Goldsmith Press, 1984).
Béasa an Túir (Dublin: An Clóchomhar Tta, 1984).
Craobhóg Dán (Dublin: An Clóchomhar Tta, 1986).

NUALA NÍ DHOMHNAILL

An Dealg Droighin (Dublin and Cork: Mercier Press, 1981).
Féar Suaithinseach (Maynooth: An Sagart, 1984).
Selected Poems/Rogha Dánta (Dublin: Raven Arts Press, 1988; repr. 1991).
Pharaoh's Daughter (Loughcrew: Gallery, 1990).
Feis (Maynooth: An Sagart, 1991).
The Astrakhan Cloak (Loughcrew: Gallery, 1993).
Cead Aighnis (An Daingean: An Sagart, 1998).

GENERAL

Alington, Revd. C. A., *The New Standard Encyclopedia and World Atlas* (London: Odhams Press, 1932).

Andrews, Elmer (ed.), *Contemporary Irish Poetry: A Collection of Critical Essays* (Houndmills: Macmillan Press Ltd., 1992).

Auden, W. H., *Secondary Worlds* (London: Faber and Faber, 1968).

—— *Collected Shorter Poems: 1927–1957*, 2nd edn. (London: Faber and Faber, 1969).

—— *W. H. Auden: Collected Poems*, ed. by Edward Mendelson (London: Faber and Faber, 1976).

Bakhtin, Mikhail, *Rabelais and his World*, trans. Hélène Iswolsky (Bloomington: Indiana University Press, 1984).

Barthes, Roland, *Writing Degree Zero*, trans. Annette Lavers and Colin Smith (New York: Hill and Wang, 1968, repr. 1981).

—— 'From Work to Text', in R. Rylance (ed.), *Debating Texts*, 117–22.

Basho, *The Narrow Road to the North and Other Travel Sketches* (Harmondsworth: Penguin, 1966, repr. 1977).

Baudelaire, Charles, *The Painter of Modern Life and Other Essays*, ed. Jonathan Mayne (London: Phaidon, 1965).

Beckson, Karl, and Arthur Ganz, *Literary Terms: A Dictionary*, 3rd edn. (London: André Deutsch Ltd., 1990).

Berman, Marshall, *All That Is Solid Melts Into Air: The Experience of Modernity* 2nd edn. (London: Verso, 1983, repr. 1995).

Berresford Ellis, Peter, *Celtic Inheritance* (London: Frederick Muller, 1985).

—— *A Dictionary of Irish Mythology* (London: Constable and Co. Ltd., 1987).

—— (ed.), *James Connolly: Selected Writings* (London: Pluto Press, 1988).

Blake, William, *Blake: Complete Writings (with variant readings)*, ed. Geoffrey Keynes (London: Oxford University Press, 1966).

Blok, Alexander, *Alexander Blok: Selected Poems*, ed. by Jon Stallworthy and Peter France (Harmondsworth: Penguin, 1974).

Boland, Eavan, *Object Lessons: The Life of the Woman and the Poet in Our Time* (London: Vintage, 1996).

Bolger, Dermot, and Gabriel Fitzmaurice (eds.), *An Tonn Gheal/The Bright New Wave* (Dublin: Raven Arts Press, 1986).

Bowie, David, *Hunky Dory* (London: RCA Records, 1971).

Boyle Haberstroh, Patricia, *Women Creating Women: Contemporary Irish Women Poets* (Dublin: Attic Press, 1996).

Bristol, Evelyn, *A History of Russian Poetry* (Oxford: Oxford University Press, 1991).

Brodski, Joseph, 'How to Read a Book', *The Times* (Monday 21 October 1996), 17.

Burkman, Katherine H. (ed.), *Myth and Ritual in the Plays of Samuel Beckett* (Mississauga: Associated University Presses, 1987).

Burns, Robert, *Selected Poems* (London: Penguin Popular Classics, 1996).

Carson, Ciarán, *The New Estate: and Other Poems* (Loughcrew: Gallery, 1988).

—— *First Language* (Loughcrew: Gallery, 1993).

Chagall, Marc, *My Life* (Oxford/New York: Oxford University Press, 1989).

Cheney, Sheldon, *The Story of Modern Art* (London: Methuen and Co. Ltd., 1958).

Cole, Ian, 'Brokering Madness'. Programme notes for the exhibition *Louise Bourgeois: Sculpture*, 22 November to 19 December 1996 at the Museum of Modern Art Oxford. Essay ref. no. DH/g.

Conrad, Joseph, *Heart of Darkness* (Harmondsworth: Penguin, 1982).

na gCopaleen, Myles, *An Béal Bocht* (Dublin: An Preas Náisiúnta, 1941).

Copeman, Christopher (ed.), *Living and Writing: Dylan Thomas* (London: Dent and Sons Ltd., 1972).

Corkery, Daniel, *The Hidden Ireland: a Study of Gaelic Munster in the Eighteenth Century* (Dublin: Gill and Macmillan, 1924, 1970).

Cronin, Michael, *Translating Ireland: Translations, Languages, Cultures* (Cork: Cork University Press, 1996).

Davitt, Michael, *An Tost A Scagadh* (Dublin: Coiscéim, 1993).

de Blacam, Aodh, *Gaelic Literature Surveyed*, 2nd edn. (Dublin: Talbot Press, 1929, 1973).

de Fréine, Celia, 'Translator's Licence—A Look at Translation in Relation to the Poetry of Nuala Ní Dhomhnaill', *Honest Ulsterman*, 103 (Spring 1997), 25–9.

de Man, Paul, 'The Dead-end of Formalist Criticism', in R. Rylance (ed.), *Debating Texts*, 101–9.

Denvir, G., *Litríocht agus Pobal* (Indreabhán: Cló Iar-Chonnachta, 1997).

de Paor, Pádraic, *Tionscnamh Filíochta Nuala Ní Dhomhnaill* (Dublin: An Clóchomhar, 1997).

Derrida, Jacques, 'Structure, Sign and Play in the Discourse of the Human Sciences', in R. Macksey and E. Donato (eds.), *The Structuralist Controversy*, 247–65; and/or R. Rylance (ed.), *Debating Texts*, 123–36.

Dinneen, Patrick S., Revd. (ed.), *Foclóir Gaedhilge agus Béarla/An Irish–English Dictionary*, 2nd edn. (Dublin: Irish Texts Society/Educational Company of Ireland, 1965).

Donne, John, *Selected Poems of John Donne*, ed. James Reeves, 7th edn. (London: Heinemann, 1969).

Dorgan, Theo (ed.), *Irish Poetry Since Kavanagh* (Blackrock: Four Courts Press, 1996).

—— and N. Duffy (eds.), *Watching the River Flow: A Century in Irish Poetry* (Dublin: Poetry Ireland, 1999).

Douglas, Keith, *Keith Douglas: Complete Poems*, ed. D. Graham (Oxford: Oxford University Press, 1990).

Eagleton, Mary (ed.), *Feminist Literary Theory: A Reader* (Cambridge MA and Oxford UK: Blackwell, 1986; repr. 1994).

Eccleshall, Robert (ed.), *Political Ideologies: An Introduction* (London: Hutchinson & Co., 1984).

Elfyn, Menna, *Cell Angel* (Newcastle: Bloodaxe, 1997).

Eliot, T. S., *Collected Poems 1909–1962*, 2nd edn. (London: Faber and Faber, 1963, 1974).

—— *Poems 1909–1925* (London: Faber and Faber, 1988).

Emerson, R. W., *Ralph Waldo Emerson: Essays and Poems*, ed. Tony Tanner (London: J. M. Dent Ltd./Everyman's Library, 1992).

Fitzmaurice, Gabriel. See Kiberd, *An Crann faoi Bhláth*.

Forsyth, James, *Listening to the Wind: an Introduction to Alexander Blok* (Oxford: Seacourt Press Ltd., 1977).

Foster, R. F., *Modern Ireland 1600–1972* (London: Penguin, 1988, repr. 1989).

Frost, Robert, *Complete Poems of Robert Frost*, 7th edn. (London: Jonathan Cape, 1966).

Frye, Northrop, *Fables of Identity: Studies in Poetic Mythology* (New York: Harcourt, Brace and World, Inc., 1963).

Gardner, Helen, *The Art of T. S. Eliot* (London: The Cresset Press, 1949, repr. 1968).

Garrat, Robert F., *Modern Irish Poetry: Tradition and Continuity from Yeats to Heaney* (London: University of California Press, 1986).

Genet, Jacqueline (ed.), *Rural Ireland, Real Ireland?*, Irish Literary Studies, 49 (Gerrards Cross: Colin Smythe, 1996).

Gibbons, Luke, *Transformations in Irish Culture* (Cork: Cork University Press, 1996).

Gibson, Lloyd, 'Pleasures of the Interface', paper given at the conference *Fabulous Transgressions: Defining the Grotesque in Contemporary Literary and Visual Culture* (University of Sunderland, 11 September 1997).

Gordon, John, *James Joyce's Metamorphoses* (London: Gill and Macmillan, 1981).

Grant, Patrick, *Personalism and the Politics of Culture: Readings in Literature and Religion from the New Testament to the Poetry of Northern Ireland* (Houndmills: Macmillan Press, 1996).

Greene, David, *Writing in Irish Today*, Irish Life and Culture Series, 18 (Cork: Mercier Press, 1972).

Greene, Miranda J., *Dictionary of Celtic Myth and Legend* (London: Thames and Hudson Ltd., 1992).

Hall, Donald (ed.). See Whitman, *A Choice of Whitman's Verse*.

Harris, Nathaniel, *The Life and Works of Chagall* (London: Parragon, 1994).

Hartley, L. P., *The Go-Between* (London: Hamish Hamilton, 1953, repr. 1966).

Hartnett, Michael, *A Farewell to English and Other Poems* (Dublin Gallery Press, 1975).

Hayden, Tom (ed.), *Irish Hunger: Personal Reflections on the Legacy of the Famine* (Dublin: Wolfhound Press, 1997).

Heaney, Seamus, *Door into the Dark* (London: Faber and Faber, 1969, 1991).

—— *Preoccupations: Selected Prose 1968–78* (London: Faber and Faber, 1980).

—— 'Forked Tongues, Céilís and Incubators', *Fortnight* No. 197 (Sept. 1983), 113–16.

—— *Station Island* (London: Faber and Faber, 1984).

—— *The Government of the Tongue* (London: Faber and Faber, 1988, 1989).

—— *Seeing Things* (London: Faber and Faber, 1988).

—— 'Learning from Eliot', *Agenda* Vol. 27 No. 1 (Spring 1989), 17–31.

—— *New Selected Poems 1966–1987* (London: Faber and Faber, 1990).

—— *The Redress of Poetry: Oxford Lectures* (London: Faber and Faber, 1995).

—— *The Spirit Level* (London: Faber and Faber, 1996).

Hepburn, A. C., *The Conflict of Nationality in Modern Ireland* (London: Edward Arnold Ltd., 1980).

Herbert, George, *A Choice of George Herbert's Verse*, ed. R. S. Thomas, 5th edn. (London: Faber and Faber, 1967, 1981).

Hewitt, John, *The Collected Poems of John Hewitt* (Belfast: Blackstaff Press, 1991).

Hofheinz, Thomas C., *Joyce and the Invention of Irish History: Finnegans Wake in Context* (New York: Cambridge University Press, 1995).

Hopkins, Gerard Manley, *Selected Poems of Gerard Manley Hopkins*, ed. James Reeves, 5th edn. (London: Heinemann, 1959).

Houlihan, Con, 'An Gearrscéal—agus rudaí eile', *Comhar* (November 1968), 11–18.

Hughes, Ted, *Selected Poems 1957–1981* (London: Faber and Faber, 1982, repr. 1986).

Hughes, H. Stuart, *Oswald Spengler: A Critical Estimate* (New York: Charles Scribner's Sons, 1952).

Hutchinson, Pearse, *Watching the Morning Grow* (Dublin: Gallery Books, 1972).

Huxley, Aldous, *The Doors of Perception/Heaven and Hell* (London: Granada Publishing Ltd./Panther Books, 1977, repr. 1978).

Johnston, Dillon, *Irish Poetry After Joyce* (Portlaoise: Dolmen Press, 1985).

—— *Irish Poetry After Joyce*, 2nd edn. (Syracuse, New York: Syracuse University Press, 1997).

Joyce, James, *Portrait of the Artist as a Young Man*. See H. Levin (ed.), *The Essential James Joyce*.

—— *Ulysses* (Harmondsworth: Penguin, 1922, 1969).

Kavanagh, Patrick, *Collected Poems* (London: MacGibbon and Kee, 1964).

—*Collected Prose*, 2nd edn. (London: Martin Brian and O'Keefe, 1973).

Kearney, Richard, *Modern Movements in European Philosophy* (Manchester: Manchester University Press, 1987).

Kelly, A. A. (ed.), *Pillars of the House* (Dublin: Wolfhound Press, 1988).

Keogh, Dermot, *Twentieth-Century Ireland: Nation and State* (Dublin: Gill and Macmillan, 1994).

Keynes, Geoffrey (ed.), See Blake, *Complete Writings*.

Kiberd, Declan, *Idir Dhá Chultúr* (Dublin: Coiscéim, 1993).

—— *Inventing Ireland: The Literature of the Modern Nation* (London: Vintage, 1996).

Kiberd, Declan, and Gabriel Fitzmaurice (eds.), *An Crann faoi Bhláth/The Flowering Tree* (Dublin: Wolfhound Press, 1991).

Kinsella, Thomas, trans., *The Táin*, Dolmen Editions 9 (Dublin: Dolmen Press, 1969).

—— 'The Divided Mind', in S. Lucy (ed.), *Irish Poets in English*.

—— 'Another Country', in S. Mac Réamoinn (ed.), *The Pleasures of Gaelic Poetry*.

—— (ed.), *The New Oxford Book of Irish Verse* (Oxford: Oxford University Press, 1986).

—— *The Dual Tradition: An Essay on Poetry and Politics in Ireland* (Manchester: Carcanet Press, 1995).

Kinsella, Thomas, and W. B. Yeats, *Davis, Mangan, Ferguson?: Tradition and the Irish Writer*, The Tower Series of Anglo-Irish Studies, II (Dublin: The Dolmen Press, 1970).

Kristeva, Julia, 'A Question of Subjectivity—an Interview', in P. Rice and P. Waugh (eds.), *Modern Literary Theory*, 128–134.

Kunitz, Stanley, and Max Hayward (eds.), *Poems of Anna Akhmatova* (London: Collins and Harvill Press, 1974).

Larkin, Philip, *Collected Poems* (London: Marvell and Faber and Faber, 1988).

—— *Required Writing: Miscellaneous Pieces 1955–1982* (London: Faber and Faber, 1983).

Lee, J. J., *Ireland 1912–1985: Politics and Society* (Cambridge: Cambridge University Press, 1989, repr. 1993).

Leerssen, Joep, 'Rebuilding the Alhambra: A Discussion with Joep Leerssen', *Poetry Ireland Review*, 49 (Spring 1996), 28–36.

Levi, Peter, *The Lamentation of the Dead* (London: Anvil Press, 1984).

Levin, Harry (ed.), *The Essential James Joyce* (London: Readers Union/Jonathan Cape, 1950).

Longley, Edna, *The Living Stream: Literature and Revisionism in Ireland* (Newcastle-upon-Tyne: Bloodaxe Books, 1994).

Longley, M., 'A Going Back to Sources', *Poetry Ireland Review*, 39 (Autumn 1993), 92–6. [A review of Ó Searcaigh, *An Bealach 'na Bhaile*.]

Lucy, Seán (ed.), *Irish Poets in English*, The Thomas Davis Lectures on Anglo-Irish Poetry (Cork and Dublin: Mercier Press, 1973).

Mac Aodha, B. S. (ed.), *Cnuasach 1966* (Dublin: Scepter, 1966).

Mac Cana, Proinsias, *Literature in Irish* (Dublin: Dept. of Foreign Affairs, 1980).

Mac Giolla Léith, Caoimhín (ed.), *Cime Mar Chách: Aistí ar Mháirtín Ó Direáin* (Dublin: Coiscéim, 1993).

Macksey, Richard, and Eugenio Donato (eds.), *The Structuralist Controversy: The Languages of Criticism and the Sciences of Man* (Baltimore and London: Johns Hopkins University Press, 1970, repr. 1972).

Mac Lochlainn, Gearóid, *Babylon Gaeilgeoir* (Belfast: An Clochán, 1997).

—— *Na Scéalaithe* (Dublin: Coiscéim, 1999).

MacMonagle, Niall (ed.), *Lifelines: Letters From Famous People About Their Favourite Poem*, 2nd edn. (Dublin: Town House and Country House, 1992, 1995).

MacNeice, Louis, *Poems* (London: Faber and Faber, 1935).

—— *The Collected Poems of Louis MacNeice*, ed. E. R. Dodds, 2nd edn. (London: Faber and Faber, 1966, 1979, repr. 1986).

Mac Réamoinn, Seán (ed.), *The Pleasures of Gaelic Poetry* (London: Allen Lane/Penguin Books, 1982).

Mahon, Derek, *The Snow Party* (London: Oxford University Press, 1975).

—— *Poems 1962–1978* (Oxford: Oxford University Press, 1979).

—— *Selected Poems* (London: Penguin, 1993).

Markham, E. A., and others (eds.), *Writing Ulster*, Vols. 2 and 3, 1991/2 (Gerrards Cross: Colin Smythe Ltd. and Linda Lee Books Ltd., 1992).

Martin, Augustine (ed.), see Yeats, *Collected Poems*.

Marx, Karl, and Friedrich Engels, *Clár na Comharsheilbhe: Forógra Pháirtí na gCumannach* (Dublin & Belfast: Páirtí Cumannach na hÉireann, 1986).

McCartney, Donal, 'Education and Language, 1938–1951'. See Nowlan and Williams (eds.), *Ireland in the War Years and After*.

McDiarmid, Lucy, and Michael Durkan, 'Q. & A.: Nuala Ní Dhomhnaill', *Irish Literary Supplement* (Fall 1987), 41–3.

McDonald, Peter, 'Incurable Ache' (a review of *The Yellow Book*, Derek Mahon, Gallery, 1997), *Poetry Ireland*, 56 (Spring 1998), 117–19.

McGuckian, Medbh, *Selected Poems 1978–1994* (Loughcrew: Gallery, 1997).

Mendelson, Edward (ed.), see Auden, *Collected Poems*.

Meskimmon, Marsha, 'The Grotesque as a Feminist Visual Strategy'. Conference paper, see Gibson, L.

Meyer-Thoss, Christiane, *Louise Bourgeois: Designing for Free Fall* (Zurich: Ammann, 1992).

Mhac an tSaoi, Máire, 'Scríbhneoireacht sa Ghaeilge Inniu', *Studies*, 44 (1955), 86–91.

—— *Codladh an Ghaiscigh* (Dublin: Sáirséal agus Dill, 1973).

—— *An Cion go dtí Seo* (Dublin: Sáirséal—Ó Marcaigh, 1987, repr. 1988).

Milner-Gulland, Robin, and Peter Levi (eds.). See Yevtushenko, *Selected Poems*.

Milosc, Czeslaw, *The History of Polish Literature* (London: Macmillan, 1969).

Molony, John Neylon, *A Soul Came Into Ireland: Thomas Davis, 1814–1845: A Biography* (Dublin: Geography Publications, 1995).

Montague, John, *Smashing the Piano* (Loughcrew: Gallery Press, 1999).

Moran, Gerard (ed.), *Galway History and Society: Interdisciplinary Essays on the History of an Irish County* (Dublin: Geography Publications, 1996).

Morgan, Stuart, 'Louise Bourgeois: Nature Study'. Programme for the exhibition *Louise Bourgeois: Serpentine Gallery London 18 May–23 June 1985* (London: Arts Council of Great Britain, 1985).

Morrison, Blake, and Andrew Motion (eds.), *The Penguin Book of Contemporary British Poetry* (London: Penguin, 1982).

Muldoon, Paul, *Mules* (London: Faber and Faber, 1977).

—— *Selected Poems 1968–83*, 5th edn. (London: Faber and Faber, 1986).

—— (ed.) *The Faber Book of Contemporary Irish Poetry* (London: Faber and Faber, 1986).

—— *Prince of the Quotidian* (Loughcrew: Gallery Press, 1994).

—— *New Selected Poems 1968–1994* (London: Faber and Faber, 1996).

Ní Cheallaigh, Pádraigín, 'An Nuala Rua is Dual . . .', *Comhar* (May 1992), 211–13.

Ní Chuilleanáin, Eiléan, 'The Borderlands of Irish Poetry'. See Andrews, *Contemporary Irish Poetry*, 25–40.

Ní Dhomhnaill, Nuala, 'Mis and Dubh Ruis: A Parable of Psychic Transformation', in R. Welch (ed.), *Irish Writers and Religion*, 194–201.

—— 'The English for Irish', *Irish Review*, 4 (1988), 116–18.

—— 'Why I Choose to Write in Irish: The Corpse that Sits Up and Talks Back', *The New York Times* (1 August 1995), 3 and 27–8.

—— 'An Fhilíocht á Cumadh: Ceardlann Filíochta', in P. Ó Fiannachta (ed.), *Léachtaí Cholm Cille XVII*, 147–79.

—— 'A Ghostly Alhambra', in T. Hayden (ed.), *Irish Hunger*, 68–78.

—— *Spíonáin is Róiseanna*, cassette and booklet (Indreabhán: Cló Iar-Chonnachta, 1993).

—— *Cead Aighnis* (An Daingean: An Sagart, 1998).

Ní Dhuibhne, Eilís, ' "The Old Woman as Hare": Structure and Meaning in an Irish Legend' (re: 'The Robber that was Hurt'), *Folklore*, Vol. 104, Nos. 1–2 (1993), 77–85.

Nietzsche, Friedrich, *Thus Spoke Zarathustra: A Book for Everyone and No One*, trans. R. J. Hollingdale (Harmondsworth: Penguin, 1961, repr. 1978).

—— *The Birth of Tragedy, and, The Genealogy of Morals* (New York/Toronto: Doubleday Anchor Books, 1956).

Nowlan, Kevin B., and T. Desmond Williams (eds.), *Ireland in the War Years and After: 1939–1951* (Dublin: Gill and Macmillan Ltd., 1969).

Ó hÁinle, C. G., ' "The Inalienable Right of Trifles": Tradition and Modernity in Gaelic Writing Since the Revival', in *Eire-Ireland*, Vol. 19 (Winter 1984), 59–77.

Ó hAnluain, Eoghan, 'The Twentieth Century: Prose and Verse'. See de Blacam, *Gaelic Literature Surveyed*, 387–405.

—— 'Nóta faoi Bhlianta an Chogaidh le Máirtín Ó Direáin', *Scríobh 2* (Dublin: An Clóchomhar Tta., 1975), 21–9.

O'Brien, Darcy, 'Piety and Modernism: Seamus Heaney's "Station Island" ', *James Joyce Quarterly*, 26, No. 1 (Fall 1988), 51–65.

O'Brien, Frank, *Filíocht Ghaeilge na Linne Seo* (Dublin: An Clóchomhar Tta, 1968).

—— *Duanaire Nuafhilíochta* (Dublin: An Clóchomhar Tta, 1969).

O'Carroll, Íde, and Eoin Collins (eds.), *Lesbian and Gay Visions of Ireland: Towards the Twenty-first Century* (London: Cassell, 1995).

Ó Coigligh, Ciarán, *An Fhilíocht Chomhaimseartha 1975–1985* (Dublin: Coiscéim, 1987).

Ó Coileáin, Seán, *Seán Ó Ríordáin: Beatha and Saothar* (Dublin: An Clóchomhar Tta, 1982, repr. 1985).

Ó Conghaile, Micheál (ed.), *Sláinte: Deich mBliana de Chló Iar-Chonnachta* (Indreabhán: CIC, 1995).

O'Connor, M., 'Lashings of the Mother Tongue: Nuala Ní Dhomhnaill's Anarchic Laughter', in T. O'Connor (ed.), *The Comic Tradition in Irish Women Writers* (Gainesville: University Press of Florida, 1996), 149–70.

Ó Doibhlin, Breandán, *Aistí Critice and Cultúir* (Dublin: Foilseacháin Náisiúnta Teoranta, n. d.).

Ó Dónaill, Niall (ed.), *Foclóir Gaeilge–Béarla/Irish–English Dictionary* (Dublin: Oifig an tSoláthair, 1977).

O'Driscoll, D. (ed.), 'Findings', *Poetry Ireland*, 36 (Autumn 1992), 123–8.

Ó Drisceoil, Proinsias, 'À la Carte Paganism?', *Poetry Ireland*, 34 (Spring 1992), 121–4.

Ó Dúil, Gréagóir (ed.), *Filíocht Uladh 1960–1985* (Dublin: Coiscéim, 1986).

—— 'Filíocht Chathail Uí Shearcaigh: i dtreo anailíse téamúla', *An tUltach* (January 1993), 12–19.

—— 'Cathal Ó Searcaigh: A Negotiation with Place, Community and Tradition', *Poetry Ireland Review*, 48 (Winter 1995), 14–18.

Ó Dushláine, Tadhg, *Paidir File* (Indreabhán: Cló Iar-Chonnachta, 1993).

Ó hEithir, Breandán and Ruairí (eds.), *An Aran Reader* (Dublin: Lilliput Press Ltd., 1991).

Ó Fiannachta, Pádraig (ed.), *Léachtaí Cholm Cille XVII: An Nuafhilíocht* (Maynooth: An Sagart, 1986).

O'Flaherty, Tom, *Aranmen All* (Dublin: The Sign of the Three Candles, 1934).

O'Flaherty, Liam, *Dúil* (Dublin: Caoimhín Ó Marcaigh, 1953, repr. 1987).

—— *The Short Stories of Liam O'Flaherty* (London: Four Square Books, 1966).

Ó Góilidhe, Caoimhghin, *Díolaim Filíochta don Ardteistiméireacht* (Dublin: Folens and Co. Ltd., 1974).

O'Leary, Philip, 'An Agile Cormorant: Poetry in Ireland Today', *Éire-Ireland*, No. XXIV: 4 (Winter 1989), 39–53.

—— 'A Night with Nuala', *Irish Literary Supplement* (Spring 1990), 22–3.

Ó Mórdha, S., 'Seán Ó Ríordáin ag caint le Seán Ó Mórdha', *Scríobh 3* (Dublin: An Clóchomhar Tta, 1978), 163–84.

Ó Muirthile, Liam, *An Peann Coitianta* (Dublin: Comhar, 1991).

—— 'Rebuilding the Alhambra: A Discussion with Joep Leerssen', *Poetry Ireland Review*, 49 (Spring 1996), 28–36.

Ormsby, Frank (ed.), See Hewitt, *Collected Poems*.

Ó Tuairisc, Eoghan (ed.) *Rogha an Fhile/The Poet's Choice* (Dublin: Goldsmith Press, 1974).

—— *Poet's Choice*, RTE Radio 1, 23–8–1982.

Ó Tuama, Seán (ed.), *Nuabhéarsaíocht: 1939–1949*, 5th edn. (Dublin: Sáirséal agus Dill, 1950, 1974).

—— 'Seán Ó Ríordáin agus an Nuafhilíocht', *Studia Hibernica*, 13 (1973), 100–67.

—— *Filí faoi Scéimhle: Seán Ó Ríordáin agus Aogán Ó Rathaille* (Dublin: Oifig an tSoláthair, 1978).

—— 'Seán Ó Ríordáin', in S. Mac Réamoinn (ed.), *The Pleasures of Gaelic Poetry*, 129–41.

—— 'Filíocht Nuala Ní Dhomhnaill: "An Mháthair Ghrámhar is an Mháthair Ghránna" ina Cuid Filíochta'. See Ó Fiannachta (ed.), *Léachtaí Cholm Cille XVII*, 95–116.

—— *Repossessions: Selected Essays on the Irish Literary Heritage* (Cork: Cork University Press, 1995).

Pasley, Malcolm (ed.), *Nietzsche: Imagery and Thought* (London: Methuen, 1978).

Paulin, Tom, *Writing to the Moment: Selected Critical Essays 1980–1996* (London: Faber and Faber, 1996).

Pearse, P., *Short Stories of Padraic Pearse: A Dual Language Book*, selected and adapted by Desmond Maguire (Cork: Mercier Press, 1968, repr. 1979).

Pirie, Donald (ed.), *Young Poets of a New Poland: an Anthology* (London: Forest Books, 1993).

Plath, Sylvia, *Ariel* (London: Faber and Faber, 1965).

Price, Alan (ed.), *J. M. Synge Collected Works Vol. 2: Prose* (Gerrards Cross: Colin Smythe Ltd., 1982).

Prút, Liam, *Máirtín Ó Direáin: File Tréadúil* (Maynooth: An Sagart, 1982).

Pushkin, Alexander, *Pushkin Threefold: Narrative, Lyric, Polemic, and Ribald Verse*, ed. and trans. by Walter Arndt (London: George Allen and Unwin Ltd., 1972).

Pyman, Avril, *The Life of Alexander Blok: Volume 1: The Distant Thunder 1880–1908* (Oxford: Oxford University Press, 1979).

—— *The Life of Alexander Blok Vol. 2: The Release of Harmony 1908–1921* (Oxford: Oxford University Press, 1980).

Read, Christopher, *Religion, Revolution and the Russian Intelligentsia 1900–1912* (London: Macmillan Press, 1979).

Reeves, James (ed.), see Hopkins, G. M. and Donne, J.

Rice, Philip, and Patricia Waugh (eds.), *Modern Literary Theory: A Reader* (London: Edward Arnold, 1989).

Robinson, Tim, *Stones of Aran: Pilgrimage* 3rd edn. (London: Penguin, 1990).

—— 'Listening to the Landscape', *The Irish Review* (Special Issue—*An Ghaeilge: The Literature and Politics of Irish*), 14 (Autumn 1993), 21–32.

Rosenstock, Gabriel, 'Gabriel Rosenstock Reviews Nuala Ní Dhomhnaill', *Poetry Ireland*, 39 (Autumn 1993), 102–9.

—— 'Searcach na Seirce', interviewing Cathal Ó Searcaigh, *Feasta* (July 1996), 4–5.

Rumens, Carol (ed.), *Brangle: New Writing from the School of English, QUB* (Belfast: Brangle Publishing, 1993).

—— *Brangle: Essays, Reviews and Poetry from N. Ireland and Beyond*, 2 (London: Brangle Publications, 1997).

Rylance, Rick (ed.), *Debating Texts: A Reader in Twentieth-century Literary Theory and Method*, 3rd edn. (Milton Keynes: Open University Press, 1987, 1990).

Said, Edward W., *Culture and Imperialism* (London: Chatto and Windus, 1993).

Sampson, George (ed.), see Wordsworth and Coleridge, *The Lyrical Ballads*.

Sayers, Peig, *Peig: A Scéal Féin*, 3rd edn. (Dublin: Talbot Press, 1939).

Schlossman, Beryl, *Joyce's Catholic Comedy of Language* (University of Wisconsin Press, 1985).

Schweitzer, Viktoria, *Tsvetaeva* (London: Harvill Press, 1993).

Sdorow, Lester, *Psychology*, 3rd edn. (Madison: Brown and Benchmark, 1995).

Sealy, Dúghlas, Untitled review of *An Bealach 'na Bhaile*, *Comhar* (July 1993), 21–2.

Sewell, Frank, 'Medbh McGuckian talks to Frank Sewell', in C. Rumens (ed.), *Brangle 1*, 51–60.

—— 'Subconscious Voyager', a review of *The Astrakhan Cloak*, *Fortnight*, 316 (April 1993), 49.

—— 'Seán Ó Ríordáin: Joycery-Corkery-Sorcery', *The Irish Review* No. 23 (Winter 1998), 42–61.

Shklovsky, Viktor, 'Art as Technique', in R. Rylance (ed.), *Debating Texts*, 48–56.

Simic, Charles, 'Secret Maps: Holly Wright's Photographs of Hands', *The Yale Review*, Vol. 84, No. 4 (October 1996), 26–36.

Skelton, Robin (ed.), *Poetry of the Thirties* (London: Penguin, 1964).

Somerville Aryat, Gillean, and Rebecca E. Wilson (eds.), *Sleeping with Monsters: Conversations with Scottish and Irish Women Poets* (Edinburgh: Polygon, 1990).

Spark, Muriel, *The Driver's Seat*, 2nd edn. (London: Penguin, 1974; repr. 1988).

Stahlberger, Lawrence Leo, *The Symbolic System of Majakovskij* (The Hague: Mouton and Co., 1964).

Stallworthy, Jon, and Peter France (eds.), see Blok, *Selected Poems*.

Stallybrass, Peter, and Allon White, *The Politics and Poetics of Transgression* (London: Methuen, 1986).

Stephens, James, 'The Outlook for Literature with Special Reference to Ireland' (1922), in M. Storey (ed.), *Poetry and Ireland since 1800*, 178–88.

Stevens, Wallace, *The Collected Poems of Wallace Stevens* (New York: Alfred A. Knopf, 1957).

Stewart, R. J., and Robin Williamson, *Celtic Bards, Celtic Druids* (London: Blandford/Cassell, 1996).

Storey, Mark (ed.), *Poetry and Ireland since 1800: A Source Book* (London: Routledge, 1988).

Tanner, Tony (ed.), see Emerson, *Essays and Poems*.

Thomas, R. S. (ed.), see Herbert, *A Choice of George Herbert's Verse*.

Thwaite, Anthony (ed.), *Philip Larkin: Collected Poems*, 2nd edn. (London: Marvell Press and Faber and Faber, 1990).

Titley, Alan, *Chun Doirne: Rogha Aistí* (Belfast: Lagan Press, 1996).

Tobin, Fergal, *The Best of Decades* (Dublin: Gill and Macmillan Ltd, 1984).

Todd, Albert C., and Max Hayward with Daniel Weissbort (eds.), *Twentieth Century Russian Poetry: Selected with an Introduction by Yevgeny Yevtushenko* (London: Fourth Estate, 1993).

Tomashevsky, Boris, 'from Thematics', in R. Rylance (ed.), *Debating Texts*, 57–65.

Tripp, Edward, *The Handbook of Classical Mythology* (London: Arthur Barker Ltd., 1970).

Waddell, Helen, *Mediaeval Latin Lyrics*, 4th edn. (London: Constable and Co. Ltd., 1935; repr. 1939).

Walshe, Éibhear (ed.), *Sex, Nation and Dissent in Irish Writing* (Cork: Cork University Press, 1997).

Warner, Marina, *Managing Monsters: Six Myths of Our Time*, The 1994 Reith Lectures (London: Vintage, 1994).

—— *From the Beast to the Blonde: On Fairy Tales and Their Tellers* (London: Chatto and Windus, 1994).

Welch, Robert, *Irish Poetry from Moore to Yeats*, Irish Literary Studies 5 (Gerrards Cross: Colin Smythe Ltd., 1980).

—— 'The Loutishness of Learning: the Presence of Writing', in E. A. Markham (ed.), *Writing Ulster.*

—— (ed.), *Irish Writers and Religion*, Irish Literary Studies, 37 (Gerrards Cross: Colin Smythe Ltd., 1992).

—— *Changing States: Transformations in Modern Irish Writing* (London: Routledge Press, 1993).

Weldon, Fay, *Letters to Alice: On First Reading Jane Austen* (London: Sceptre, 1993).

Whitman, Walt, *A Choice of Whitman's Verse: Selected with an Introduction by Donald Hall* (London: Faber and Faber, 1968).

Williams, John Ellis Caerwyn, and Máirín Ní Mhuiríosa, *Traidisiún Liteartha na nGael* (Dublin: An Clóchomhar Tra, 1979).

Williams, William, Carlos, *Paterson* (New York: New Directions Paperbook 1952, 1963).

Wordsworth, William and S. T. Coleridge, *William Wordsworth and Samuel Taylor Coleridge: The Lyrical Ballads 1798–1805*, ed. George Sampson (London: Methuen and Co. Ltd., 1903, repr. 1965).

Yeats, W. B., *W. B. Yeats: Collected Poems*, ed. Augustine Martin (London: Vintage, 1992).

Yevtushenko, Y., *Yevgeny Yevtushenko: Selected Poems*, ed. by R. Milner-Gulland and P. Levi, S. J. (Middlesex: Penguin Books, 1962, repr. 1964).

—— *A Precocious Autobiography*, trans. Andrew R. MacAndrew (Harmondsworth: Penguin Books Ltd., 1965).

Zenkovsky, V. V., *A History of Russian Philosophy*, 2 vols. (London: Routledge & Kegan Paul Ltd., 1953).

Index

Agostini, R. 146 n.
Akhmatova, A. 81
Alexander, Pope 75
Alhambra 8, 58, 147, 187 n., 201, 202
Alington, C. A. 8 n.
Apocalypse, 65
Artaud, A. 105 n.
Auden, W. H. 39, 49 n., 60, 61, 74,
    75 n., 88, 90, 114 n.
St Augustine 22

Bakhtin, M. 164, 165
St Barra 22, 23
Barthes, R. 57
Basho 5
Baudelaire, C. 11, 52, 141–2, 144
Bealtaine 63, 67, 70
    see also Samhain
Beckett, S. 11, 164 n., 166 n., 167,
    168 n.
Beckson, K. and Ganz, A. 68 n.
Berdyaev, N. A. 113
Berman, M. 105 n., 128–31 n., 133–7 n.,
    141–4, 202
Berresford Ellis, P. 63 n., 71
Berryman, J. 79
Blake, W. 85
Blok, A. 7, 120, 138, 139 n.
Boland, E. 1, 96 n.
Bolger, D. and Fitzmaurice, G. 150 n.
Botticelli, A. 79
Bourgeois, L. 6, 96, 155, 158 n., 162–3,
    167 n., 168–71, 187–8
Bowie, D. 191 n.
bricolage 57–8, 192, 200
Brodski, J. 1, 162
Burkman, K. 164 n., 166–8 n.
Burns, R. 87, 166 n.
Byron, G. G. 75

Cardinal, M. 163
Carson, C. 51, 58, 60, 181
Cavafy, C. 97

Céitinn, S. 33
Celan, P. 79
centre 54–57, 106–7, 141, 144, 167
    see also island
Chagall, M. 52
Chekhov A . 33
city 4, 65–9, 79–80, 85, 92–4, 104, 110,
    118, 121, 126–9, 131–41, 146
Cole, I. 194 n.
Comhar 127 n., 140, 151 n.
Connolly, J. 32, 134, 141
Conrad, J. 168 n.
Corkery, D. 3, 12–16, 21, 26, 29, 32, 39,
    45, 47
Corso, R. 152 n.
Cronin, M. 2 n.
cummings e e 18, 33
Czekanowicz, A. 1

Dante 33
Davis, T. 127
Davitt, M. 1, 51, 150 n., 196 n.
de Blacam, A. 10 n., 104 n., 137 n.
de Fréine, C. 7
de Man, P. 57, 131
Denvir, G. 58 n.
de Paor, P. 153 n., 169, 175–6 n., 178 n.,
    180, 186 n., 190, 192
Derrida, J. 54–7, 116 n., 146 n., 200
de Valera, E. 129n., 134
Devlin, B. 32
Dinneen, P. S. 80 n.
Donne, J. 19, 49, 182
Dorgan, T. 7, 103 n.
Douglas, K. 68 n.
Dylan, B. 130, 191 n.

Eagleton, M. 154 n.
Eagleton, T. 165
Easter (1916) Rising 125
Eccleshall, R. 57
Eckhart, J. 97
Elfyn, M. 150 n.

Eliot, T. S. 4, 7, 18, 19, 33, 52, 66, 114 n.,
    117 n., 129, 134, 141, 147, 187
Emerson, R. W. 60–1, 78, 105–6 n., 121
Empson, W. 57
Engels, F. 134 n.
Feasta 29, 43, 132
Fiacc, P. 1 n.
Flaherty, R. J. 127 n.
Folklore 154 n.
Forsyth, J. 138–9 n.
Foucault, M. 173–4
frasca 36
Freud, S. 55
Frost, R. 7, 18, 19, 106
Frye, N. 56, 68 n., 141 n.
Funge, P. 38

Gandhi, M. 199 n.
Gardner, H. 4 n., 134 n.
Genet, J. 146 n.
Ghost Dance 117
Gibbons, L. 129 n.
Gibson, L. 183
Giese, R. 59, 76
Gogol, N. 66
Gordon, J. 60, 63 n., 64 n.
Govinda, L. A. 99 n.
Gramsci, A. 177
Greene, D. 10 n.
Greene, M. J. 67 n., 72, 189

Han Shan 70
Haraucourt, E. 110n., 124
Hardy, T. 63, 115
Hartley, L. P. 118 n.
Hartnett, M. 7, 191 n.
Heaney, S. 6, 29, 51, 60, 63, 77, 82, 102,
    133 n., 146, 173, 177
  on Kavanagh 22, 81 n., 85
  'Field of Vision' 76, 97–8
  'Forked Tongues' 11, 26, 43, 45, 52
  'Joy or Night' 114–15 n.
  'Making Strange' 78, 79, 104 n.
  'Squarings' 54, 70 n., 79, 85
  'Station Island' 19, 26, 49
Heidegger, M. 55, 100 n., 130–1
Herbert, G. 20, 27
Hewitt, J. 105
Hitler, A. 10
Hölderlin, J. C. F. 130–1
Holmes, T. 69

homecoming 5, 12, 32–4, 41, 46, 52, 59,
    62, 65–6, 79–83, 85, 91–4, 101,
    130–1, 135, 139–40, 143, 145–6, 163,
    175, 192, 202
Hopkins, G. M. 14, 18, 33, 47, 100
Houlihan, C. 126 n.
H. U. (The Honest Ulsterman) 148 n.
Hughes, H. S. 109 n.
Hughes, T. 124
Huxley, A. 97–100
Hy-Brazil 117

Ibsen, H. 33
INNTI 4, 147, 150
Irish Review 151 n.
Irish Times 11
island 23, 33, 45, 54–5, 83, 110, 116–26,
    144–6, 186–8,

Jackson, M. 136
Jenkinson, B. 1
Johnston, D. 2
Joyce, J. 58, 60–4, 71, 73, 77, 107, 113
  influence on Ó Ríordáin 3, 12, 14–16,
    21, 26–9, 33, 39, 45, 47, 50, 52, 57
Jung, K. 190, 196

Kafka, F. 65
Kavanagh, P. 2 n., 17, 22, 24, 25, 60, 62,
    81, 85, 113, 121, 126 n., 127, 146
Kearney, R. 131 n.
Keats, J. 33
Kerouac, J. 5, 69, 73, 77, 114
Kiberd, D. 2 n., 12, 19, 22 n., 44–5
Kiernan, V. G. 155
Kinsella, T. 1 n., 2 n., 50–51, 179 n., 201
Kirsánov, S. I. 84 n., 102
Krisnamurti 87, 99 n.
Kristeva, J. 105, 106, 177

Lacan, J. 106
Laing, R. D. 106
Land League 107, 112
Larkin, P. 39, 40, 43, 67, 114, 116, 138 n.,
    200 n., 202 n.
Leach, E. 183
Leerssen, J. 8
Lemass, S. 129 n.
Lenin, V. I. 52
Lévi-Strauss, C. 56, 57, 200
Lichtenberg, G. C. 60 n.

Longley, E. 52 n.
Longley, M. 59 n., 60
Lordán, E. 7
Lowell, R. 88

Mac Aodha, B. S. 12 n.
MacCana, P. 47, 49
McCartney, D. 127 n.
Mac Conghail, M. 121 n.
McDiarmid, L. and Durkan, M. 133 n.,
    151 n., 164 n., 165 n., 172 n., 181
    n., 182 n., 200 n.
Mac Donagh, T. 58
McDonald, P. 3 n., 7 n.
Mag Fhiongaill, C. 104 n.
McGuckian, M. 7 n., 201
McLaverty, M. 60
Mac Lochlainn, G. 50 n., 180 n.
MacMonagle, N. 160 n., 166 n., 197 n.
MacNeice, L. 50, 85, 133
Mac Réamoinn, S. 10 n.
Mac Síomóin, T. 108, 116
Mac Thòmais, R. 86
Macksey, R. and Donato, E. 54 n., 58 n.
Mahon, D. 7 n., 38, 60, 85, 161
Mangan, J. C. 58
Mann, T. 110
Marcuse, H. 66
Marx, K. 134 n., 141 n.
Mayakovski, V. 52
Meskimmon, M. 185
Metaphysical poets 19, 27, 28, 35, 49
Meyer-Thoss, C. 6 n., 96 n., 162 n., 163
    n., 167 n., 168 n., 169 n., 170 n.,
    183, 188 n.
Mhac an tSaoi, M. 1, 2, 9, 11, 18, 29, 45,
    47–8, 58
Milosc, C. 36 n., 199 n.
Mitchell, J. 154 n.
modernity 3, 4, 6, 9–12, 14, 35, 47–58,
    104–7, 119–20, 126–147, 150–3,
    160, 175, 179, 185, 192–3, 200, 202
Molony, J. N. 127 n.
Montague, J. 51
Moore, M. 76 n.
Moran, G. 120 n.
Morgan, S. 155 n., 170 n., 197 n.
Morrissey, S. P. 49
Morrisson, B. and Motion, A. 86 n.
Muldoon, P. 6, 12, 50, 60, 130, 174 n.,
    180, 186

Namjoshi, S. 159
News of the World 75
New York Times 151 n.
Ní Cheallaigh, P. 151 n.
Ní Chuilleanáin, E. 102, 103 n.
Ní Dhomhnaill, N. 1, 5–6, 7, 52 n., 58,
    88, 91, 97, 103 n., 133 n., 147–98,
    200
    Féar Suaithinseach 150, 153, 154–74
    Feis 150, 153, 174–94
Ní Dhuibhne, E. 154 n.
Nietzsche, F. 55, 108, 114, 185, 192
No Loitering! 27, 34, 39, 41
Nowlan, K. B. and Williams, T. D.
    127 n.
Norwid, C. 199 n.

Ó hAnluain, E. 9 n., 49, 126–7 n., 140
O'Brien, D. 50 n.
O'Brien, F. 47
Ó Coileáin, S. 3 n., 7 n., 11 n., 14, 27 n.,
    30 n., 33–4 n., 37 n., 39 n., 41 n.,
    43, 45, 48 n., 75 n., 79 n., 85 n., 88
    n., 96 n., 107 n., 138 n., 140 n.,
    196 n.
Ó Conaire, P. 58
O'Connor, M. 18 n., 153 n., 171 n., 172
    n., 177 n., 193 n., 195, 197 n.
O'Connor, T. 173 n.
Ó Dalaigh, M. A. 105
Ó Direáin, D. 119
Ó Direáin, M. 1, 3–4, 7, 9, 10, 47, 51, 56,
    58, 90, 104–148, 188, 200, 202
    Ó Morna 107–128
    Ár Ré Dhearóil 128–145
Ó Driscoll, D. 159 n., 175 n.
Ó Drisceoil, P. 152 n., 174 n.
Ó Dúill, G. 63, 64, 71–2
Ó Dúshláine, T. 34
Ó hEithir, B. and R 120 n., 126 n.,
    127 n.
Ó Fiannachta, P. 196 n.
O'Flaherty, J. 107, 112
O'Flaherty, L. 115, 120 n., 146–7
O'Flaherty, T. 107 n., 118, 120 n., 127 n.,
    202 n.
O'Leary, P. 178, 179, 193, 196, 201 n.
Oliver, M. 88
Ó Mórdha, S. 10 n., 28 n.
O'Neill, T. 32
Ó Rathaille, A. 49, 178

Ó Ríordáin, S. 1, 2 n., 3, 6, 7, 9–58, 60,
    73, 75, 79, 82, 85, 88, 90, 92, 96,
    99, 100 n., 104–7, 110, 123, 130,
    138, 140 n., 147 n., 155–6, 162, 178,
    186 n., 188, 192, 196, 200
  Brosna 28–37
  Eireaball Spideoige 11, 12–28, 34
  Línte Liombó 37–43
  Tar Éis Mo Bháis 43–46
Ó Searcaigh, C. 1, 4–5, 7, 51–2, 58–104,
    138, 150, 176 n., 200
  An Bealach 'na Bhaile 91–95
  Miontráigéide Cathrach 65, 76, 77, 79
  Na Buachaillí Bána 95–100
  Súile Shuibhne 59–77
  Suibhne 77–91
Ostriker, A. 171
Ó Súilleabháin, E. 33
Ó Tuairisc, E. 1, 6 n., 24 n., 51 n., 151 n.,
    153 n., 163 n., 173 n.
Ó Tuama, S. 3 n., 9–12, 20–1, 37, 48–9,
    104–7 n., 178 n., 195–7
Ó Tuathail, E. 115 n., 129 n., 146 n.
Ó hUiginn, M. 137 n.

Paisley, I. 32–3
Paulin, T. 115–16
Pearse, P. 32, 58, 123, 134, 141
Picasso, P. 41
Pirie, D. n., 191 n.
Plath, S. 166 n., 192, 197
Plato 97
Poetry Ireland 152 n.
Polkowski, J. 191
pope 41
post-structuralism 106
Pound, E. 52
primitivism 115–16, 133
Prút, L. 111, 112, 114
Pushkin, A. 20, 138

Rabelais, F. 160, 164
Raftery, A. 5
Reardon, V. 185
religion 16, 19–26, 38, 71–5, 90–1, 153,
    155–7, 183
Rice, P. and Waugh, P. 105 n.
Rich, A. 7, 96 n.
Robin, R. 65
Robinson, T. 118 n., 119–20, 146 n.,
    202 n.

Rosenstock, G. 51, 99 n., 195
Rousseau, J. J. 56, 133
Rumens, C. 102 n., 192 n.
Rushdie, S. 173 n.
Ruskin, J. 68
Rylance, R. 9 n., 200 n.

Said, E. 155 n.
Samhain 67, 70
Santayana, G. 74
Schlossman, B. 16 n.
Schneiders, S. 193
Schnyder, L. Dr. 159
Schweitzer, V. 153 n.
Scríobh 18, 43, 127 n.
Sealy, D. 62, 74, 108, 116
Sewell, F. 197 n.
Shakespeare, W 33
Shelley, P. B. 33
Shklovsky, V. 16–17
Simic, C. 76 n.
Skelton, R. 114 n.
Smiths, The 49 n.
Somerville Aryat, G. and Wilson, R. E.
    159 n., 164–5 n., 176 n., 185 n.,
    190 n.
Sontag, S. 194 n.
Spengler, O. 109–110, 112, 114–16, 119,
    129
Stallybrass, P. and White, A. 159 n.,
    160 n., 163 n., 165, 174 n.
Stephens, J. 201
Stevens, W. 68 n., 79
Stewart, R. J. and Williamson, R.
    5 n.
Storey, M. 201 n.
Strindberg, A. 33
Strong, E. 7
Suibhne 63, 194
Sweeney, *see* Suibhne
Synge, J. M. 118, 122, 146 n.

Tanner, T. 78 n., 106 n., 121 n.
Titley, A. 51
Tolstoi, L. 33
Tomashevski, B. 48
tradition 1–7, 199–202
    and Ní Dhomhnaill 152–3, 156, 160,
        163–4, 173, 177–8, 185, 186, 195
    and Ó Direáin 105, 107, 118, 121,
        126–131, 137, 139–41, 143–8

and Ó Ríordáin 11, 13–15, 17–19,
    23–4, 26, 34, 47–9, 51
and Ó Searcaigh 58, 60, 63, 71–2, 75,
    79–91, 94–5
transgression 2, 3, 6, 151, 155–7, 160, 166,
    170, 173–4, 183–8, 194–5, 197–8
transition 50 n.
Tsvetaeva, M. 7, 153
Turgenev, I. 33
Tynyanov, Y. 9, 79, 200 n.

Vico, G. 60, 63
Virgil 18

Walshe, É. 2 n.
Warner, M. 152, 155n., 157 n., 159, 160 n.,
    162, 166 n.
Weber, M. 128–9

Welch, R. 5 n., 37, 57 n., 64 n., 100 n.,
    115 n., 156 n.
Weldon, F. 146 n.
Whitman, W. 122, 152
Williams, J. E. C. and Ní Mhuiríosa, M.
    51 n.
Williams, T. 36
Wordsworth, W. 62, 96, 97 n., 99
Wright, H. 76 n.

Yale Review 76 n.
Yeats, W. B. 28, 45, 49, 85, 107, 122 n.,
    135–6, 191
Yevtushenko, Y. 5, 7, 59, 83–6, 87 n., 94,
    95, 101–2, 137 n.

Zenkovsky, V. V. 113 n.